STORMING
THE
Heavens

STORMING THE *Heavens*

AFRICAN AMERICANS AND THE EARLY FIGHT FOR THE RIGHT TO FLY

GERALD HORNE

BLACK CLASSIC PRESS
Baltimore

Storming the Heavens: African Americans and the Early Fight for the Right to Fly

Library of Congress Control Number: 2017964699

Print book ISBN: 978-1-57478-151-9
e-Book ISBN: 978-1-57478- 152-6

Printed by BCP Digital Printing (www.bcpdigital.com), an affiliate company of Black Classic Press, Inc.

To review or purchase Black Classic Press books, please visit: www.blackclassicbooks.com.

You my also obtain a list of titles by writing to:
Black Classic Press
c/o List
P.O. Box 13414
Baltimore, MD 21203

STORMING THE Heavens

TABLE OF CONTENTS

John Robinson. This Chicagoan volunteered to fight alongside Ethiopian forces in the 1930s after this nation was invaded by Italian legions; became a founder of Ethiopian Airways, the continent's major carrier to this day. (Courtesy Chicago History Museum).

INTRODUCTION

One minute, John Robinson was soaring through the skies of Ethiopia. The next, his hopes for surviving were plummeting precipitously.

It was late 1935, and this southern-born son of Black Chicago had chosen to take his immense piloting skills to Addis Ababa to assist the beleaguered regime of Emperor Haile Selassie I, His Imperial Majesty, the Conquering Lion of Judah, in foiling a brutal invasion by Benito Mussolini's Italian legions. Soon, Il Duce's incursion came to be viewed as a harbinger of what was to be termed World War II.

Robinson had just departed from the city of Adowa in northern Ethiopia after it was bombarded twice. He was *en route* to Addis Ababa with some important papers when two Italian airplanes attacked him. As he noted later in a dispatch to the Associated Negro Press, the agency that had sponsored his volunteer journey: "[The] Italians started shooting. I will never forget that day and the day after....I really had the closest call I have ever had," he added with relief, "One part of the wing on the airplane I was flying had ten holes when I landed."[1]

---

1 John Robinson to Claude Barnett, 21 November, 1935, Box 169, Folder 9, Claude A. Barnett/Associated Negro Press (ANP) Papers, Chicago History Museum [hereafter denoted as CAB-CHM]. The ANP was one of the most important institutions in Black America in the 20th century. See, e.g., Gerald Horne, *The Rise and Fall of the Associated Negro Press: Claude Barnett's Pan-African News and the Jim Crow Paradox* (Urbana: University of Illinois Press, 2017).

1

2

The man known as Colonel John Robinson of the Imperiale Ethiopenne Air Force was only one example of African Americans' extraordinary interest and involvement in aviation years before the 1957 launching of the Soviet satellite Sputnik. In his case, Ethiopia and Emperor Selassie were the beneficiaries of that attention. Whenever Selassie had important documents to dispatch speedily to his generals or when he himself wished to travel by air, Colonel Robinson, and he alone, was given that position of trust.[2] Robinson could well be considered one of the founders of Ethiopian Airways—a carrier that, by 2015, was deemed to be perhaps the best and most reliable airline on the continent and, as one periodical stated, "the main generator of foreign exchange" in this sprawling East African nation.[3]

African Americans' early interest in aviation reflected a longing for modernity and cosmopolitanism, especially since, as one analyst maintained, "Afro-diasporic people," to their painful detriment, "have been popularly constructed as backward and anti-technology".[4] Though Wilbur and Orville Wright have been credited widely for the invention of the airplane in 1903,[5] a Negro, Thomas Crump of Fisk University, invented a flying contraption as early as 1889. A Negro by the name of John Pickering reportedly developed an "airship" around 1900.[6] The Negro inventor W. F. Johnson conceived the idea of an electrically powered biplane as early as 1910 while another Negro,

2 Press Release, May 1936, Reel 12, #986, Part I, Series A, CAB-CHM. See also Reto Hofmann, *The Fascist Effect: Japan and Italy, 1915-1952* (Ithaca, New York: Cornell University Press, 2015).

3 Isma'il Kushkush, "Ethiopia, Long Mired in Poverty, Rides an Economic Boom," *New York Times*, March 4, 2015, A9.

4 Naima J. Keith, "Looking for the Invisible," in *The Shadows Took Shape*, ed. Naima J. Keith and Zoe Whitley (New York: Studio Museum in Harlem, 2013), 13-17, 15-16.

5 See, e.g., John D. Anderson Jr., *Inventing Flight: The Wright Brothers and their Predecessors* (Baltimore: The Johns Hopkins University, 2004). See also Julie Jedgepeth Williams, *Wings of Opportunity: The Wright Brothers in Montgomery, Alabama—America's First Civilian Flying School and the City that Capitalized On It.* (Montgomery, Alabama: New South Books, 2010). With regards to this latter citation; it may not have been coincidental that this pioneering flying school was established in the so-called "Cradle of the Confederacy."

6 Enoch P. Waters, *American Diary: A Personal History of the Black Press* (Chicago: Path Press, 1987), 195.

3

William Polite, patented an anti-aircraft gun in 1917—taking time away from his day job as headwaiter at a hotel in Wilmington, North Carolina.[7]

These Black inventors were not alone in this quest. One writer credits the Wright Brothers' relationship to the poet Paul Laurence Dunbar with helping to spark early Negro interest in aviation.[8] This fascination with aviation was also viewed as evidence of an enlightened self-interest on the part of Negroes in that airplanes were widely viewed early on as the "winning weapon"[9] and yet another tool to be deployed to subjugate African Americans and their colonized cousins in Africa and the Caribbean. The better part of wisdom dictated that Blacks learn more about flying. The airplane fed militarism and allied conservatism, which in turn buoyed a closely related colonial mentality and Negro-phobia.

As early as 1906, Sir Hiram Maxim—whose invention of a fully automatic machine gun had won him pride of place among colonialists—acknowledged the "potency" of aviation "as an instrument of warfare." He added ominously that "it behooves all the civilized nations of the earth to lose no time in becoming acquainted with this new means of attack and defence."[10] Lord Robert Baden–Powell, a leading British colonialist in Africa, concurred in 1908, just a few years after the Wright Brothers illustrated the value of flight, that London was "in possession of a power which controls the fate of nations"—namely, aviation.[11]

---

7 Thomas C. Parramore, *First to Fly: North Carolina and the Beginnings of Aviation* (Chapel Hill: University of North Carolina Press, 2002), 143, 192.
8 Jill D. Snider, "Flying to Freedom: African-American Visions of Aviation, 1910 to 1927" (PhD diss., University of North Carolina, 1995), 9.
9 See, e.g., Gregg Herken, *The Winning Weapon: The Atomic Bomb in the Cold War, 1945-1950* (New York: Knopf, 1980).
10 Gordon Hancock, October 1939, Reel 19, #799, Part I, Press Release, CAB-CHM.
11 Alfred Gollin, "The Wright Brothers and the British Authorities, 1902-1909," *English Historical Review*, 95(375), (April 1980), 292-375, 296, 311. See also Alfred Gollin, *No Longer an Island: Britain and the Wright Brothers, 1902-1909* (Redwood City, CA: Stanford University Press, 1984).

4

That same year, when the prolific and progressive H. G. Wells chose to novelize aviation in *The War of the Air*, he opted not to avoid the odiousness of the "Yellow Peril concept,"[12] suggesting a close tie between white supremacy and the new era of flight. This poisonous discourse did not escape the attention of African Americans. The twin towers of oppression—slavery and Jim Crow—had long confined them on slave ships, plantations, jails, and neighborhoods. However, the forces of production in U.S. society began to erode this shackling and racist social relationship. The advent of steamships and railroads, and later airplanes, provided people of African descent with a motorized escape from their Earth-bound oppression. This conflict between social relations and productive forces induced strains within the system of iniquity—Jim Crow in particular—causing it to buckle as African Americans deployed these forces to their benefit.[13]

* * *

In 1939, the then-reigning celebrity, Paul Robeson, beamed proudly that his son was "already interested in aviation engineering" and that he had bundled him off to Moscow for flight training. Robeson cautioned astutely that one could only imagine "what a chance a Negro aviation engineer would have in the United States or in England."[14] Tellingly, just before the Moscow's launching of the Sputnik satellite into outer space in 1957, another Negro pilot, 26-year-old Howard B. Spears Jr., who had flown earlier for the U.S., applied for Soviet citizenship

12 H. G. Wells, *The War in the Air* (Lincoln: University of Nebraska Press, 2002). See also Robert Wohl, "The Prophets of the War," *MHQ: Quarterly Journal of Military History*, 7(2), (Winter 1995), 81-91.
13 Elizabeth Stordeur Pryor, *Colored Travelers: Mobility and the Fight for Citizenship Before the Civil War* (Chapel Hill: University of North Carolina Press, 2016).
14 Lawrence Lamphere, "Paul Robeson: 'Freedom' Newspaper and the Black Press" PhD diss., Boston College, 2003), 27. See also Gerald Horne, *Paul Robeson: The Artist as Revolutionary* (London: Pluto, 2016).

because, as he said, "I want to be treated like a human being" and he was disgusted with lingering Jim Crow.[15]

The U.S. would be compelled to take halting steps away from Jim Crow, not least because of the national security implications exposed by Spears' defection. Indeed, the departure of Robinson and others to far-flung global sites was a resonant symbol of the leakage of talent that represented a leakage of national security that conceivably could be quite harmful to Washington. Assuredly, the ease of traveling to Moscow from the Americas, instigated by aviation, was a signal factor in the erosion of Jim Crow. As aviation helped to break the boundaries of segregation and second-class citizenship, the U.S. was compelled to adjust accordingly.

A similar process was unfolding in colonized Africa. By the 1920s, as a direct result of aviation developments and African Americans' concomitant mastery of this new technology, a riveting notion took hold in southern Africa: that a liberating air force of U.S. Negroes would descend on that benighted region and eviscerate colonialism as pilots dropped balls of burning charcoal upon the colonizers.[16] The fear that the airplane could become a tool of liberation soon became a reality.

Like Jim Crow, colonialism and apartheid were designed to confine Black bodies, but confinement hardly defined the reality experienced by Alex La Guma, a leader of the African National Congress (ANC) and the South African Communist Party. Writing from London in 1973, La Guma informed his leadership in Tanzania that "while in Moscow, having just departed Cairo," he received a message from Helsinki asking him to participate in a meeting in Hanoi. It was an invitation he quickly accepted, then jetted off to Vietnam to forge an important alliance.[17]

---

15 Press Release, January 1956, Reel 59, #17, Part I, Series B, Claude Barnett/Associated Negro Press Papers, North Carolina State University, Raleigh, North Carolina [hereafter denoted as CAB-NCSU].
16 Robert Edgar, "Garveyism in Africa: Dr. Wellington and the 'American' Movement in the Transkei," *Ufahamu: A Journal of African Studies*, 6 (1976), 31-57, 41.
17 Alex La Guma to "Dear Brother," 30 January 1973, Box 16, Folder 78, Part I, Lusaka

6

If the steady advancement in air transportation technology could facilitate the ability of the colonized to leapfrog their confinement and mobilize across borders, the colonizers feared that aviation could also operate to the detriment of apartheid and colonialism in other ways. The ANC paid close attention when, in the dying days of apartheid, South African Airways was compelled to end flights to the U.S.[18] It later was denied permission to enter a good deal of African airspace.[19] Both *demarches* hastened the suffocating isolation and subsequent demise of the Pretoria regime.

* * *

Of course, just as fire tempers steel for construction on one hand while fomenting destruction on the other, aviation too could be harnessed in malignant fashion. The Nazi chief of the Air Staff in Berlin, General Karl Koller, argued passionately for the eminence of aviation for his diabolical government. In words deemed worthy of retention by U.S. General Hoyt Vandenberg, former Chief of Staff of the Air Force and former Director of Central Intelligence, Koller proclaimed:

> Everything depends on air supremacy, everything else must take second place. The supremacy of the sea is only an appendage of air supremacy [since] the country that has air supremacy and vigorously strengthens its air power over all other forms of armament to maintain its supremacy, will rule the lands and the seas, will rule the world.[20]

Koller further stated that "all plans for the defense of a country, a continent or a sphere of interest or for offensive operations must be

Mission, African National Congress Archives, Fort Hare University–Alice, South Africa [hereinafter denoted as ANC Archives].

18 *The West Australian*, 17 November 1986, Box 64, Folder 112, Lusaka Mission, ANC Archives.

19 *Sydney Morning Herald*, 29 December 1988, Box 65, Folder 115, Lusaka Mission, ANC Archives.

20 "The Memoirs of General Koller, the German Chief of Staff," no date, Box 34, Hoyt S. Vandenberg Papers, Library of Congress, Washington, DC [hereafter the Vandenberg Papers].

in the hands of the Air Force Command." In any case, he reasoned, "naval officers will rarely, and army officers almost never, be able to keep pace with the large-scale thoughts and wide horizon which the men of all air forces in the world have more or less acquired."[21]

Understandably, U.S. Negroes were hardly indifferent to this Nazi's way of thinking. When the "Black Wall Street" of Tulsa, Oklahoma, was bombed from the air in a racist pogrom in 1921, many Blacks came to believe that their very survival depended on the study of aviation becoming a priority.[22] James Peck, an African American pilot lent his aviation skills to the besieged republic of Spain when that nation came under fire in the late 1930s. He summed up the gathering consensus among Blacks in the U.S. thusly: "[T]he advent of airpower has changed the world's conception of military strategy in general and U.S. defense in particular—all of which most certainly affects the darker citizenry."[23]

The U.S. Negro press was likewise alert when the then-avatar of aviation, Charles Lindbergh, was said to have declared in late 1939 that "if the white race is ever seriously threatened, it then may be time for us to take our part in its protection, to fight side by side" with Europe against its numerous colonized subjects. "But not," Lindbergh added, "with one against the other for our mutual destruction."[24] This attitude, according to the moderate Negro journalist Gordon Hancock, made "Lucky Lindy" one of "Hitler's stooges."[25]

The prevalence of lynch laws in the United States—yet another weapon in the arsenal of racism deployed against African Americans—

21 Ibid.
22 Snider, "Flying to Freedom," iii.
23 Column by James Peck, 10 April 1940, Reel 20, #743, Part I, Press Releases, CAB-NCSU. (This is the microfilm edition of the source cited.)
24 Column by Gordon Hancock, October 1939, Reel 19, #799, Part I, Press Releases, CAB-NCSU.
25 Column by Gordon Hancock, June 1941, Reel 22, #552, Part I, Press Releases, CAB-NCSU.

meant that Lindbergh's rancidness could not be ignored easily. Indeed, those sentiments heightened the need to counteract the advantage in the skies held by those who shared Lindbergh's views.

Negro pilot Chauncey Spencer, who fought alongside U.S. forces during World War II, seemed to take Lucky Lindy's words as a personal affront. He threw down the gauntlet, angrily assessing the celebrity's idea that flying was "one of those priceless possessions which permit the white race to live at all in a pressing sea of Yellow, Black and Brown" and thus "a tool especially shaped by western hands."[26] Spencer knew well that this wrongheaded notion was not Lindbergh's alone. "[T]he public's attitude," he added, was also "extremely hostile to Negro flyers."[27] Indeed, the very existence of Black aviators contradicted the prevailing notion of Black people's inherent ineptitude while adumbrating the belief that the plane, as a weapon of war, could be turned sharply against white supremacy.

Another apparent connection between aviation and retrograde attitudes occurred when Lindbergh's aviator peer—the pilot Edward "Eddie" Rickenbacker—was hailed by the fascist Gerald L. K. Smith and denounced by union leader Walter Reuther for his questionable political leanings.[28] Rickenbacker and Lindbergh exemplified the once-prevalent idea that enthusiasm for aviation and fascism were linked tightly.[29] Aviators reportedly formed a disproportionate component of the British Union of Fascists.[30] Unsurprisingly, the leading African

---

26 Michael Laris, "Freedom Flight," *Washington Post*, February 16, 2003, https://www.washingtonpost.com/archive/lifestyle/magazine/2003/02/16/freedom-flight/6bac72d9-eff2-4fc4-88d5-39ec92044dcf/?utm_term=.4810107515de.

27 Chauncey E. Spencer, *Who is Chauncey Spencer?* (Detroit: Broadside, 1975), 30.

28 Statement, 8 February 1943, Box 108, Edward Rickenbacker Papers, Library of Congress.

29 Rex Warner, *The Aerodome: A Love Story* (Boston: Little, Brown, 1966). Originally published in 1941, this novel associated aviation with the rise of fascism. See also Thomas Hippler, *Bombing the People: Giulio Douhet and the Foundations of Air-Power Strategy, 1884-1939* (Cambridge, UK: Cambridge University Press, 2013). Douhet was a proponent of total war, which—he thought—was facilitated by aviation; he was also an ardent fascist. He was a close student of the aerial bombing of Libya in 1911; and it is striking that this man, considered to be one of the world's most important theorists of air power, drew upon events in Africa to arrive at his deadly conclusions, which were then applied promiscuously in Ethiopia.

30 David Edgerton, *England and the Aeroplane: Military, Modernity and Machines* (London:

American intellectual Alain Locke predicted in 1940 that the U.S. "will no doubt pass through a brief period of fascism in the near future,"[31] an opinion he did not connect to the ascendancy of aviation. That connection, however, was made by others—Lindbergh, for example— who foresaw the rising tide of fascism and colonialism as part and parcel of the ascendancy of aviation as the so-called winning weapon.

* * *

The idea of flight had captivated the human imagination for centuries before materializing in the early 20th century.[32] Thereafter, this captivation accelerated rapidly, with some in the U.S. coming to view the plane as a kind of messiah, perhaps because it penetrated the heavens where a deity was believed to reside. After Lindbergh's groundbreaking trans-Atlantic flight in 1927, an elderly Negro woman reportedly asked him, in all apparent seriousness, how much he would charge her to fly her to heaven and leave her there.[33]

The idea of escaping an earthbound hell occurred to numerous people of African descent. Johnny Griffin (1928–2008)—a leading jazz tenor saxophonist who just happened to be a Negro—offered a cosmically grounded philosophy to explain Black people's desire to transcend their earthly plight in America and elsewhere:

> ...the main thing is I'm here because I did something wrong on my planet. I'm not really from this planet. I did something wrong on my planet and they sent me here to pay my dues. I figure pretty soon my [dues] will be paid and they're going to call me home so I can rest in peace....I can't be from this place [for] there is no love here and I love people. All I see is hate

Penguin, 2013), xxiii, 77.

31   Release, August 1940, Reel 21, #400, Part I, Press Releases, CAB-NCSU.

32   Phil Scott, *Pioneers of Flight: A Documentary History* (Princeton, NJ: Princeton University Press, 1999).

33   Joseph Corn, *The Winged Gospel: America's Romance with Aviation* (Baltimore: The Johns Hopkins University Press, 2001), 11, 13, 35.

10

around me…..that's what's wrong with the earth today. Black
and white on this planet, there is no love, there is only hate.[34]

Strikingly, this desire to transcend was reflected in the work of other
musicians most notably Sun Ra, who was raised in the hellhole that
was Birmingham, Alabama, during the height of Jim Crow.[35]

Proponents of the contemporary Afro-Futurist movement, in
refiguring the metaphoric rendering of the horrors of the Trans-Atlantic
Slave Trade as akin to an alien abduction, have also alluded to Black
people's long history of looking upward to the sky for salvation and
inspiration.[36] This reflection on cosmology is rooted distantly in African
conceptions of the cosmos. Thus, Afro-Baptist hymns and sermons
posit an awareness of one's place in the cosmos and the possibility of
spiritual travel within it—an awareness transferable not only to music
but also to an interest in flight.

Others saw flight as an instrument of reform, regeneration, and
salvation—as a substitute for politics, revolution, or even religion.
"Aerial liberation through flight" was more than a slogan for certain
women, who argued that flying served to spur, if not reinforce,
their confidence and independence.[37] A similar feeling arose among
American Negroes. Not to be discounted in determining why Blacks
were attracted early to aviation was the sense of liberation provided
when soaring above the clouds. Moreover, flying reinforced and
enhanced the historic tendency of African Americans to engage in
flight from atrocious conditions. Entering the cockpit and taking off

34 John Szwed, *Space is the Place: The Lives and Times of Sun Ra* (New York: Pantheon, 1997), 136. See also Art Taylor, *Notes and Tones: Musician-to-Musician Interviews* (New York: Da Capo, 1966), 69-70.
35 Szwed, *Space is the Place.*
36 Ytasha L. Womack, *Afro-Futurism: The World of Black Sci-Fi and Fantasy Culture* (Chicago: Lawrence Hill, 2013), 32. See also Laurence Douny, *Living in a Landscape of Scarcity: Materiality and Cosmology in West Africa* (Walnut Creek, CA: Left Coast Press, 2014); Jon Willis, *All These Worlds Are Yours: The Scientific Search for Alien Life* (New Haven, CT: Yale University Press, 2016); Charles Wohlforth and Amanda Hendrix, *Beyond Earth: Our Path to a New Home in the Planets* (New York: Pantheon, 2016).
37 Corn, *Winged Gospel*, 11, 13, 35.

into the clouds helped to bolster the idea that by so ascending, the depravity of the oppression that too often characterized the facts on the ground were left behind.

Perhaps because of her dual identity as a Negro and a woman, Willa Brown came to be pre-eminent in introducing aviation to African Americans. Brown's ascendancy was steeper than that of most in that she co-founded, with Cornelius Coffey, what was then the "largest privately owned Negro aviation school in the country"[38]: the Coffey School of Aeronautics. So renowned was she for her aviation accomplishments that in November 1941, Enoch Waters of the Chicago-based National Airmen's Association of America sought to nominate her for the Spingarn Medal, the highest honor of the National Association for the Advancement of Colored People (NAACP).[39] As Waters maintained in his nomination statement, Brown, "more than any other single individual [is] responsible for the present interest of Negroes in aviation." This was quite an accolade since Black women typically faced a kind of double jeopardy with regard to flight and aviation. As of 1929, when the first Women's Air Derby was held, only 34 of the reported 4,690 licensed pilots in the U.S. were women. Some men mocked their inaugural aerial competition, dubbing it the "Powder Puff Derby."[40]

Similarly, Black women were not welcomed at Alabama's Tuskegee Institute, where a generation of Negro pilots were being trained there to support the U.S. war effort in the 1940s. In 1942, Janet Harmon Bragg, the first Negro woman to earn a full commercial pilot's license, was turned down by Tuskegee Institute's pilot training program, even though she passed the airborne part of the test, presumably because

38 Enoc Waters to Claude A. Barnett, 7 November 1941, Technical Files–Willa Brown, National Air and Space Museum, Washington, DC [hereafter denoted as NASM].
39 Ibid.
40 Peter J. Westwick, "Photo Essay: An Album of Early Southern California Aviation," in *Blue Sky Metropolis: The Aerospace Century in Southern California*, ed. Peter J. Westwick (Berkeley: University of California Press, 2012), 15-33, 20.

12

she was a woman. During World War II she was turned down again—apparently because she was a Negro—when she sought to join the Women's Air Force Service Pilots, which ferried equipment for the military.[41] Born in Griffin, Georgia, in 1912, Bragg had bought her own plane by the 1930s. She later became president of the Challenger Air Pilots, a group of ebony aviators.[42]

But before Brown and Bragg, there was Bessie Coleman. Generally acknowledged as the first person of African descent worldwide to become a licensed pilot, Coleman achieved this feat by fleeing the U.S. for France in late 1920 to receive flight training. There, she walked nine miles a day for ten months to and from flight school. Coleman's trailblazing accomplishments were later cited as the source of Willa Brown's inspiration and aspirations to fly.[43]

Despite the demonstrated competence of Brown, Bragg, and Coleman, a reporter observed in early 1940 that "female students have not been accepted in some of the Negro institutions authorized by the government to teach aeronautics to colored students." "In one large university," the reporter continued, "the girls flocked to the class seeking admission [but] they were gently turned away."[44] At a 1949 ceremony honoring the disappearance of the now-celebrated Euro-American pilot Amelia Earhart, a Negro journalist lamented that no similar efforts had been made to preserve the names of Coleman and other ebony pioneers of her gender. According to his article, there were "only 37 Negro women in the air transportation industry in 1940," and by 1949 there were "at least 50 Negro women aviators

41 Funeral Program, April 1993, Box 2, Files on Janet Harmon Bragg, Vivian Harsh Research Collection on Afro-American History and Literature, Carter G. Woodson Regional Library, Chicago Public Library.
42 Paul Sloan, "Aviator Janet Harmon Bragg, 86" (Obituary), *Chicago Tribune*, April 13, 1993, http://articles.chicagotribune.com/1993-04-13/news/9304130038_1_air-force-service-pilots-mrs-bragg-nursing. See also "Janet Waterford Bragg," Technical Files, NASM.
43 Press Release, "General Aviation News" (published by the U.S. Department of Transportation), no date, FAA-Great Lakes Technical Files–Bessie Coleman, NASM.
44 Press Release, January 1940, Reel 20, #212, Part I, Press Releases, CAB-NCSU.

[yet] it was disappointing that none of them were invited to the Earhart celebration."[45]

Willa Brown, pictured in the early 1940s: She too, was responsible for training many of the earliest African-American pilots.
(Chicago History Museum)

* * *

The immensity of the horror that was Jim Crow inexorably caused some African Americans to consider drastic remedies, many of which

---

45 Press Release, October 1949, Reel 41, #959, Part I, Series B, CAB-NCSU.

led to musings unmoored by earthly forces. Thus, the man with his feet firmly planted on *terra firma*, W. E. B. Du Bois, mused that the problems of Negroes worldwide were so deeply and historically entrenched that the eradication of their miseries could be imagined only through the intervention of a catastrophic natural force—on the cosmic level, no less.[46] Just as indigenous South Africans figured correctly that the invention of flying machines would have profound implications for their plight, a similar trend proved to be the case for African Americans. The advancement of the productive forces reflected in aerial, then cosmic, developments proved to be inimical to the social relationship that was Jim Crow.

Aviation also encouraged a long-term trend among African Americans: expatriation. Lieutenant General Benjamin O. Davis Jr., a leading pilot and son of an illustrious Negro military man, did not muse about reaching the cosmos; however, despite his fame, fortune, and patriotism, he conceded that his father "was always happiest overseas, where black people were treated far better than they were by most of their own countrymen at home…failing to find that respect in the United States." His father, the younger Davis noted, "escaped the problem by spending as much time as he could out of the country."[47] Similar thoughts apparently occurred to other Negroes, who saw aviation as a means to their desired ends. Aviation enhanced a more permanent expatriation, allowing Negroes to reside more easily abroad, where they could then become sterner critics of their homeland while reclining in the bosom of that republic's staunchest foes.[48]

Aviation additionally facilitated the ability of Negro artists to attain celebrity abroad. The tenor Roland Hayes was just one of many African

---

46 See W. E. B. DuBois, *Darkwater: Voices from Within the Veil* (New York: Schocken, 1969), 253-274. See also Diana Rebekkah Paulin, *Imperfect Unions: Staging Miscegenation in U.S. Drama and Fiction* (Minneapolis: University of Minnesota Press, 2012), 236.

47 Davis Jr., *Benjamin O. Davis Jr., American*, 4.

48 See, e.g., Ernest Dunbar, *The Black Expatriates: A Study of American Negroes in Exile* (New York: Dutton, 1968).

American performers who attained stardom in Europe before gaining a modicum of acclaim in the U.S.[49] Aviation allowed these artists to accumulate more wealth and build global networks that could then be enlisted in the anti-Jim Crow struggle.

Though facilitated by advances in aviation, the Black expatriation trend was no simple matter. Aviation and expatriation came with a price tag that some were unwilling or unable to pay, and poverty and bigotry consigned many Blacks to a flightless existence just as it dialectically motivated others to explore the contested realm of the skies. By the 1930s, U.S. Negroes were adjudged "the most earthbound people in the country,"[50] with various Jim Crow restrictions barring them from airplanes and airports alike. In 1960, the man who was to become the world's foremost boxing champion, Muhammad Ali, was so reluctant to fly to the Rome Olympics that later catapulted him to fame and fortune that he boarded the plane carrying an army surplus parachute, which he donned before kneeling in the aisle and praying.[51] As late as 1962, aviation industry estimates indicated that only two percent of U.S. Negroes had flown anywhere, either domestically or abroad.[52] The Haitian American performer Wyclef Jean recalled that while growing up on his home island in 1982, an "airplane was as strange as a UFO." [53]

* * *

The experience of James Peck in Spain illustrates why political reactionaries early deemed it so important to bar Negroes from the heavens. Aviation facilitated a global war against Jim Crow, colonialism,

---

49 Christopher A. Brooks and Robert Sims, *Roland Hayes: The Legacy of an American Tenor* (Bloomington: Indiana University Press, 2015).

50 David T. Courtwright, *Sky as Frontier: Adventure, Aviation and Empire* (College Station: Texas A&M University Press, 2005), 137.

51 Ibid., 199.

52 Jenifer Van Vleck, *Empire of the Air: Aviation and the American Ascendancy* (Cambridge, MA: Harvard University Press, 2013), 270.

53 Wyclef Jean, *Purpose: An Immigrant's Story* (New York: HarperCollins, 2012), 24.

and fascism—and African Americans were well positioned to take part in those struggles. During the Spanish Civil War, Peck, flying for the Spanish Republican Air Force, launched an aerial strafing expedition against that nation's fascist foes. As Peck recalled, evincing little pity: "I watched the trapped fascist soldiers run pell-mell in all directions like groups of wild confused mice...the fools!" With a dash of faux sympathy, however, he added, "If they lie still on the ground, they've a chance. Peculiar how one can feel sorry for a sworn foe"[54] Though Peck felt compelled to choose temporary exile in Spain to help fight the ultra-right forces there, he was also warring against the comrades of those in the U.S. who bolstered the Jim Crow laws that had chased him from North American shores.

This position was not peculiar to Negroes of the left, like Peck. This paradoxical combination of African Americans feeling compelled to assume an earthbound status by racism, chauvinist restrictions, and poverty while simultaneously taking a deep interest in aviation was connected dialectically. That is, what is often forbidden is often believed to be most alluring. The desire to bar Negroes from the heavens may have driven them to consider the stratosphere even more. Predictably, given a reigning Jim Crow and the increasing use of planes as instruments of warfare, concomitant with the idea that Negroes should be kept away from technological sophistication, special measures were taken to keep this persecuted minority far distant from airplane manufacturing, airports, and, not least, commercial air travel.

* * *

In 1941, as the U.S. stood on the brink of a war with existential implications for it as a nation, J. H. Kindleberger, president of the North American Aviation Company, aroused the ire of U.S. Negroes when he stated that his plant in Kansas City, Missouri, was hiring but

---

54   James L. H. Peck, *Armies with Wings* (New York: Dodd, Mead, 1940), 92.

that African Americans would be employed solely as janitors, "no matter how well trained." His position was not an outlier. Swallow Aircraft's plant in Wichita, Kansas—then well on its way to becoming a center for aircraft manufacturing—produced and distributed a handbill requesting that only "White American Citizens" register for its training courses.[55]

That same year, Fairchild Aircraft, headquartered in supposedly liberal New York, adamantly and bluntly refused even to consider the presumably bizarre notion of hiring a Negro. At Boeing, soon to become an industry giant, the lily-white unions stood alongside management's pre-existing bias. This recalcitrance continued even after the White House issued an Executive Order mandating otherwise,[56] and even though the U.S. was so desperate for aircraft workers that the blind, the deaf, and what one scholar termed "the deformed" were sought avidly for employment.[57] By July 1943, Boeing employed a miniscule 44 African American men and a paltry 285 African American women out of a workforce of nearly 30 thousand.[58] Of the approximately 250,000 people working in the flight-related field of aerospace between 1945 and 1950, African Americans represented only about 1.6 percent of this total. As a recent study accurately concluded in 2015, "there appear to have been few industries more openly contemptuous toward the idea of racial equality at this time than the aerospace industry."[59]

Worse, from the viewpoint of U.S. national security, was that Jim Crow practices apparently facilitated the ability of German agents to penetrate its aviation and aeronautics factories during the immediate pre-war era and during wartime itself. Presumably, those agents'

---

55 Press Release, 1 May 1941, Box II: A233, NAACP Papers, Library of Congress.
56 Memorandum, 10 September 1941, Box II: A234, NAACP Papers.
57 Courtwright, *Sky as Frontier*, 118.
58 Polly Myers Reed, *Capitalist Family Values: Gender, Work and Corporate Culture at Boeing* (Lincoln: University of Nebraska Press, 2015), 81.
59 Richard Paul and Steven Moss, *We Could Not Fail: The First African Americans in the Space Program* (Austin: University of Texas Press, 2015), 63, 64.

whiteness allowed them entry into buildings from which Negroes were barred. For example, the specifications for every plane built at the Farmingdale, New York, Sikorsky Aircraft Company plant fell into Berlin's hands. The confiscated plans included the blueprints for the U.S. Navy's new carrier-based scout bomber, the designs for a new Boeing-built bomber, the acquisition of classified maps of the U.S., plus a classified report on the U.S. Army Air Corps tactical air services conducted at Long Island's Mitchell Field. The success of Berlin's penetration of sensitive U.S. facilities was so significant that one German official boasted that the United States "cannot plan a warship, design an airplane, [or] develop a new device" without those secrets being passed on to his nation's intelligence service. Arguably, hiring more Negro workers, who were indisputably less likely to be swayed by fascism, would have eroded the possibility of such damaging coups.[60]

This industry-wide bigotry was of maximum importance. W. Stuart Symington, who had served as Secretary of the U.S. Air Force before becoming a U.S. Senator, observed that in 1944, during the peak of World War II airplane production, the nation produced 96,000 airplanes, of which 75,000 were destined for combat.[61] Prior to Symington's pronouncements, W. Gerard Tuttle, manager of industrial relations at Vultee Aircraft in California, brusquely informed Robert Robinson of the left-leaning National Negro Congress (NNC) that "the policy of this company [not] to employ people other than of the Caucasian race," was inviolable and "consequently we are not in a position to offer your people employment at this time."[62] The NNC's response was an exacting and furious one. The organization pointed out that, as of 1940, aircraft building was the nation's largest defense industry

60 Ladislas Farago, *The Game of Foxes: The Untold Story of German Espionage in the United States and Great Britain During World War II* (New York: McKay, 1971), 36.
61 Remarks by W. Stuart Symington, 18 September 1948, 2 P.M., at Selfridge Air Force Base, Box 35, Vandenberg Papers.
62 W. Gerard Tuttle to Robert Robinson, circa 1941, Box 60, *Herbert Hill Papers, Library of Congress.*

and that southern California was "the center" of that boom. The profits from that industry, it went on to state, "stagger the imagination"[63]:

> For example, the war has zoomed Lockheed's profits more than 397 percent. During the first six months of 1940, Lockheed had a net profit of $2,022,619 as compared with $508,860 for the first six months of 1939. Bendix Aircraft Corporation made profits of $4,295,419 for the first six months [of 1940] as against $2,168,210 for the corresponding period of 1939. Similarly, Curtiss-Wright profits almost doubled during the first six months of 1940, as compared with 1939: $6,235,969 as compared with $3,370,804.[64]

All this profit taking was occurring, the NNC response noted, not only as war clouds loomed dangerously above but also as "aircraft moguls started complaining that they couldn't find enough skilled workers" and Negroes with a fervent passion for aviation languished on the sidelines.[65]

What came to be called the military-industrial complex was becoming a formidable force in the political economy of the U.S. during this era, and Negroes could hardly afford to be marginalized in that crucial sphere. Lockheed's sales revenues rocketed from $10 million in 1938 to almost $700 million by 1943. This behemoth corporation produced more than 19,000 aircraft from 1939 to 1945, necessitating a rise from 7,000 employees in 1939 to 28,000 by May 1941 and 94,000 by 1944.

After World War II, aircraft manufacture became what was by certain measures the largest industry in the world, with much of it centered in southern California. The plants headquartered in the South employed a whopping two million workers, who built a staggering

---

63 Ibid.
64 Ibid.
65 Ibid.

20

300,000 planes during the war.[66] By 1954 Lockheed was the third-largest U.S. aircraft firm in terms of revenue with $733 million in sales, trailing only Boeing and Douglas. By 1957—as the Russian satellite Sputnik was about to redefine aerospace—this giant had revenues of $879 million; by 1961 its sales were up to $1.45 billion.[67]

Banning Negroes from working in the U.S. aviation industry was akin to banning them from the future. Matters hardly differed at the nation's airports. As of 1956, no U.S. airline had ever hired a Negro flight attendant. In 1954, an American Airlines supervisors' manual expressly disqualified applicants with "broad noses" and "coarse hair."[68] Pan American Airways, the principal airline connecting the U.S. to the world, was accused in 1945 of separating Negro family members based on their skin color, with the lighter-skinned allowed to sit among those defined as white while the darker-complexioned members were relegated to the plane's "Siberia."[69] Negroes repeatedly reported being refused service when they sought to purchase airline tickets, proving once again that the corporate executives of that era obeyed other gods beyond profit.

Those Negroes who were fortunate enough to board an aircraft, with or without contention, often were compelled to sit in separate rows, and flight attendants treated them rudely—when they deigned to notice them at all. Their discriminatory practices were no boon for flight safety. In emergencies, such as when encountering turbulence during a flight, it is doubtful that a racist attendant would have a magical change of heart and civilly request civilized cooperation from those whom she had treated so discourteously only moments before.

66   Westwick, "Photoessay," 15-33, 30.
67   Sherman N. Mullin, "Robert E. Gross and the Rise of Lockheed: The Creative Tension Between Engineering and Finance," in *Blue Sky Metropolis: The Aerospace Century in Southern California*, ed. Peter J. Westwick (Berkeley: University of California Press, 2012), 57-78, 64, 68, 73.
68   Victoria Vantoch, *The Jet Sex: Airline Stewardesses and the Making of an American Icon* (Philadelphia: University of Pennsylvania Press, 2013), 59, 60.
69   Claude A. Barnett to Pan American Airways, 29 August 1945, Reel 8, #430, Part III, Subject Files on Black Americans, 1918-1967, Series I, Race Relations, CAB-NCSU.

A problem for the airlines and their employees' Jim-Crow mania was that NAACP staff members often had to travel by air to accomplish their national objectives; thus, they were keenly positioned to object sternly to such praxis. In August 1945, for example, the NAACP's leading attorney, Robert Carter, a future federal judge, departed New York City for Detroit. As he irritably related in a letter sent to the offending carrier, Northwest Airlines, after his flight:

> When I boarded the plane, the stewardess led me to one of the seven single seats which was the only seat with a reserve sign and requested [that I be seated]. The rest of the passengers were white and were told to take any seat they cared to occupy. [This was] the first instance of this type that I have encountered in air travel.[70]

Carter went on to state that this occurrence was made all the more unacceptable to him coming on the heels of a war supposedly designed to extirpate such toxicity. He maintained that the experience was "most humiliating,"[71] before inquiring why the airline allowed Jim Crow to persist when Dixie was not the destination.

Gloster Current, another NAACP staffer, had a similar experience in spring 1952. He was headed to Denver when stormy weather diverted the flight to Salt Lake City, arriving near midnight. There, a United Airlines executive provided the disgruntled passengers with hotel accommodation slips, but as the dark-skinned Current was about to board the airport limousine heading toward the designated hotel, his name was scratched from the list. He was informed that the hotels in Salt Lake City "practiced discrimination" and would not accommodate him. Current then returned to United's desk at the airport, where he was ignored interminably, then dispatched impolitely to what he described as a "third-rate 'colored'

---

70   Robert Carter to J. J. Fauteux, Traffic Manager of Northwest Airlines, 24 August 1945, Box II: A9, NAACP Papers.
71   Ibid.

hotel."[72] There, he was given an unheated room, which led to his contracting a severe case of influenza that left him bedridden for several days. Thus, when Jim Crow reached the heavens, it touched directly an NAACP staff trained in litigation—and litigate they did—which did not bode well for this archaic system of crude indignities.

The ability to take commercial flights was, by its very nature, a matter of class and income, and as such only Negroes of financial means had the ability to afford air travel. By subjecting middle-and what few upper-class Negro airline passengers there were to such discriminatory practices as those described by Carter and Current, African Americans were forced to storm the heavens in pursuit of justice.

As Joyce Chaplin claims in her history of round-the-world travel, by the time Sputnik took flight, aviation had shrunk the planet and altered the atmosphere in favor of various anti-Jim Crow measures.[73] Euro-American aviation mogul Eddie Rickenbacker reportedly surmised that flying had reduced the size of the U.S. to the size of Pennsylvania and perhaps had reduced the size of the world to the size of the U.S.[74] Air travel made it possible to zip from North America to distant continents in hours instead of weeks, thereby helping to forge what came to be called "the global village" in which the peculiar racial folkways of the U.S. were not necessarily embraced. This complicated Washington's attempt to win hearts and minds in a worldwide contest with competing ideologies, the manifold consequences of which have yet to be grasped fully.

* * *

Before 1941 no more than 300 or 400 passengers traveled by air in either direction between the U.S. and Africa. (This represented an abrupt

72   Walter White to D. P. Magarell, Vice President, United Air Lines, 2 April 1952, Box II: A233, NAACP Papers.

73   Joyce C. Chaplin, *Round About the Earth: Circumnavigation from Magellan to Orbit* (New York: Simon & Schuster, 2012).

74   Courtwright, *Sky as Frontier*, 197.

turnabout from the African Slave Trade, which resulted in thousands of transatlantic crossings by sea and the depositing of hundreds of thousands in North America.[75]) By 1941, airmail service between New York and West Africa and the Congo had been inaugurated.[76] Months earlier, the U.S. granted South African pilots permission to conduct test flights at U.S. facilities, thus heightening cooperation between the two powers and increasing Pretoria's aviation capacity in a manner that was to prove inimical to the interests of Africans.[77] When direct air service was initiated between the U.S. and South Africa in 1948, U.S. official William C. Foster chortled that it would "bring these two democracies [sic] closer in every sense of the words." "Travel and friendship will be facilitated," he maintained, and "South Africa has now been brought within easy range of American travelers and outsiders."[78] The reality was that this air link facilitated the growing revulsion felt in the U.S. toward apartheid. It illuminated uncomfortable parallels between the Afrikaners' system of hate and its North American cousin Jim Crow and had gigantic consequences hardly envisioned at the time.

In 1951, segregationists at Miami's airport were reduced to accepting both the absence of Jim Crow washrooms and the non-enforcement of the quotidian "White Passengers Seated in Front, Colored Passengers Seated in Rear" signs on airport buses. Why? According to press reports, a "fear of antagonizing West Indian visitors who are also black" had emerged as Jamaica, Barbados, and other U.S. neighbors in the Caribbean began to surge to independence from colonialism.

75　Petition "Before the Civil Aeronautics Board," Docket #1171, "In the Matter of the Applications for Certification of Public Convenience and Necessity Between the United States and Africa.....Brief [by Pan Am], 8 March 1945, The Records of the Pan American World Airways, Inc.–University of Miami [hereafter denoted as Pan Am Papers].

76　Press Release, 4 December 1941, Box 317, Folder 28, Pan Am Papers.

77　R. Walton Moore to Secretary of State Henry Stimson, 23 July 1940, Record Group 59, Decimal Files, 848A.221/4, Box 5123, General Records of the Department of State, National Archives and Records Administration, College Park, Maryland.

78　Statement of William C. Foster, Acting Secretary of Commerce, circa 1948, Box 200, Folder 19, Pan Am Papers.

These uprisings created the possibility of the formerly colonized island nations becoming closer to Moscow if maltreated by Washington.[79] By 1955, one journalist was beaming that "many Coloured Americans were choosing 'God's Little Country' [Jamaica] as the ideal summer vacation spot."[80] An increasing number of air links fueled that trend. Left unsaid was how the Miami authorities could distinguish between "coloured" Jamaicans and "coloured Americans." Their difficulties in accomplishing this contributed to the ongoing pressure to desegregate, and then decolonize, that island. A persistent problem for the U.S. during the Cold War was maintaining a "color bar" to oppress African Americans while lifting that bar for Africans, Indians, and others among the dark-skinned within its borders. Ultimately, the U.S. was unable to tap dance successfully on this irrational tightrope and was forced to lift its color bar for all.[81]

Arguably, the increase in air travel facilitated both the decline of Jim Crow and colonialism alike, but the problem of maintaining that bar abroad remained a stubborn issue nonetheless. By 1956, an executive at the premier U.S. global air carrier, Pan-American Airways (PAA or "Pan Am," for short), was fretting about the "danger that may exist to PAA's investment should some of the predictions of native uprisings and riots" in apartheid South Africa bear fruit. He likewise worried that the numerous prognostications made in the U.S. press about the circumstances within that nation might "become true." W. H. Lyons, Pan Am's regional director for the Iberian Peninsula and Africa, questioned if the Pretoria government had "the means effectively to check anything more widespread [than] broken windows." It was hardly consoling to him that, for Pan Am, "any risk involved does not compare, for example, with our present exposure in the Middle and Far East."[82]

---

79 Release, September 1951, Reel 46, #850, Part I, Series B, CAB-NCSU.
80 "Spotlight News Magazine," July-August 1955, Box 372, Folder 22, Pan Am Papers.
81 Release, August 1955, Reel 57, #1070, Part I, Series B, CAB-NCSU.
82 W. H. Lyons to Executive Vice President, 14 December 1956, Box 320, Folder 40, Pan

The color bar broke into pieces in 1957, when Moscow set aloft a satellite into outer space. Sputnik's launch took place just as Ghana was surging to independence and Little Rock, Arkansas, was erupting in racist riots as a result of school desegregation—allowing the astute to link these supposedly disparate events and view them as contributing to a national crisis for the U.S. At the time, many believed Washington was falling behind in the Cold War due to its failure to utilize its human capital of African descent, thereby alienating the rising nations in Asia, Africa, and the Caribbean and jeopardizing its national security. The Sputnik launch also implicated aerospace in that the field of aeronautics, viewed by many as the key to global hegemony, loomed as an even more gargantuan challenge, contributing both to frazzled nerves and a resoluteness to change.

C. D. Jackson, a confidante of President Dwight D. Eisenhower, confided to influential press baron Henry Luce that if he (Jackson) were still working in Washington, he would have advised the President to act immediately after the satellite launch. In his view, Sputnik was an "overwhelmingly important event—against our side." "In the Middle East, in Africa, in Asia, where it will be exploited to the hilt by the Communists," he bemoaned, "it will have tremendous impact...no comfort should be derived from the fact that it has shoved Little Rock off the front page of the world." He concluded that "the successful impact" of Sputnik was "considerably heightened" by the turmoil in Little Rock."[83]

Jackson's connections were easily grasped by U.S. Negroes, who were pressing aggressively for across-the-board change. There certainly was something both serendipitous and inexorable about the

---

Am Papers.

83 C. D. Jackson to Mr. Luce, 6 October 1957, Log-1957 (4), Box 69, General File or Time Incorporated File, 1933-1964, Subseries A, Alphabetical File, 1933-1964, C. D. Jackson Papers, Dwight Eisenhower Presidential Library, Abilene, Kansas. See also Howard C. McCurdy, *Space and the American Imagination* (Washington, DC: Smithsonian Institution, 1997).

collision of Sputnik and Little Rock. Like so many others, African Americans flocked to the gospel of aviation; yet, their central reason for doing so was to erode the brutal force of Jim Crow. When it appeared that the U.S. was falling behind in aerospace and that its national security was being threatened, Negroes hammered home the point that Jim Crow was a co-factor in that enervating process in hopes of weakening the monster of segregation. Sputnik, in their view, exposed the contradiction between the growth of the productive forces in aerospace and the iniquitous social relation that was Jim Crow.

L. D. Reddick, an advisor to Dr. Martin Luther King Jr., harrumphed upon learning of the Sputnik launch. As he contended, "Perhaps our country [the U.S.] did not put a man into outer space first because so much of our thought and energy are consumed in holding the colored man down."[84] W. E. B. Du Bois concurred with Reddick's view, charging hotly that the U.S. had engineered a "vast intellectual waste of human ability in the past 60 years by depriving Negroes of equal educational advantages,"[85] making its lag in the space race inevitable. The moderate Negro leader Gordon Hancock upped the ante, noting an awkward dilemma that was a direct result of racism:

[E]ither this country must let the Negro go or succumb to the triumph of Communism. America must make its choice! ...so much time is spent holding the Negro back...Russia threatens to run away with the world.[86]

Congressman Adam Clayton Powell of Harlem also concurred, averring that "America must become a second-class power as long as she tolerates the concept of a second-class citizenship."[87] Another

---

84 Remarks of L. D. Reddick, 22 April 1961, Reel 4, #525, Part III, Subject Files on Black Americans, 1918-1967, Series I, Race Relations, CAB-NCSU.
85 Remarks by W. E. B. DuBois, Reel 64, #188, Part I, Press Releases, CAB-NCSU.
86 Column by Gordon Hancock, October 1957, Reel 63, #1125, Part I, Press Releases, CAB-NCSU.
87 Release, January 1958, Reel 64, #474, Part I, Press Releases, CAB-NCSU.

commentator in the Negro press proclaimed that Sputnik was a "bigger defeat than Pearl Harbor. And that is an understatement."[88] To many, Washington was more interested in the "race race" than the "space race"—and thus bound to be vanquished on both fronts.

* * *

In 1945, W. E. B. Du Bois spoke rhapsodically about crossing the Atlantic by plane:

> It was but yesterday when flying was for birds and angels [but now] what was superman for [Charles] Lindbergh, I did as a passing chore. Nothing is impossible. One of these mornings we will breakfast in New York, lunch on the moon and after dinner shake hands with God.[89]

In more earthbound fashion, Du Bois also noted that the "ease and swiftness" of air travel would also make the upcoming 1945 meeting of the Pan-African Congress "a simple and feasible matter."[90] More than most, Du Bois understood the value of aviation as a tool in promoting his ample goals, notably those of an anti-colonial and anti-Jim Crow variety. In early 1944, to present a series of lectures and attend several conferences, he flew from Atlanta to Texas, then on to Kansas City and Chicago, then back to Atlanta. One can only speculate on what fertile thoughts occurred to that leading intellectual and activist as he mused about peering from on high at the "flaming lights of Birmingham and the red and gold of New Orleans." "During the day we rode above the clouds," Du Bois later wrote, "which looked like a great white snow field below us."[91]

The sentiments of the premier African American intellectual of his day were mirrored by the premier fictional creation in the African

---

88 Release, December 1957, Reel 64, #332, Part I, Press Releases, CAB-NCSU.
89 W. E. B. Du Bois, "The Winds of Time," *Chicago Defender*, November 5, 1945, 7.
90 Ibid.
91 W. E. B. Du Bois to Du Bois Williams, 14 March 1944, W. E. B. DuBois Papers, University of Massachusetts-Amherst, Amherst, Massachusetts.

American canon: Richard Wright's iconic Bigger Thomas. In *Native Son*, Thomas gazes in wonder at the heavens then muses, "God, I would like to fly up there in that sky." That Wright was rooted in Black Chicago, the headquarters of Black aviation, doubtlessly influenced his shaping of the perambulating thoughts of his fictional protagonist. As one perceptive critic observed, Thomas' words signify that he wanted to be free in a wide space and escape his narrow place—a persistent theme of Africans since they first began arriving in North America, and a reality that aviation brought ever closer.[92]

It is reasonable nonetheless to assume that the advent of aviation encouraged activists like Du Bois and writers like Wright to conceive ever bolder dreams. As aviation facilitated others like them to become more productive in pursuing their political objectives, it enabled other activists and thinkers to travel more speedily. Air travel made it easier for them to reach allies, no matter how far away, and plan jointly against mutual foes.

Thus, the rise of aviation should be considered when contemplating how and why Jim Crow and colonialism began to crumble when it did. This connection is the animating idea behind this book, which focuses on the precursors of African peoples' extra-terrestrial contemplations as well as the decades of African-descended peoples' interest and involvement in aviation and aeronautics leading up to the turning point that was the Sputnik launch. It is about Black people from all over the world who demanded the right to fly, the opportunity to soar into the heavens, and the ability to participate in modernity—be it by captaining an airship, building such a vehicle for private or commercial use, or simply occupying a seat on board a plane or rocket.

---

92 Meryem Ayan, "The Cultural Logic of Racism in Richard Wright's *Native Son*," *African Journal of History and Culture*, 3(9) (December 2011), 135-139, 136; Richard Wright, *Native Son* (New York: Harper and Row, 1940.

CHAPTER 1

TAKING OFF

The ability to take to the air was deemed quite useful to the United States—and to U.S. Negroes—as early as the Civil War. Rudimentary flight vessels such as aerial balloons, when used for reconnaissance and intelligence gathering, contributed an ultimately triumphant tactical and strategic advantage for both the Union and Confederate sides.[1] Many African Americans of that era also came to view soaring above the clouds as a highly desirable practice to cultivate.

As the Wright Brothers were moving toward their engagement with destiny at Kitty Hawk, U.S. Negroes (and, to be fair, others around the globe) were moving similarly to invent airplanes of their own.[2] Charles Wesley Peters of Pittsburgh (though born in Virginia) is regarded as the first U.S. Negro to pilot "heavier-than-air" craft, this occurring in 1911.[3] Pittsburgh, along with Chicago and France, were viewed at the time as the cradles of aviation for Black people. Peters had flown a glider as early as 1906, and he is regarded as the first Black designer and builder of an airplane, an event that also occurred in 1911.[4]

---

1 Tom D. Crouch, *The Eagle Aloft: Two Centuries of the Balloon in America* (Washington, DC: Smithsonian Institution Press, 1983).

2 Snider, "Flying to Freedom," 27.

3 George Edward Barbour, "Early Black Flyers of Western Pennsylvania, 1906-1945," *Western Pennsylvania Historical Magazine*, 69(2) (April 1986), 95-119, 97.

4 Samuel Broadnax, *Blue Skies, Black Wings: African American Pioneers of Aviation*,

Bessie Coleman, pictured in the 1920s alongside Tony Fokker, was one of the first African-American aviators.
(Courtesy Chicago History Museum)

The year in which Peters first took to the air (1911), was also the year in which the first documented instance of aerial bombing was recorded. Not coincidentally, this destruction occurred in Africa—Libya, in this case—at the instigation of Italian colonialists. The British, the French, and the Spanish soon followed suit, bombing their respective African colonies.[5] The following year (1912), Harriet Quimby, considered one of the most famous of the U.S.'s women pilots, became one of the earliest victims of what historians regard as an epidemic of plane crashes. That fatal encounter took place in Quincy, Massachusetts.[6]

African Americans took to the skies not only for the adventure of it but also because they sensed that those with possibly malevolent

(Westport, CT: Praeger, 2007), 17.
5 Van Vleck, *Empire of Air*, 139.
6 Courtwright, *Sky as Frontier*, 31.

intentions toward them were acting similarly. By 1908, the Wright Brothers were moving aggressively to sign a contract to deliver planes to the U.S. Army.[7] By 1911, tracts hailing aviation as a boon for reconnaissance and direct attack on the colonized began circulating in Britain, then the world's leading colonial power. As the British Colonel J. E. Capper argued, "every flying machine must be armed with a quick-firing, small-bore gun or rifle, and the aeronaut [pilot] must be trained to use it whilst in rapid flight."[8] His recommendation was adopted rapidly.

By the onset of World War I, an increasing number of African Americans were becoming ever more intrigued by aviation. That growing list included a young Eugene Bullard of Columbus, Georgia, who, in 1895, escaped Jim Crow by stowing away on a merchant ship bound to Europe. Bullard first settled in Paris, where he became a boxer. In 1916, he joined the French air force, and quickly rose to renown as an acclaimed aviator.[9] U.S. military intelligence, however, regarded Bullard as a notorious figure—a Negro who had left the U.S. and joined a foreign fighting force. Prematurely, inaccurately, and perhaps as a matter of wish fulfillment, those intelligence operatives were the first to report Bullard's death as a result of a vicious blow inflicted outside a Paris café by a U.S. officer.[10]

Then there was Chauncey Spencer, a future Tuskegee Airman. It was in Lynchburg, Virginia, in 1917 that Spencer espied a plane overhead. "I was eleven years old," he recalled. "The very next day I began building my own plane."[11] In 1918, in a pasture near Quitman, Texas, Thomas

---

7   Copy of the Wright Brothers' 1908 contract with the U.S. Army, Orville and Wilbur Wright Papers, University of North Carolina–Chapel Hill.

8   Colonel J. Capper, "The Aeroplane in Warfare," in *The Aeroplane*, ed. Claude Grahame–White and Harry Harper (London: Laurie, 1911), 166-196, 168, 169, 183

9   Craig Lloyd, *Eugene Bullard: Black Expatriate in Jazz Age Paris* (Athens: University of Georgia Press, 2000).

10   Memorandum, undated, Reel 25, File 10128-338, 1-4, Record Group 165, Name Index to Correspondence of Military Intelligence Division of the War Department, General Staff, 1917-1941, National Archives and Records Administration, College Park, Maryland.

11   Chauncey Spencer, *Who is Chauncey Spencer?* (Detroit: Broadside, 1975), 12.

Allen—widely viewed as the first Negro aviator to cross the U.S.—got an advanced case of what he termed "airplane fever."[12] Allen's trailblazing flight took place in 1932, but because of employment discrimination he found it difficult to find work as a pilot. He nonetheless spent three decades working as a mechanic with Douglass Aviation.

By 1919, "airplane fever" had infected the U.S. military, as its planes crushed rebels in the then-U.S.-occupied Dominican Republic by dropping bombs on that island from on high.[13] This enhanced use of and the immense publicity associated with airplanes—often armed with bombs and guns designed to suppress Africans and other colonized and subject peoples—helped to propel African Americans' study of aviation. Their lengthening roster included the likes of Bessie Coleman, born in 1893 in Texas. Her father, she often claimed, was three-quarters Native American. Her mother, Susan Coleman, was Negro and, by the pinched U.S. rules of the day, this meant that Bessie Coleman too was defined as Negro. Coleman further explained that her politicization intensified early when she "learned of Harriet Tubman at Mother's knee." She was baptized in the Missionary Baptist Church when she was about 12 years old. Her father later took the liberty of returning his family to "Indian Territory," out west, which facilitated young Bessie's attending Langston College, a historically Black institution in what had become the state of Oklahoma.

Tellingly—and this was the case for a number of the early Negro pilots—Coleman was first taught to fly by a European rather than a Euro-American. In her case, her flight teacher was the head pilot for Fokker, a corporation founded in Germany before relocating to the Netherlands. Also like many of the early Negro pilots, she honed her aviation skills in Chicago. She also trained in France, like Bullard.

---

12 Clipping, no date, Black Americans in Flight Collection, Missouri Historical Society, St. Louis, Missouri.

13 "Comment," *The Dominican Republic Reader: History, Culture, Politics*, ed. Eric Paul Roorda, Lauren Derby, et al. (Durham, NC: Duke University Press, 2014), 243.

Robert Abbott, the affluent publisher of the *Chicago Defender*, the leading organ of the Negro press, backed her financially as she studied the French language: her meager earnings as a manicurist were insufficient to pay for this endeavor. Also, like other Negro pilots, Coleman sought to open her own flying school to spread the proliferating gospel of aviation further.

When Bessie Coleman obtained her international pilot's license, she became one of the first women in the world to fly an airplane and, most likely, the only Negro woman so qualified. She was also a celebrity of sorts and frequently exhibited her daredevil skills in Gary, Indiana, and Houston, Texas. In Austin, Texas, she once was entertained by Governor Miriam "Ma" Ferguson, a social rarity for that Jim Crow bastion.[14]

Bessie Coleman's celebrity, however, was earned by dint of hard work. On February 21, 1922, she departed New York for France, arriving a week later. She stayed in France until late April, when she flew to Holland, staying until late May. Then she was off for three months in Germany, before returning to Amsterdam and then to Manhattan in early August.[15]

As so often happened with women pilots who had entered a field dominated by men, Coleman's physical appearance was a focus of interest. Harlem's *Negro World*, the news organ of Marcus Garvey's growing organization, found her to be a "bright and attractive young lady" with "brilliant conversationalist gifts and charming manners." Despite her being the "only colored aviatrix in the world," the report further noted that she was "very modest and unassuming in manner."[16] Coleman's admiring biographer describes her as "beautiful, articulate and shrewd," with a "slim, shapely figure."

14 "Memoirs of the Late Bessie Coleman, Aviatrix, Pioneer of the Negro People in Aviation," 1969, Technical Files, NASM.
15 Passport of Bessie Coleman in Technical Files, NASM.
16 *Negro World*, August 26, 1922.

Coleman was, like so many of the early Negro pilots, also a very principled person. She once stormed out of a New York City movie studio where she was starring in a film because she considered the script demeaning to Negroes.[17] Fearless and widely recognized, she was extended an invitation from Bolshevik Russia to teach women to fly. That invitation may have been motivated by her telling a Paris reporter that she sought to "cause the Negro to change Uncle Tom's Cabin into a hangar"[18] and by her attendance at the heralded Pan-African Congress in France. The *Negro World*, hailed her as the "Negro Girl Aviator" who was determined to "teach [the] race to fly."[19] Even though that organ encouraged Negro men to "pattern" their piloting after such British woman flyers as Elsie Mackay, it was evident that Coleman was their beacon.[20] Naturally, the U.S. authorities requested that Coleman be investigated after she was spotted in the company of Negro soldiers.[21]

On April 30, 1926, Coleman was enticed by the Elite Circle and Girls De Luxe Club to come to Jacksonville, Florida, for a flying exhibition. The man charged with arranging this intrepid display was John Thomas Betsch, the 21-year-old son of a German brick mason and a Negro woman. A graduate of Howard University and aviation enthusiast, Betsch subsequently became well known as the father of one of today's leading African American intellectuals: Dr. Johnetta Cole, former president of Atlanta's Spelman College.[22]

The event was touted as one in which the locals could witness firsthand the new-fangled invention that was the airplane—and

---

17 Doris Rich, "My Quest for Queen Bess," August-September 1994, *Technical Files*, NASM.
18 Jill D. Snider, "Flying to Freedom," 157.
19 *Negro World*, October 4, 1921.
20 *Negro World*, January 30, 1926.
21 Memorandum, undated, Reel 48, File 10315-362, Record Group 165, M1194, Name Index to Correspondence of Military Intelligence Division of the War Department, General Staff, 1917-1941, National Archives and Records Administration, College Park, Maryland.
22 Doris L. Rich, *Queen Bess: Daredevil Aviator* (Washington, DC: Smithsonian, 1993), 49, 107. See also Lillian M. Fisher, *Brave Bessie: Flying Free* (Dallas: Hendrick-Long, 1995).

flown by a woman at that. "Expect you and your friends to enjoy 'An Aerial Frolic' honoring Miss Bessie Coleman," the event's promoters announced.[23] Accompanied by the music of the Imperial Jazz Orchestra, Coleman was to perform curlicues and other audacious maneuvers. As fate would have it, however, Coleman also exhibited another disturbing trait of early Negro pilots: while flying through the air in a swashbuckling manner before an admiring crowd, she crashed and perished. Tellingly, though she offered no evidence, another Black woman pilot—Marie St. Clair Thompson—argued that because Coleman was "envied" and "hated," her plane had been sabotaged. She claimed that Coleman's control cable "was sawed in half" and "tampered with" by nefarious "white people."[24]

Bessie Coleman's heroic promise did not die with her on that field in Florida. A few years later, the Black Congressman Oscar De Priest of Chicago commended the formation of the Bessie Coleman Aero Clubs, whose female members flew planes over the train that brought him to Los Angeles in 1929.[25] As Marcus Garvey's aviation specialist stated in 1932, "I can truly say that Bessy [sic] Coleman in her short career did more to promote aviation among colored people than all the Negro aviators in the world combined."[26]

Coleman's dauntlessness in the air was a reflection—to a veritable madcap degree—of the distorted perceptions and horrid conditions U.S. Negroes were experiencing on the ground in the early 20th century. In Oklahoma, as a front-page banner headline in the *Negro World* blared in 1921, "Home Guards Set Fire to Buildings While Airplanes

23   Herman "Skip" Mason Jr., *African-American Life in Jacksonville* (Dover, NH: Arcadia, 1997), 51.
24   Interview with Marie St. Clair Thompson, September 9, 1996, Box 3, Betty Gubert Papers, Vivian Harsh Research Collection of Afro-American History and Literature, Carter G. Woodson Regional Library, Chicago Public Library [hereafter denoted as Gubert Papers].
25   Press Release, August 1929, Reel 1, #977, Part I, CAB-NCSU.
26   *Negro World*, 5 March 1932.

Dropped Bombs on Homes in Negro District in Tulsa."[27] Black Tulsa was bombarded from the air in the midst of a racist pogrom in what one analyst has termed "the airplane's first known appearance in a racially motivated attack on American soil."[28] Two weeks before that dastardly incident, another Negro news service announced worriedly that the "U.S. Army Air Force was being taken over by the Ku Klux Klan."[29] When the bigoted regime in South Africa later took to the air to attack its antagonists, Marcus Garvey, the leading Black Nationalist, was said to have bemoaned that disturbing reality. Garvey subsequently proposed that U.S. Negro pilots travel forthwith to the beleaguered continent to build planes for the indigenes.

African Americans of Garvey's day were haunted by the frightening, almost surreal image of what was termed the "vampire plane," a contraption that was used by oppressors to hunt down and slaughter fleeing Negroes.[30] In a front-page editorial published in the *Negro World*, Garvey told of how "Christian Boers of South Africa Use Aeroplanes to Bomb Hottentots." As he surmised, "[I]f Africa is to be redeemed, the western Negro must help with scientific and technical skill" [i.e., aviation] "the Hottentots [who] have no aeroplanes and because of that the Boers and the British can bomb them out of their holes and huts." He further asserted that this outrage was occurring even though "around these American cities and this Western World, we have many Negroes who can fly in aeroplanes." "Why not build some [planes]," the article asked, "and when the Hottentots need aeroplanes to combat aeroplanes, why not give them of our technical ability?" After all, concluded Garvey, "we can build aeroplanes anywhere for that matter, even in South West Africa"—today's Namibia—where his

---

27 *Negro World*, June 18, 1921, 1.
28 Dominick A. Pisano, ed. *The Airplane in American Culture* (Ann Arbor: The University of Michigan Press, 2003), 105.
29 Ibid., 111.
30 Snider, "Flying to Freedom," 88.

United Negro Improvement Association chapters were beginning to flower.[31] Garvey worried that planes would be the final nail in the coffin of the Negro globally. "Italian Aviators Bomb African Arab Village" was yet another detailed story that appeared in the *Negro World* about this unsettling trend. It reported that the people in Benghazi were experiencing, as a result, "warfare more brutal than that of savages considered proper by the civilized powers."[32]

The proximity of North African colonies to European colonizers tended to facilitate the use of planes as a weapon. The *Negro World* thus focused considerable attention on what was then termed the "Rif Rebellion" in what is now Morocco. It detailed the carnage as "French airplanes kill[ed] fifty women and children to one Riffian." Yet, as the leader of the Moroccan rebels, Abd El-Krim, wrote for Garvey's audience: "I am reluctant to resort to airplane reprisal [but] we will retaliate by sending a fleet of airships to [French] cities" unless the French halted their barbarism immediately. "We can do comparatively more damage to them," El-Krim promised, "than they have been doing to us" by assaulting France's "built cities."[33]

Perversely inspiring to Garveyites was the curious example of Euro-American pilots such as Charles Sweeney, who enlisted in the forces of the Moroccan colonizers. "Six other military aviators are going to Morocco to see how many Riffians they can kill," the *Negro World* reported angrily.[34] As El-Krim maintained, "no less than one hundred American aviators" were involved in bombing his forces and people.[35] Weeks later, he announced that all captured mercenaries would be "shot instantly." One among this group, a Charles Kerwood, in a dire signal to his comrades, was able to retreat to Paris after nearly three

---

31 *Negro World*, June 17, 1922, 1.
32 *Negro World*, November 8, 1924, 3.
33 *Negro World*, June 27, 1925.
34 *Negro World*, August 3, 1925.
35 *Negro World*, August 22, 1925.

months of combat in North Africa. He escaped with a mere broken right arm and a four-inch scar running from his left eye to his mouth.[36]

Perhaps the images of the injured Kerwood that appeared in newspapers around the world explain why, a few months later, the *Negro World* reported that the number of U.S. nationals in combat in Morocco had dwindled to just 40. More disturbing, however—and similarly perversely inspiring—was that one of this group was Daniel Cole of Detroit, a Negro and graduate of both the University of Michigan-Ann Arbor and the Massachusetts Institute of Technology. Like Bullard and Coleman, he too had gone to France for training, as an airplane designer in his case. Yet, after vainly seeking to become a martial pilot for France, Cole joined the infamous Foreign Legion, where, in four months he had become a corporal and in nine months a sergeant. His, however, was an unusually speedy ascent coupled with a lethal descent. His plane crashed, and he was buried in Casablanca.[37]

The audience of Garvey's *Negro World* periodical was Pan-African—comprised of readers in the Caribbean and Africa not least [38]—with many then enmeshed in incipient anti-colonial struggles. Although Garvey was encouraging African Americans to enter this fray, in some ways those outside North America were better positioned to take advantage of his counsel as they were battling for sovereignty or struggling to maintain it, as in Ethiopia's case. "When black men conquer distance by ships and airplanes, what then?" the *Negro World* queried its readers. "Black men were the first to sail the seas in ships and are the originators of the aeroplane, or ships with wings," it contended. It further cited the edifying words of the influential U.S. journalist Arthur Brisbane, who posited: "[W]hen you see a Zulu chief flying through the African sunlight on a

---

36 *Negro World*, October 24, 1925.
37 *Negro World*, December 12, 1925.
38 Tony Martin, *Race First: The Ideological and Organizational Struggles of Marcus Garvey and the Universal Negro Improvement Association* (Dover, MA: Majority Press, 1986).

motorcycle, and realize that any average human being can be taught to run a flying machine in eight hours, you wonder how long 'white supremacy' will last."[39]

This staunch approach to white supremacy may explicate Garvey's stance toward Charles Lindbergh, whose 1927 trans-Atlantic journey catapulted him into the global spotlight. The impact of Lindbergh's startling feat could be compared to the landing and settling of humans on Mars in the 21st century. It helped to drive more Negroes into the ionosphere, however; yet another turning point in this elongated process.[40]

One of the world's leading Negro pilots, William Powell, happened to be in Paris when "Lucky Lindy" landed.[41] Envisioning a gigantic industry of Black-owned and constructed airplanes, all operating under Black control, Powell stated that "Negroes must take a lesson from Lindbergh's example of pluck, determination and self-confidence," adding, "Marcus Garvey [is] a man of the Lindbergh type."[42] Garvey's UNIA certainly paid careful attention to aviation, deeming planes a complement to the shipping vessels that were the basis of the organization's Black Star Line. Powell's comments echoed Garvey's view.[43]

Powell's positive description of Garvey also could have applied to Clarence Lorraine of Jersey City, a Negro pilot who in 1927 initiated a flight to Africa—that is, from New York to the Congo.[44] It also could have applied to Mary Daughtry of New York, described in 1931 as "the only colored aviatrix and parachute jumper in the world."[45] That year,

39   *Negro World*, 27 June 1925.
40   Snider, "Flying to Freedom," iii.
41   Von Hardesty, *Black Wings: Courageous Stories of African American Aviation and Space History* (Washington, DC: Smithsonian, 2008), 23.
42   *Negro World*, May 28, 1927.
43   Joseph Corn, *The Winged Gospel: America's Romance with Aviation* (Baltimore: The Johns Hopkins University Press, 2001).
44   *Negro World*, August 27, 1927.
45   *Negro World*, August 8, 1931.

as aviation feats had become a form of entertainment rivaling baseball, vaudeville, and radio, Daughtry jumped from an altitude of over 8,000 feet before an awestruck audience of 25,000.

It is unclear if Dr. A. Porter Davis became interested in aviation because of Lindbergh's 1927 flight, as so many others had. The fact remains that this prosperous Kansas City African American physician first took to the air in that year and, for several years thereafter, not a day passed when Dr. Davis was not airborne. Though Davis was in the unique position of having his own plane, he faced difficulty with regard to taking off and landing since white supremacists in his vicinity refused to allow him to use their airports. Even the city-owned facility barred him from its landing strips. Davis was instrumental in efforts to organize an aviation-manufacturing corporation nevertheless. In 1929, he collaborated with Chicago-based promoter Rupert Simmons to stage an air show in which he (Davis) was the featured flyer. Thousands showed up for the event, one of the first exhibitions of its kind, which then led to the formation of the Chicago Girls Flying Club. The club, comprised of young Black women aviation students and a few licensed pilots, included such stalwarts as Janet Waterford, Willa Brown, Marie St. Clair, and Lola Jones. Most of its members were nurses, stenographers, clerks, waitresses, and maids who spent nearly every available penny of their meager incomes to pay for their flying lessons.[46]

Fitting right into this riveting scenario was Hubert Fauntleroy Julian (1897-1983) of Trinidad and Tobago, another of Garvey's followers, who was to be a fixture on both the U.S. and world aviation scenes for decades to come. In 1923, he leapt from a plane with his pockets filled with circulars about his proposed flight to Africa.[47] That same year, a report noted that thousands of people, gathered in New Jersey

46 Clipping, circa 1935, II: K19, NAACP Papers, Library of Congress, Washington, DC.
47 See Death Certificate of Hubert Julian, 19 February 1983, Box 6, Gubert Papers; Clarence D. Chamberlin, *Record Flights*, (Philadelphia: Dorrance, 1928), 232, 233.

to witness Julian's latest aeronautical performance. Onlookers were thrilled when he jumped from a plane 2,500 feet in the air, descending about 200 feet before opening his parachute.

UNIA member Edison McVey performed a similar stunt at that exhibition. McVey had served with the 95th Air Squadron of the United States Army, where he had been attached to the squad's pursuit group and earned the rank of sergeant first class. The Brooklyn division of the UNIA, to which McVey belonged, had purchased a plane, an action that was becoming increasingly more frequent.[48] Once again signaling the importance of aviation to Garvey, McVey was made the *Negro World*'s regular aviation columnist.[49]

Hubert Julian, the son of an affluent man in his island home, was a colorful figure who sought to build Garvey's Air Service as a complement to the Black Star shipping line. Wily, well-dressed, and pugnacious, the six-foot, two-inch, 200-pound Julian quickly came into conflict with Garvey, as he did with pilot John Robinson in Ethiopia more than a decade later. He also had been charged in court with assaulting a former partner.[50] Julian was nonetheless the exemplar of the Negro who was able to traverse the globe repeatedly as a direct result of aviation. He would turn up Zelig-like in multiple scenarios, from the Finnish-Soviet conflict that took place after the Ethiopian conflict, to meeting with top fascist leaders in Rome, to running guns in Guatemala a decade later, to acting similarly in the Congo, and more before his death in 1983. Though often portrayed as such, Julian was no buffoon. This was an unfortunate mischaracterization that may have been influenced by one of his early parachuting stunts in which he played "I'm Running Wild" on a saxophone during his descent.

---

48 *Negro World*, July 7, 1923.
49 *Negro World*, January 13, 1932.
50 *Topeka Plain Dealer*, August 31, 1923.

Julian claimed to speak fluent French, Italian and Spanish, adding that he could "get by in half a dozen more languages." He also claimed that he neither smoke nor drank and that he had "an obsession with water, which he [drank] incessantly." Once a week, the abstemious pilot averred, he fasted completely. He further claimed credit for a patent for a combination parachute and propeller that allowed a disabled plane to land safely.

Julian recalled that in Trinidad at the age of 12, he watched agape as a plane crashed with the pilot perishing. While crying unashamedly in the aftermath, he became enchanted with aviation. His father later made him promise not to fly to the U.S., then notorious for its depredating Jim Crow laws and for the racial hatred and prejudice which existed there. He promptly disobeyed and even went so far as to become a youthful U.S. citizen, where he became close friends with another man of the Caribbean: Marcus Garvey.

"I regularly supported Marcus and his movement in its aims, and he in turn did much for me," Julian said later. Like many others, he also detected "bitterness, envy and even hatred" between immigrants like himself and the U.S. Negro population, which may have accounted for some of the pushback the UNIA received from this latter group. Nevertheless, when Julian performed a tricky flyover of the group's Liberty Hall in Harlem, he "could see every face craned up to watch" and could not perceive any distinction in birthplace, only beaming pride. Although he was able to wrangle a meeting with the NAACP's leader, James Weldon Johnson, that organization, which was dominated by U.S. Negroes, refused to support Julian's various ventures. Conversely, when Julian met with UNIA delegates at an important gathering of the group, Garvey himself rose to hail him as a distinguished "fighter for our race."

Julian encountered both advantages and disadvantages as a derivative of his birthplace. "Another thing which always stood me in good stead," he confessed, was his British accent. This, he indicated, allowed him to escape the obloquy routinely heaped upon descendants of mainland-enslaved Africans. Yet, like U.S. Negroes, he too found that hiring planes was "twice as difficult...as it was for a white aviator," requiring a "bigger deposit and bigger fees"[51] Undaunted and unafraid of confrontation, Julian persisted. Despite his later conflicts with Garvey—he was virtually excommunicated from the UNIA in the 1920s—he likewise did not fear reconciliation, returning to address the group in 1932.[52]

Julian often skirted the boundaries of ethics and the law. For example, in 1920 it was alleged that he sold some automobiles illegally in Grenada before escaping with the proceeds to New Brunswick, Canada.[53] More questions surround the controversial Julian's reputation, including those raised about his possible collaboration with the Italian invaders in Ethiopia in the 1930s. He also was reported to have collaborated with the so-called "Black Hitler" of that day—Sufi Abdul Hamid—in taking his aviation talents to East Africa. Additionally, Julian attracted the skeptical attention of the U.S. Federal Bureau of Investigation, which claimed he was not a pilot but a "parachute jumper." The FBI scrutinized his efforts to finance a proposed flight across the Atlantic in 1924. The object of the trip, Julian claimed, was to "stimulate interest [in aviation] among Negroes...] [which] would result in a colored aeronautical school where the science of aviation could be studied," thus facilitating Negroes' entrance into "various branches" of aviation. It was also on the Fourth of July in 1924 that Julian was rescued from Flushing Bay in New York after an ill-fated parachute jump that had begun inauspiciously in Harlem.[54]

---

51   Colonel Hubert Julian, *Black Eagle, as told to John Bulloch* (London: Jarrolds, 1964), 10, 12, 23, 23, 43, 44, 45.

52   *Negro World*, January 2, 1932.

53   Memorandum, 20 July 1920, Record Group 59, Decimal File, Box 348, PI 157, E200 HM 1991, 150.44c6/8, Records of U.S. State Department, National Archives and Records Administration, College Park, Maryland [hereafter denoted as NARA-CP].

54   Memorandum, 15 November 1940, Reel 17, #915, J. Edgar Hoover Official and

Despite his murky past and though derided as the clown prince of aviation, Hubert Julian was also an inspiring figure for many. This included the heralded Tuskegee Airman, Louis Purnell, who completed an astonishing 1,578 combat missions during World War II that included being shot down and taken prisoner.[55] Purnell admiringly claimed that Julian was early on his "chief inspiration." He spoke glowingly of the confident master pilot as a "dashing figure" who once visited his church in Wilmington, Delaware, "to deliver a speech about aviation and collect funds toward the purchase of an airplane for a solo nonstop flight from New York City to Rome." Julian, he claimed, later invited the parishioners to an airshow, whereupon he promised to repeat his signature parachuting stunt of playing the saxophone while descending.[56] Thus, in his various forms of inventiveness, Hubert Julian was not terribly unique among Africans in the Diaspora—fully embodying their ability to adapt to new inventions, even those that portend potentially catastrophic consequences while seeking to adapt to modernity and thereby refute the naysayers who believe this to be beyond their competencies.

* * *

In 1925, William Hale, an African American from West Virginia, obtained a patent on an airborne vehicle that could hover in the air, then ascend and descend, not unlike a helicopter.[57] A few years later, a Detroit Negro named Timothy Glenn was praised by the *Negro World* for actually building planes.[58] In 1931, the U.S. Negro journalist and NAACP activist William Pickens found himself in Los Angeles, where

---

Confidential File, Library of Congress, Washington, DC.

55   Bart Barnes, "Curator and Tuskegee Airman Louis Purnell Dies," *Washington Post*, August 16, 2001.

56   Louis Purnell, "The Flight of the Bumblebee," October 1989, Technical Files, NASM.

57   Clipping, no date, Reel 7, #467,Part III, Subject Files on Black Americans, 1918-1967, Series A, Agriculture, CAB-NCSU.

58   *Negro World*, September 26, 1931.

he encountered J. H. Montgomery. This Negro inventor, wrote Pickens, "sent a dead vulture flying head-on into an electrically produced thirty-five mile gale," thereby demonstrating a "new principle in aviation"—namely, that "the same principle by which birds soar could be applied to a new type of airship."[59]

Invention—and flying—are often preceded by trial and error before the perfection of various safety mechanisms. This reality, combined with the ugly reality that Negroes' planes were generally the most primitive, led to justifiable complaints by African Americans about the peril of aviation.[60] As Pickens complained in 1929 referring to the all-too-frequent air crashes of his day, such as the one that claimed the life of Bessie Coleman, Blacks were "falling out of the sky too fast." "There is a difference between courage and foolhardiness," he advised. Adding that being Black in the U.S. was itself, to a degree, life threatening, he also noted that it was easy to ignore his wise counsel.[61]

Other Negroes suspected that there may have been factors beyond mechanical misfires or even simple error that contributed to the rash of crashes experienced by Black aviators. The case of "Ace" Foreman, a Negro aviator who died by drowning, is a curious one. A son of Texas, Foreman worked in an airplane factory in New York—a prized post—and there learned the rudiments of mechanics and plane building. With that foundation, Foreman decided to take to flight, yet later crashed and died. A Negro reporter raised a note of suspicion about possible sabotage of Foreman's attempt, observing that "the fact that he was a good swimmer introduced an element of mystery into his death."[62]

---

59 Press Release, November 1931, Reel 4, #1035, Part I, Press Releases, CAB-NCSU.
60 See, e.g. Letter from Edna Sheldon, no date, circa 1922, Box 100, John Toland Papers, Library of Congress. It states that the "Roma Disaster" in "Feb[ruary] of 1922," involved the crash of an airship; "it was our first lighter than air ship major disaster," occurring in Norfolk; "it was a horrible scene, the bodies with arms raised fending off the flames..."
61 Press Release, November 1929, Reel 2, #21, Part I, Press Releases, CAB-NCSU.
62 Press Release, August 1929, Reel 1, #977, Part I, Press Releases, CAB-NCSU.

Just before the Foreman tragedy, the announcement that "No Negro Aviator in America holds [a] Commercial Pilot's License" was broadcast throughout the land.[63] This was, to be sure, a reflection of the bigotry of that era, which meant that Blacks not only had the flimsiest aircraft and the least flight training but also were barred from landing strips and airplane hangars, It also was a clarion call to U.S. Negroes to continue their steep ascent toward flight competency, as evidenced by the large crowds that gathered to watch Bessie Coleman as she made her final flight.

Further complicating this scenario, and contributing to the danger surrounding it, is the fact that aviation was seen early on as entertainment and a frolic. A case in point is the notoriety of the U.S. Negro daredevil known as Willie "Suicide" Jones. Jones once fell 28,000 feet—intentionally—after jumping from an airplane before pulling the cord of his parachute and floating to safety. At one point, Jones held the dubious record for a delayed parachute leap.[64] Arguably, the Negro fascination with aviation combined with their often parlous financial plight to drive them into such perilous ventures. Even without the potential of sabotage or other dangers, piloting back then was inherently dangerous. John Robinson who soared to prominence as a pilot in Ethiopia, made his initial flight in 1930, but he too had to be lifted out of that plane by his comrades after it returned to the ground. As a mirror image of a latter-day Icarus, he had flown too high and his arms and legs had virtually frozen in the cold elevations; he had to endure medical intervention to survive. Like too many Negroes, he did not have sufficient income to support his ambition and consequently built a plane from spare automobile parts—the invention that almost killed him.[65]

63 Press Release, circa 1928, Reel 1, #59, Part I, Press Releases, CAB-NCSU.
64 "Willie 'Suicide' Jones Breaks Air Leap Record," *Chicago Defender*, September 11, 1948, 1.
65 Press Release, January 1930, Reel 2, #383, Part I, Press Releases, CAB-NCSU.

What Beryl Markham experienced flying in colonial Kenya in the 1930s was akin to what Negroes like Colonel John Robinson endured. In the frail, unsteady machines flown by these pilots, often buffeted by fierce gales, Markham claimed that "there was no radio, nor any system...designed to check planes in and out of their points of contact." This, she wrote, "made it essential for a pilot either to develop his [sic] intuitive sense to the highest degree or to adopt a fatalistic philosophy toward life. Most of the men I knew in Africa managed to do both."[66] Similar words could have been said about their African American counterparts.

Colonel Robinson's travails were indicative of the obstacles faced by Negro pilots. According to one report, Robinson had been "repairing bootleggers' cars in Chicago" in the 1920s, "but the heat was on him, so he had to go to Detroit."[67] This was hardly a step upward, wrote his aviation partner Cornelius Coffey: "Back then if a black man wanted to fly a plane, he had to buy it first."[68] This was no easy feat. Hence, Robinson's ingenuity turned to constructing one from spare auto parts. With a similar dose of creativity, Coffey became one of two black licensed aircraft mechanics in the U.S. (along with John Greene) by 1932. By the time he died in 1994, Coffey too had joined Robinson in the pantheon, given that his school of aeronautics trained more than a thousand Negro pilots to fly between 1938 and 1945. Some of his trainees became anti-fascist fighters of the highest order, despite their dearth of income.[69]

When the future pilot, Chauncey Spencer, arrived in Chicago in the early 1930s to visit Robinson's newly founded flying school, he was decidedly unimpressed. As Spencer recalled later, however:

66 Beryl Markham, *West with the Night* (San Francisco: North Point Press, 1983 [originally published 1942]), 187.
67 John Robinson to P. L. Prattis, 6 February 1930, Reel 11, #203, Part III, Subject Files on Black Americans, 1918-1967, CAB-NCSU; Clipping, circa 1935, II: K19, NAACP Papers.
68 Henry Allen, "To Fly, to Brave the Wind," *Washington Post*, September 26, 1979, B1.
69 "Cornelius Coffey, Aviator," *Washington Post*, March 6, 1994, B5.

> I sensed something was wrong when I walked into the garage. There were two car engines, an aircraft propeller but nothing that resembled an aircraft school. Colonel Robinson [the honorific he carried as a result of his service with the Ethiopian military] seemed [too] eager for my nine hundred dollars that my father had given me to study, but, leery of the school, I left.

Spencer was aware that "the Negro flyers…were all supporting themselves with other kinds of jobs" and suspected that Robinson was in that downscale category.[70]

Nevertheless, Robinson was upbeat in the early 1930s, lauding the "opportunities for young colored men in aviation," which he believed were bound to increase. He had just completed a 12-month course in aviation mechanics and had even constructed a plane in his garage. He had also approached Curtiss–Wright Aeronautical University seven times—before being admitted in the early 1930s.[71] Robinson lived to fly several other days—to Addis Ababa, in his case—neatly illustrating why aviation was so attractive to so many Negroes. It was a field that allowed one to fly past the quotidian racial chauvinism that afflicted African Americans.

Shortly after Robinson's brush with death, Jack Teat of Los Angeles was thousands of miles away toiling as an aviator for the Brazilian Mining Company. After Teat was delayed in Buenos Aires after what was called the Brazilian Revolution, a reporter for the U.S. Negro press noted approvingly that this "young colored aviator is the first pilot of his race to complete a regular course in aeronautics" in Brazil and, as was becoming common, he was willing to fight in a foreign air service "if called upon."[72]

Many U.S. Negroes were able to take advantage of this incipient globalization. Coleman and Bullard both learned how to fly, or had

---

70 Chauncey E. Spencer, *Who is Chauncey Spencer?* (Detroit: Broadside, 1975), 28.
71 Press Release, November 1931, Reel 4, #1075, Part I, Press Releases, CAB-NCSU.
72 Press Release, October 1930, Reel 3, #398, Part I, Press Releases, CAB-NCSU.

their skills honed, abroad. Others gained knowledge of aviation from recent immigrants to the U.S. C. Alfred "Chief" Anderson, born in 1908, was taught to fly by a German pilot who migrated to the U.S. after World War I.[73] Ernest Buehl persuaded a reluctant government certifying pilot to fly with Anderson when the latter was trying to get his commercial license. Anderson passed, and in 1932 became the first Black pilot to hold an air transport license.[74] Anderson later credited Buehl with refining his piloting technique and with twisting the arm of the federal examiner on his behalf. Speaking in thickly accented English, Buehl recalled that the official "took me aside and he called me everything under the sun because I would even attempt to get that man into an airplane." "I finally tell him," Buell said, "'Look, I'm a foreigner. I'm a citizen by the paper. That guy's born here.'" Buehl also sold a useful plane to one of Anderson's comrades, which marked a step forward in the story of Black aviators.[75] Buehl apparently did not realize his actions were part of the reason why attempts were made to "blackball" him in his field.[76]

Thanks to him, however, Anderson was able to join Dr. Alfred Forsythe on a major aviation journey. Of a polyglot background—African, Scottish, and South Asian—Forsythe also had roots in the Bahamas and Jamaica. He had attended Tuskegee Institute and the University of Toledo. By 1923, he was in medical school at McGill University in Quebec and, like Hubert Julian, was attracted to Garvey. (His brother, Roger, was an interpreter for General Smedley Butler's U.S. occupation forces in Haiti).[77]

It was July 17, 1933, at 3:00 AM, when a small blue-and-gold monoplane carrying Forsythe and Anderson soared into foggy darkness

---

73 *Washington Star*, January 11, 1980.
74 David Stout, "Charles Anderson Dies at 89," *New York Times*, April 17, 1996, B7.
75 Interview with C. A. Anderson, 4 April 1976, Technical Files, NASM.
76 Clipping, no date, Technical Files, NASM.
77 Roger A. Forsyth, *Black Flight: Breaking Barriers to Blacks in Aviation* (Los Angeles: All Court, 2001), 9. 10, 64, 105, 147, 241, 283.

at the airport in Atlantic City, New Jersey. The plane headed westward on what was to become a coast-to-coast journey that both epitomized and captured the proliferating Negro interest in aviation. Twelve days later, the two aviators returned to New Jersey. Suggestive of the impact and import of what they had accomplished, whereas a scant two hundred people had watched their departure, a massive two thousand hailed their return. When they soared over the Hollywood Bowl, not only were they saluted by thousands more, but radio broadcasts saluted their feat before an even larger audience.

The two intrepid pilots flew without parachutes and over country wholly unknown to them in a plane so small that refueling stops were necessary every two or three hundred miles. This was an organized voyage, sponsored by the National Negro Aeronautical Society, which earlier had supported the same two pilots in a flight from Philadelphia to Montreal. The Society's purpose was to improve the Negro's image, which its members believed had been defamed on stage and screen to their global detriment. It further proposed and supported flights across the world, with a journey to the Caribbean, soon to follow, seen as only the beginning. Behind its efforts was a powerhouse of political support, including that of Congressman Oscar De Priest, Eugene K. Jones of the National Urban League, and, suggestive of the group's panoramic vision, Gabriel Dennis, a leading official who served in numerous positions in Liberia.[78] The subsequent flight to twenty-five nations in the Caribbean and South America was a landmark in the history of Negroes in aviation.[79]

As evidenced once again, aviation allowed Negroes to evade certain Jim Crow barriers in that Anderson's secondary intention in that trans-Caribbean nation flight was to import coffee to be sold in the

---

78 Mary J. Washington, "A Race Soars Upward," *Opportunity*, 10 (October 1934)), 300-301, National Urban League Papers, Library of Congress.

79 "Note," *The Crisis*, 41(12), (December 1934), 353.

U.S. by Black merchants.[80] His flight, perhaps more than the Lindbergh venture, demonstrated the potential of aviation to many U.S. Negroes, and led to an increase in the number of Blacks who sought to learn how to fly.

As Anderson and Forsythe flew their monoplane—informatively named in honor of the icon of self-help that was Booker T. Washington— into Haiti after landing in Jamaica, they were greeted warmly at the presidential palace by President Stenio Vincent himself and all the members of his cabinet. *En route*, they were entertained similarly and elaborately in Nassau, Havana, and Kingston. In the Bahamas, the largest crowd in the history of the island assembled to meet "the men who could fly." In Cuba, the powerful military man, and eventual dictator, Fulgencio Batista, greeted them.[81]

Though heralded like conquering potentates as they landed, the greeting the two pilots received in Haiti may have been the most enthusiastic of all. In honor of their warm greeting, they circled the presidential palace 21 times, in an aerial version of the multi-gun salute accorded dignitaries.[82] Haiti, straining against the effects of a lengthy U.S. occupation, thus became a site for Pan-African solidarity via the air. This epic flight, coming in the wake of Thomas Allen's 1932 trans-continental flight across the U.S. itself, signaled that a new era in mobility had arrived among Negroes. This perception was buoyed when another Negro pilot announced soon after that he planned to fly around the world.[83] Undaunted, Forsythe and Anderson kept heading

---

80 Martia Graham Goodson, ed., *Chronicles of Faith: The Autobiography of Frederick D. Patterson* (Tuscaloosa: University of Alabama Press, 1991), 73.

81 Press Release, 19 November 1934, Reel 1, #657, Part III, Subject Files on Black Americans, Series A, CAB-NCSU. See also *Nassau Daily Tribune*, November 10, 1934.

82 Press Release, November 1934, Reel 9, #965, Part I, Press Releases, CAB-NCSU.

83 Press Release, 8 August 1949, Reel 1, #664, Part III, Subject Files on Black Americans, Series A, CAB-NCSU. See also, Press Release, October 1934, Reel 9, #712, Part I, Press Releases, CAB-NCSU: "...the first Pan-American Inter-Racial Goodwill Fight....Tuskegee Institute one of the most enthusiastic sponsors of the goodwill flight," i.e. the "'projected flight to twenty-five Latin American and West Indian countries..."

southward, traveling as far as the northern coast of South America.[84] Their 12,000 mile journey was one of a number of critical turning points in the history of Black aviation.[85]

* * *

Beyond the bigotry and poverty of the era, still other factors bedeviled aspiring Negro pilots in the U.S. In the early 1930s, the NAACP's William Pickens made note of what he called "the usual American Negro complex," which, he contended, "makes them more afraid of a black air pilot than of a white one." As he continued dishearteningly, "White people," on the other hand, "will risk it with a black man quicker than the blacks will." To display his own rebuke of this complex, Pickens noted, he chose to fly from Los Angeles to Mexico with Hubert Julian at the controls. Pickens concluded happily that the Trinidad-born pilot, who had joined the Canadian Air Force in 1917, was not the "clown prince of aviation" but a talented aviator. "[No eagle was ever more at home in the air than is Hubert Julian," he wrote. He was quick to point out, however, that unlike the national bird, Julian's winged device "cost as much as $18, 000." For that reason, he surmised, "Julian is more careful than the average white pilot," thus reassuring him further. He added that "if a Negro aviator would kill anybody, it would get even extra space and sensational notice—especially in the Negro papers."[86]

Despite the burst of enthusiasm for aviation in certain Negro circles by the 1930s, Pickens noted that it was nonetheless still unusual for Negroes to take to the air. "It is so unusual for colored people to fly," claimed the quizzical leader after taking a flight from San Francisco to Los Angeles with stops in Oakland, Fresno, and Bakersfield, "that when the committee came out to meet me in Bakersfield ….they say that the Air Port people did not want to let them into the field." Simple

---

84   Press Release, November 1934, Reel 9, #965, Part I, Press Releases, CAB-NCSU.
85   Corn, *Winged Gospel*, 36.
86   Press Release, April 1932, Reel 5, #685, Part I, Press Releases, CAB-NCSU.

bigotry, rather than the unusualness of airborne Negroes, may also have been at play in that instance, Pickens noted. Still, he observed that upon returning to Texas, "I mean to fly from El Paso to San Antonio to avoid day and night in Jim Crow"—that is, he wrote, "if they will let me fly in Texas."[87]

Pickens was only one of what was fast becoming a solid corps of Negro "aviation evangelists," who chanted praise song after praise song about air travel. These enthusiasts exulted that humans finally were conquering the barrier of being earthbound. They also commended the new vistas that were opened for African Americans as a result. John Robinson, soon to distinguish himself in East Africa, was foremost among them as he hastened to underscore the opportunities that he believed were only going to increase.[88]

As with any gold rush, however, scams flowered. Such was the accusation leveled at the pioneering Black aviator William Powell, when he came to Los Angeles from Chicago purportedly to open a branch of the increasingly popular Bessie Coleman Aero Club. Powell was accused of painting "gaudy pictures of sudden wealth to investors and sudden fame to young men and women aviators" but delivered "nothing but empty hopes" and "some empty pocketbooks."[89] Still, the alleged peculations of a few could not obfuscate the wider horizons opened by the birth of aviation. By the time U.S. Negroes like Colonel Robinson found it necessary to travel to Ethiopia to fight fascism, it was evident that a new stage in the struggle against colonialism and Jim Crow had been reached—and this time, that struggle would be in the air.

---

87   Press Release, April 1932, Reel 5, #602, Part I, Press Releases, CAB-NCSU.
88   Phillip Thomas Tucker, *Father of the Tuskegee Airmen, John C. Robinson* (Washington, DC: Potomac, 2012), 2
89   Press Release, October 1930, Reel 3, #397, Part I, Press Releases, CAB-NCSU.

Cornelius Coffey, This Chicagoan, pictured in the 1930s, helped to train many of the first African-American pilots.
(Courtesy Chicago History Museum)

CHAPTER 2

FROM ETHIOPIA TO TUSKEGEE

Despite African Americans' pulsating interest in aviation, reportedly none held a commercial aviation license as of 1928.[1] Of course, gaining official credentials, which implicates a ruling by an official body, should be distinguished from actually possessing the skill involved (just as a beautician can be talented without holding a license). Yet, the lack of licensing surely hampered the ability of African Americans to soar heavenward.

For example, budding Negro pilots were barred routinely from airports across the nation and, after formal bars were lifted, many encountered difficulties gaining access to planes and air travel.[2] The advantage of aviation, however, was that it was a field eminently suitable for pursuit overseas. This tendency merged with another trending phenomenon in the 1930s—the drift toward war or, more specifically, the Italian invasion of Ethiopia, followed by the Spanish Civil War—all of which created both opportunity and impetus for U.S. Negro pilots to take their skills abroad and thereby circumvent the Jim Crow barriers strewn in their paths at home.

Thus it was that James Lincoln Holt Peck, born in about 1913, crossed the Pyrenees mountain range while making a 14-hour march

---

1 Press Release, circa 1928, Reel 1, #59, Part I, Press Releases, CAB-NCSU.
2 Press Release, March 1933, Reel 7, #113, Part I, Press Releases, CAB-NCSU.

to Valencia, Spain, in 1937. There, he flew planes and fought alongside the Spanish republicans for four months, bombing Majorca once in his more than 40 convoy missions. By December 1937, the five-foot, eight-inch, 167-pound pilot was back in the U.S. gaining experience that not only was difficult for persons of his ancestry to obtain in their land of birth but that became harder to utilize even after the U.S. entered the war against the fascists he had been fighting.[3] One researcher has dubbed Peck "the first American since World War I to shoot down a German plane in aerial combat," noting that he "had become an ace in Spanish skies with the destruction before his guns of two German and three Italian warplanes." Peck, that writer claims, was unimpressed with the U.S.'s "Chato biplanes" and secretly hoped that U.S. pilots would "someday have opportunity to fly the newer, faster Russian monoplanes." He later joined others of the time in leaning toward Moscow politically.[4]

"For the first time I [received] a clear picture of just what happens when a bullet meets man," said Peck of his combat experience, "I want[ed] to fly away home." Nonetheless, his performance was sufficiently sterling for a Chinese envoy to try to recruit him to fight Tokyo's forces in Asia.[5]

The Negro's interest in aviation was both prescient and timely. As early as 1920, many in the U.S. had acknowledged that the "next war will be fought in the air." Despite this realization, the human capital represented by U.S. Negro pilots such as Peck often was shunted aside as conflicts erupted, forcing Black aviators to take their fascism-fighting talents overseas.[6] Just as the thought had occurred to the adversaries of U.S. Negroes that airplanes could be used effectively

---

3   "Current Biography," 1942, Box 7, Gubert Papers.
4   Martin Caidin, *The Ragged, Rugged Warriors* (New York: Dutton, 1966), 28.
5   James L. H. Peck, *Armies with Wings* (New York: Dodd, Mead, 1940), 89, 95, 97.
6   *Baltimore American*, January 30, 1920, Box 28, William Mitchell Papers, Library of Congress.

to subjugate them and other oppressed people further, it also dawned on African Americans that aviation could be an effective weapon on their behalf. Practically speaking, that weapon was more likely to be used abroad against colonial and fascist invaders (or by colonial and fascist invaders), but imaginative Negro writers did not rule out the combative use of airplanes at home.

George Schuyler, otherwise known as the godfather of Negro conservatism, was one who wrote along those lines. In his affecting 1930s novel, *Black Empire*, Schuyler depicted airplane hangars and aviation workshops and described "two big machine shops, [in which] more than a score of young colored men and women were…engaged in the making and repairing of aircraft." In that fictional rendering, U.S. Negroes had "trained five hundred colored pilots, men and women, and manufactured one hundred pursuant planes and fifty bombing planes" named after heroines like Sojourner Truth and Bessie Coleman. The book's hero, Carl Slater, is enamored with a Negro woman named Patricia Givens, described as a "beauty who superintended an aircraft industry, piloted planes across the country and talked of conditioning the masses, world revolution and such."[7]

Schuyler had an active imagination but, in penning *Black Empire*, he was indeed drawing upon the ever-escalating events and sentiments swirling about in the air around him. The same could be said for the Pan-Africanist pioneer, Duse Mohamed Ali, whose novel during the same era portrayed U.S. Negro aviators defending their country against a joint Russian-Japanese attack.[8]

When Harlem's Sufi Abdul Hamid, derided as the "Black Hitler" of the 1930s, was killed in a plane crash while taking flying lessons,

---

7   George S. Schuyler, *Black Empire*, Boston: Northeastern University Press, 1991 [originally published in the 1930s], 43, 45, 70, 86, 103.

8   Alex Lubin, *Geographies of Liberation: The Making of an Afro-Arab Political Imaginary* (Chapel Hill: University of North Carolina Press, 2014), 61.

the direction of the winds of change became further evident.[9] When A. W. Sinclair, speaking from New Orleans, stressed the importance of "developing an air-mindedness within the ranks [of] Negro youth,"[10] he was knocking on an open door. When the religious grouping that came to be known as the Nation of Islam was organized during this period, it is no wonder that the "mother plane" was at the center of their theology and cosmology.[11]

* * *

Nonetheless, it was Ethiopia—not Spain—that captured the imagination of African Americans in the war against fascism. The U.S. Negro Daniel Alexander was a missionary from Chicago who arrived in East Africa about 1905. He married an Abyssinian woman and lived there for decades with their son. While there, he reported on how airplanes had reduced the time it took government officials to reach far-flung provinces from thirty to forty days to a few hours. As the impending invasion of Italian forces crept closer, Alexander—along with many in Addis Ababa—worried about the loyalties of the Ethiopians' European pilots and wondered if that nation would be better served by African American flyers.[12]

Alexander was not alone in expatriation. Augustinian Bastian of the U.S. Virgin Islands and Harlem also resided in Ethiopia in the 1930s. Bastian was a Garveyite who had traveled to the Horn of Africa in a delegation led by Rabbi Arnold Ford, a leader of Harlem's "Black Jews." There, he encountered others from his Caribbean homeland.[13]

---

9 Press Release, August 1938, Reel 17, #452, Part I, Press Releases, CAB-NCSU. See also Press Release, June 1935, Reel 10, #1006, Part I, Press Releases, CAB-NCSU: Hamid, who was thought to be "Egyptian" or "Sudanese," was actually born in Philadelphia—though some said Georgia was his birthplace.

10 Press Release, September 1938, Reel 17, #758, Part I, Press Releases, CAB-NCSU.

11 Claude Clegg, *An Original Man: The Life and Times of Elijah Muhammad* (New York: St. Martin's Press, 1997).

12 Press Release, November 1930, Reel 3, #475, Part I, Press Releases, CAB-NCSU.

13 Press Release, January 1936, Reel 11, #1124, Part I, Press Releases, CAB-NCSU.

Claude Barnett's Associated Negro Press (ANP) took the initiative to concretize Alexander's sentiments. He received encouragement from the likes of C. A. Scott of the *Atlanta Daily World*, who suggested that it "would be a fine thing" if the ANP sent a correspondent to Ethiopia. Scott insisted further that periodicals like his "would be willing to pay" for reports from that part of the world. So moved, Barnett responded that "Ethiopia, as represented in the Emperor [Haile Selassie I], will welcome well-trained Americans." "The Emperor," he claimed, "is aware of the undeveloped resources of his country" and "he prefer[s] that his development should be made by blood brothers. But they can do nothing about putting the whites out until they have blacks who can do the job."[14]

Echoing Selassie's awareness that a "qualified man must know more than a trade" and "must also be prepared to sacrifice, to work hard and to go to that country without stirring up ill feelings among the whites there," the ANP's Barnett advocated strongly for the Ethiopian initiative.[15] "I was personally responsible" for that far-reaching venture, he claimed with accuracy.[16] He further asserted that "our [the ANP's] man," U.S. Negro pilot John Robinson "has a job with the Ethiopian government which we helped him obtain."[17]

Barnett was not exaggerating. Typical of the wider Negro press, an operative of the Harlem-based *New York Amsterdam News* confessed that his publication could not afford the "Ethiopian proposition" on its own since it was "broke," "insolvent," and, adding for emphasis, "there is no money."[18] What he did not intend was for ANP's effort

---

14   C. A. Scott to Claude Barnett, 26 August 1935, Reel 14, #543, Part II, Organizational Files, CAB-NCSU.

15   Press Release, July 1935, Reel 6, #935, Part 3, Subject Files on Black Americans, CAB-NCSU.

16   Claude Barnett to P. L. Prattis, 23 November 1935, Reel 7, #211, Part II, Organizational Files, CAB-NCSU.

17   Claude Barnett to Carl Murphy, 18 July 1935, Reel 17, #78, Part II, Organizational Files, CAB-NCSU.

18   P. L. Prattis to Claude Barnett, 3 December 1936, Box 170, Folder 9, CAB-CHM.

to be a solo one. "If two or three papers agreed to pay for from two to three hundred words once or twice a week from Addis," he wrote, promising "truthful coverage,"[19] they could all publish Robinson's dispatches—and support his role in air combat too (though the latter went unmentioned). By then, the Ethiopian issue had struck a chord of intense popularity with African Americans and the organized left in the U.S. The Communist Party news organ had sent its own correspondent to the Ethiopian war zone and, according to Barnett, was asking "$500 from colored newspapers" to receive its dispatches.[20]

Barnett, however, had his thumb on the pulse of his community and thus was able to launch successfully his own venture, thereby circumventing the Communists. By summer 1935, mass public meetings, at which expressions of solidarity with Ethiopia proliferated, were rocking Harlem and Black Chicago. "Large numbers of colored Americans eagerly seek an opportunity to do their bit to help Ethiopia," was one observer's conclusion.[21]

By 1935, Harlem was seething with anger about Benito Mussolini's adventurism and invasion of Ethiopia. In August, more than a thousand Harlem clergy pledged to engage in a Sunday of prayer against the war.[22] Tens of thousands marched through Harlem's streets, forming a phalanx that included in its frontline both Communist leaders and Father Divine, a wildly popular cleric. "Harlem hasn't seen so impressive a parade [sic] in many years," wrote one awed reporter.[23] (Not to be undone, Father Divine's peer and competitor, Daddy Grace, later called upon his reported 200,000 followers to pray for Emperor

19 Associated Negro Press to Carl Murphy, 2 November 1935, Reel 17, #99, Part II, Organizational Files, CAB-NCSU.
20 Claude Barnett to Carl Murphy, 18 July 1935, Reel 17, #78, Part II, Organizational Files, CAB-NCSU.
21 Press Release, July 1935, Reel 10, #1089, Part I, Press Releases, CAB-NCSU.
22 Press Release, August 1935, Reel 11, #43, Part I, Press Releases, CAB-NCSU.
23 Press Release, August 1935, Reel 11, #67, Part I, Press Releases, CAB-NCSU.

Selassie.[24]) The NAACP's William Pickens reported seeing "at least five miles" of marchers. Pickens added ominously that the march was "the raw stuff out of which revolutions are made."[25] Others observed that the biggest-selling and most in-demand item in Harlem was the "tri-color [flag] of Ethiopia."[26]

Another factor that propelled this mass protest was the reaction of New York's Italian Americans, many of whom donated ambulances to Rome's forces and offered to volunteer in its armed forces.[27] By December 1935, the Italian American community had raised $100,000 for the invading Italian forces.[28] John Robinson's Chicago church upped the ante by sending an entire field hospital to the warfront in East Africa.[29] The newly minted "Chicago Society for the Aid of Ethiopia," planned to send 10,000 cablegrams to the League of Nations in protest of Italy's aggression.[30] By July 1935, two large mass meetings had taken place in Black Chicago, with a sizeable number of African Americans indicating a willingness to sacrifice to aid Ethiopia. About 3,500 Blacks jammed into the Roseland Ballroom at 47th Street and South Parkway. A comparable crowd amassed subsequently, erupting into loud cheering, hand clapping, and the like when asked to show their support for assisting Addis Ababa.[31]

The fervor of Black Chicago and Harlem was matched elsewhere in the nation. Reportedly, more than 50 North Carolinians enlisted in the Ethiopian armed forces; strikingly, most of those recruits were former members of the U.S. military.[32] Addis Ababa's consul in Manhattan traveled south to thank the Negroes of Winston-Salem,

24   Press Release, May 1936, Reel 12, #1043, Part I, Press Releases, CAB-NCSU.
25   Press Release, August 1935, Reel 11, #126, Part I, Press Releases, CAB-NCSU.
26   Press Release, August 1935, Reel 11, #118, Part I, Press Releases, CAB-NCSU
27   Press Release, December 1935, Reel 11, #993, Part I, Press Releases, CAB-NCSU.
28   Press Release, December 1935, Reel 11, #1034, Part I, Press Releases, CAB-NCSU.
29   Tucker, *Father of the Tuskegee Airmen*, 168.
30   Press Release, June 1936, Reel 13, #193, Part I, Press Releases, CAB-NCSU.
31   Press Release, July 1935, Reel 10, #1089, Part I, Press Releases, CAB-NCSU.
32   Press Release, August 1935, Reel 11, #143, Part I, Press Releases, CAB-NCSU.

North Carolina, for raising funds for his nation.[33] The famed contralto, Marian Anderson, also raised funds for Ethiopia when she sang in Sweden for that purpose.[34] Walter Davis, a sergeant for the U.S. during World War I, recruited for Ethiopia among his fellow Negro soldiers in Fort Worth, Texas, and was pleased to see that hundreds attended a mass meeting to that end.[35]

This point–counterpoint—between Italians and Italian Americans on the one hand, and Africans and African Americans on the other— led the well-informed U.S. Negro columnist J. A. Rogers to conclude that a kind of grudge match was unfolding between the two camps. Rome and its acolytes, he posited, were seeking revenge against both the Ethiopians and African Americans for a lengthy list of purported sins, not the least of which included the humiliating defeat inflicted upon the mammoth Italian boxer Primo Carnera at the hands of "The Brown Bomber," Joe Louis.[36]

Certainly, emotional temperatures were rising in Harlem too. "Sepia Harlem has gone mad," was one observer's conclusion when word first circulated that Italy had annexed Ethiopia. Reportedly, every corner of Lenox and Seventh Avenues in Harlem featured milling crowds assembled to hear street-corner speakers' denunciations of Rome. A monster parade ensued, with some shouting the disturbing slogan, "Don't Buy from the Wops."[37] New Orleans erupted too, with 3,000 marching there in favor of sanctions against local pro-Rome merchants. Those protesters included future eminent scholars St. Clair Drake and L. D. Reddick (later an advisor to Dr. Martin Luther King Jr.).[38] Due south, workers in British Guiana went on strike to protest the Italian invasion. According to one commentator, the men there were "in a

33 Press Release, November 1935, Reel 11, #874, Part I, Press Releases, CAB-NCSU.

34 Press Release, November 1935, Reel 11, #893, Part I, Press Releases, CAB-NCSU.

35 Press Release, July 1935, Reel 10, #1179, Part I, Press Releases, CAB-NCSU.

36 William Scott, "Colonel John C. Robinson: The Condor of Ethiopia," *Pan African Journal*, 5(1), (Spring 1972), 59-69, 63.

37 Press Release, May 1936, Reel 12, #1056, Part I, Press Releases, CAB-NCSU.

38 Press Release, May 1936, Reel 12, #1098, Part I, Press Releases, CAB-NCSU.

Haile Salassie. Emperor of Ethiopia 1930-1974.
(Courtesy Moorland-Spingarn Research Center, Howard University)

tense mood" because of the conflict, and many seemed eager to travel to Ethiopia to fight.[39] "Ethiopia offers the greatest opportunities today for American Negroes," reports triumphantly proclaimed, particularly referring to Negroes with aviation skills.[40]

Among those journeying to Addis Ababa for that precise reason was John Robinson. The Associated Negro Press had dispatched

39 Press Release, September 1936, Reel 13, #746, Part I, Press Releases, CAB-NCSU.
40 Press Release, July 1935, Reel 6, #962, Part III, Subject Files on Black Americans, CAB-NCSU.

him there with the ostensible aim of filing reports about the conflict. Surreptitiously, Robinson's reports bore the pen name Wilson James, as the ANP, wary of alerting his adversaries to his more combative role as a pilot fighting Rome's best in the skies, "refrained from making any news of his activities."[41]

It was in early 1935 that the Ethiopian Emperor's nephew Malaku Bayen "thought of trying to acquaint American Negroes with the happenings in Ethiopia through the Negro press"[42] Bayen had studied medicine at Howard University in the early 1920s, and he identified closely with African Americans. He had married an African American—Dorothy Hadley of Evanston and Chicago—and was well versed in both the culture of the U.S. and that of its darker denizens too.[43] He was supportive of Robinson's dual role and knew when Robinson sailed eastward. He trusted that Barnett would not mention the pilot's travels in the papers until he got to Addis Ababa,[44] given that arranging for a U.S. national to engage in combat abroad was a putative violation of U.S. law.[45]

The parents of Haile Selassie Stewart, born in Mississippi in May 1936, mirrored Bayen's mutuality with regard to relations between U.S. Negroes and Ethiopians.[46] Mutuality was enhanced because Bayen too was subjected to Jim Crow—a Manhattan hotel was the culprit in the most publicized instance.

With the Ethiopian government subsidizing his travel expenses through the ANP, Robinson—as Wilson James—slipped covertly into

41 Press Release, July 1935, Reel 10, #1090, Part I, Press Releases, CAB-NCSU.

42 Malaku Bayen to Claude Barnett, 30 January 1935, Box 170, Folder 9. CAB/CHM.

43 Press Release, October 1935, Reel 11, #658, Part I, Press Releases, CAB-NCSU. See also Press Release, October 1936, Reel 13, #794, Part I, Press Releases, CAB-NCSU: "Mrs. Malaku Bayen" was in Addis with their son when the war with Italy erupted. They moved on to Palestine and Britain. She speaks Amharic. Here, it is said, her spouse is the cousin—not the nephew—of the Emperor.

44 Malaku Bayen to Claude Barnett, 6 May 1935, Box 170, Folder 9, CAB-CHM.

45 William R. Scott, "Colonel John Robinson: The Condor of Ethiopia," *Pan African Journal*, 5(1), (Spring 1972), 59-69, 61.

46 Press Release, May 1936, Reel 12, #854, Part I, Press Releases, CAB-NCSU.

the East African nation on May 29, 1935. "I told everybody here I was a tailor," he recalled, "and [that I] was born here but had been in America for 25 years. All the people believe[d] it because I look just like an Abyssinian."[47]

Robinson's arrival, of course, was no simple matter. Not only could going to a war zone be deemed illegal, some Ethiopians did not welcome the arrival of African Americans, despite Ethiopia's weakened position. Robinson registered as a mechanic and was attached to the nation's rather bare-bones air force.

The Caribbean-born pilot, Hubert Julian, arrived in Addis Ababa about the same time Robinson did, after addressing an assemblage inspired by Marcus Garvey.[48] Julian had been traveling throughout the U.S., seeking to secure $35,000 for his proposed flight across the Atlantic. Reportedly, he had raised all but $4,900 through such efforts when the affluent Negro businessman, C. C. Spaulding, head of North Carolina Mutual Life Insurance Company, thought it would be a "fine thing" if Julian were "successful." Spaulding, who found Julian "most enthusiastic, [and] very conscientious" encouraged "as many Negroes as possible, [to] send him something—at least $1.00 each."[49]

The ANP's Barnett, perhaps the most influential figure in the early years of Black aviation, was "skeptical" of Julian's "ability" and claimed that the Trinidadian pilot had "plenty of nerve" but lacked prudence.[50] He warned Spaulding about rumors he had heard about the pilot, adding that he had tried unsuccessfully to dissuade Julian "from talking too grandiloquently."[51] With the affluent Spaulding's high-level

---

47 Press Release, October 1936, Reel 13, #804, Part I, Press Releases, CAB-NCSU.
48 *Negro World*, January 2, 1932.
49 C. C. Spaulding to Claude Barnett, 15 November 1933, Reel 5, #707, Part III, Series C, Subject Files on Black Americans, CAB-NCSU.
50 Claude Barnett to C. C. Spaulding, 21 November 1933, Reel 5, #708, Part III, Series C, Subject Files on Black Americans, CAB-NCSU.
51 Ibid.

aid, Julian nonetheless made it to East Africa, but his welcome was not as effusive as Robinson's.

Reportedly, the former Garveyite was snubbed upon his arrival in Addis Ababa, though—like Robinson—he too strenuously denied the allegation that Ethiopians generally shunned U.S. Negroes and other Africans from the Diaspora. In truth, as Ethiopians increasingly stared down the barrel of the approaching Italian gun, they welcomed African Americans. According to one journalist: "The Associated Negro Press has been in direct communication with the Emperor of Ethiopia and knows that arrangements have been completed, with the active cooperation of the Emperor, for some Negroes to go to that country." The ANP was quick to point out, however, that the "Ethiopian government, through past experiences, is somewhat wary of Negro Americans"[52]

This was not the case for Malaku Bayen, the Emperor's nephew in the U.S., who was intimately involved in Robinson's journey and sought to arrange similar ventures.[53] Bayen confided to the ANP's Barnett that Ethiopia would not "get very far with the help that is rendered by the white man." As he maintained, Ethiopia "could obtain all the help that [it needed] from the United States and the West Indies." He dismissively asserted that the Emperor's government was "employing white foreigners in various departments, and that these white men have gone on year after year, doing as little as they can for us." In his view, Ethiopia needed to "carefully select" recruits with "definite training… i.e., a superior type of well qualified black men, who are not fortune hunters and who have race consciousness."[54]

Taking Bayen's cue, Barnett—a graduate and disciple of Booker T. Washington's Tuskegee Institute—contacted a dean at his alma mater

---

52 Press Release, July 1935, Reel 10, #1090, Part I, Press Releases, CAB-NCSU.
53 Malaku Bayen to Claude Barnett, 6 May 1935, Box 170, Folder 9, CAB-CHM.
54 Malaku Bayen to Claude Barnett, 31 March 1935, Box 170, Folder 9, CAB-CHM.

At Harlem Meeting for Ethiopia

Two thousand Harlem people heard Dr. Malaku Bayen, (above), Emperor Haile Sellassie's personal envoy speak Monday night at Rockland Palace under the auspices for the United Aid for Ethiopia.

Malaku Bayen. Haile Selassie's nephew, perhaps his cousin.
(Courtesy Moorland-Spingard Research Center, Howard University)

and informed him that Ethiopia "will welcome Colored Americans," especially engineers and "scientifically trained men." They wanted more men (and women) like Robinson, Barnett claimed, and they were willing to pay for those recruits' transportation and to offer them a salary.[55] One such recruit, James Alexander Harte, would become

---

55 Claude Barnett to E. G. Roberts, Dean of Mechanical Industries of Tuskegee Institute, 17 July 1935, Box 170, Folder 9, CAB-CHM.

the Emperor's chief motor mechanic. Harte, who hailed from British Guiana, spent almost six years in Addis Ababa.[56]

The rumored African reluctance to embrace U.S. Negroes and other Blacks from the Diaspora apparently did little to deter their interest in going to and fighting for Addis Ababa. Perhaps because of the bite of the Great Depression, it was reported that "scores of American aviators"—including a complement of Euro-Americans—wanted to volunteer to become pilots in East Africa. All were willing to serve under the leadership of the man who later came to be known as Colonel Robinson, "head of the Imperial Ethiopian Air Force."[57] Within months, the skilled Robinson was successfully piloting and training others, while a Negro correspondent crowed that the "English pilots" in Ethiopia were "poor flyers" and only served to "smash" the East Africans' planes.[58]

For his part, Robinson maintained that most of the resistance to non-indigenous Black fighters came from European expatriate fighters who felt threatened by the arrival of skilled African Americans. Additionally, he reported back to Barnett, "The white influence over here is very, very strong." They "have poisoned the minds of the Abyssinian against the American Negroes," to their mutual detriment, he wrote.

"All the commercial business in this country is run by white people," Robinson reported, still masking his combat role and signing his weekly dispatches as an "Official Foreign Associated Negro

56 Press Release, August 1936, Reel 13, #630, Part I, Press Releases, CAB-NCSU. Strikingly, Marcus Garvey was quite hostile to Ethiopia at this point, terming the Emperor "misguided" while adding that "neutrality was the best attitude for the Negro in the present European conflict." See Press Release, September 1936, Reel 13, #694, Part I, Press Releases, CAB-NCSU. See also Press Release, January 1937, Reel 13, #1121, Part I, Press Releases, CAB-NCSU: The Reverend Adam Clayton Powell in Harlem before a crowd of 700 says, "Black Nationalism, whatever that is, must go."
57 Press Release, October 1935, Reel 11, #666, Part I, Press Releases, CAB-NCSU.
58 Press Release, April 1936, Reel 12, #712, Part I, Press Releases, CAB-NCSU.

Press Reporter."[59] He was referring to the large numbers of Greeks in Ethiopia, finding them to predominate "more than any other white race" in that nation; and to the many "Indians from India, Turks and Egyptians" there. Notwithstanding, Robinson was determined, despite the odds, "to get some jobs for other men" back home—U.S. Negroes like himself. In his "spare time," the lowly tailor-mechanic-reporter-pilot participated in at least twelve airborne dogfights. In one, he just missed shooting down Mussolini's son.

Robinson's mission was quite dangerous. In February 1936, he barely escaped death when the plane in which he was slated to fly crashed. Of that episode, he wrote: "The big shot English pilots don't seem to be so good out here, as flying here is much different from other parts of the world." He was referring to the towering mountains, inadequate runways and landing strips, and tricky winds, adding that the "fighting is very hard in the north….Flying near Addis Ababa is extremely difficult because of the height of the city. I was the first one to reach the airplane just before it burst into fire."[60]

Still, unlike the British pilots who flew for the Ethiopians and whom, he reported, "cracked up" plane after plane, Robinson "never sustained a mishap of [that] nature." Just before he was to leave Addis Ababa in May 1936, when Robinson was chased by two speeding enemy fighting planes, he skillfully maneuvered his craft to safety without a scratch.[61]

Robinson, was not left unscathed, however. He was gassed at least three times, as the invading foreign planes promiscuously deployed chlorine and mustard gas from the air. He injured his hand in another air raid. He actually arrived in Africa with a broken arm, an injury that severely hampered his piloting.

---

59 John Robinson to Claude Barnett, 3 June 1935, Box 170, Folder 9, CAB-CHM.
60 John Robinson to Claude Barnett, 25 February 1936, Box 170, Folder 9, CAB-CHM.
61 Press Release, 12 May 1936, Reel 12, #986, Part I, Press Releases, CAB-NCSU.

Robinson faced other challenges as well. On his way to East Africa, he reportedly stopped in Port Said, Egypt, where he was followed by a suspicious character who addressed him first in Amharic, a central language of Ethiopia, then in French, and finally in English. At first, Robinson thought the man was an Ethiopian emissary. He soon realized that the region was replete with spies unhelpful to his mission.[62] He eventually eluded the spy and traveled on to Djibouti, where the excessive heat bothered him.

Three days later, Robinson was face-to-face with His Imperial Majesty, Emperor Haile Selassie I. He also got his first look at the 24 dilapidated planes of the nation's paltry air force and concluded that the planes were largely unfit for combat but useful for scouting and reconnaissance. Soon acquiring the titles of "Brown Condor of Ethiopia" and "Commander of the Royal Air Force," Robinson was accepted rather quickly into the inner and higher councils of Addis Ababa. He frequently conferred with the Emperor and his war cabinet.[63] In an early example of Pan-African skill transfer, he helped train Ethiopia's pilots and regularly patrolled what was termed the "Eritrean front" and "Italian Somaliland."[64]

Robinson also filed numerous articles for the ANP in his "undercover," reporter role. As he wrote for his many readers back home: "I have flown the heights in the [U.S.] but in flying here, I have suffered a little from 'air sickness.'" Due to the higher altitudes—16,000 feet or more—he was required "to stay a safe distance over the mountains" of East Africa. To drop bombs accurately "from such an altitude," he wrote, "one has about one chance out of six thousand to do any damage."

In his aerial dogfights with the Italians, Robinson claimed that he drew upon the wisdom of "warriors of old, who yet remember Adowa,"

---

62 Press Release, May 1936, Reel 12, #1093, Part I, Press Releases, CAB-NCSU.
63 Press Release, June 1936, Reel 13, #201, Part I, Press Releases, CAB-NCSU.
64 Tucker, *Father of the Tuskegee Airmen*, 153.

the Ethiopian site where the Italian invaders were repulsed in a major Pan-African victory in 1896.[65] As he reported dejectedly from Addis Ababa in October 1935:

> The Italians have won most every battle here. People here are beginning to realize that war today is different from the fighting in 1896 [since] the League of Nations is just another white man's bluff. White people will always stick together in the end when it comes to the color question.[66]

Robinson's reaction was an understandable one for a U.S. Negro, though it elided the then-raging ideological conflict between Moscow and Washington. He nonetheless insisted that he had done his "part" to help Ethiopia and to "let the Ethiopians know that the American Negro is not at all as bad as the white race try to picture him to be." Despite his best efforts in the air, however, Robinson concluded in late 1935 that it "looks like the beginning of the end for this country."[67]

Robinson's remarks also reflected the cascading and negative reaction to white supremacy that accompanied the Ethiopian–Italian conflict by 1935. Planes of whatever provenance were needed desperately. Hubert Julian claimed that the Ethiopians had only 12 planes left and, of those, only 7 were flyable, and those were all "small, slow and obsolete."[68] By December 1935, a British manufacturer delivered six new airplanes to Addis Ababa—at a cost of $30,000 each—but an unimpressed Robinson was cited widely in the U.S. Negro press for reporting that "Japan....has agreed to send as many airplanes or other necessities as are desired and with no strings attached."[69]

---

65 Press Release, October 1935, Reel 11, #435, Part I, Press Releases, CAB-NCSU.
66 Ibid.
67 John Robinson to Claude Barnett, 28 November 1935, Box 170, Folder 9, CAB-ANP. He added, "strange to say but it is true the Christians in the north are the worst fighters...the Italians kick them around like nothing" while the Moslems are "putting up a good fight."
68 Julian, *Black Eagle*, 104.
69 *Kansas City* [Kansas] *Plain Dealer*, December 27, 1935.

Despite the racism and perils he faced, Robinson's stint in East Africa was not all pain and angst. He was given a commodious, eight-room home; had six servants at his disposal, and a private car besides. Moreover, the married pilot confessed that he "had to fight off"" numerous potential lovers.[70]

Colonel Robinson was not the only Negro from North America who was attracted to Ethiopia. As early as 1930, a Manhattan journalist interviewed the Trinidad-born pilot Hubert Julian in that African nation. "Clad faultlessly in morning dress and swinging a heavy Malacca stick," Julian, who was then planning a flight from Harlem to Addis Ababa,[71] denied that he was then quarreling with the Emperor. He did not deny, however, that an unnamed party had attempted to poison him, nor did he fail to note that he was travelling on an Ethiopian passport. The next year, the Air Ministry in London would deny adamantly that Julian had served as an officer or in the ranks of any nation's flying corps or air force in Ethiopia, Canada, or elsewhere, as he maintained.[72]

As suggested by the alleged poison plot, Hubert Julian had more than his share of foes, one of whom was fellow pilot William Powell, who was himself already notorious for several aviation scams he was accused of perpetrating.[73] A fistfight ensued between the two in spring 1932, with a reporter-*cum*-fight-judge asserting that "Powell got a bit of the worst of it" and that he subsequently "swore out two warrants of assault and battery against Julian."[74]

---

70 *New York World-Telegram*, 19 May 1936.

71 *New York Times*, November 19, 1930, NASM.

72 Air Ministry-London to Managing Editor of *West End News*, Brooklyn, 30 July 1931, Box 171, Folder 3, CAB-CHM.

73 Press Release, May 1932, Reel 5, #744, Part I, Press Releases, CAB-NCSU.

74 Press Release, May 1932, Reel 5, #810, Part I, Press Releases, CAB-NCSU. See also Press Release, May 1932, Reel 5, #744, Part I, Press Releases, CAB-NCSU: "Some hot words passed in dispute" and "rather uncouth language used also." This occurred, though "just a week previously they had been greeted by a large crowd at Lindbergh Field at San Diego when they arrived in a new plane accompanied by Mrs. Ravastar Tellis, who was the largest contributor to the purchase fund. The plane was christened 'Ravastar' in her honor."

Upon his arrival in Ethiopia, Julian also came into conflict with Colonel Robinson, physically assaulting His Imperial Majesty's pilot at an Addis Ababa hotel the day after a spirited boxing match featuring Joe Louis took place[75] According to Robinson, Julian was miffed that the Chicagoan wielded more influence in Ethiopia. He also suspected—correctly, it turns out—that Robinson was publishing articles critical of him. As Robinson reported, he easily bested Julian in the resulting fracas.[76] For his part, Julian claimed that he had confronted the Chicagoan over the latter's newspaper articles. "[O]ne word led to another," and they "came to blows," Julian reported; "then Robinson pulled a knife. So I picked up a chair, cracked him around the head with it and laid him out."[77]

Robinson's reporting of the altercation told a different story. Julian, he claimed, "owe[d] different people nearly $500, including hotel bills, money borrowed, board, laundry and entertainment. He beats his servants and struts the streets bragging about the 60 airplanes he owns [and his] $60,000 bank account." The contumacious Julian later became embroiled in a fierce row with Ethiopian police officers, who beat him brutally after Julian was accused of interfering with an arrest.[78]

While Robinson was attempting to "pass" as Ethiopian, he claimed that Julian was "telling everybody" that he (Robinson) was a U.S. citizen, thereby placing the Chicagoan in jeopardy. Said the irked pilot of his erstwhile colleague, "the leading people" of Ethiopia "don't speak to him." Robinson was convinced that Julian's behavior contributed to the Ethiopians' disreputable opinions of African Americans. He expressed concern that, upon departing the region and returning to the

---

75 Tucker, *Father of the Tuskegee Airmen*, 99.
76 Press Release, August 1935, Reel 11, #119, Part I, Press Releases, CAB-NCSU.
77 Julian, *Black Eagle*, 106.
78 Press Release, July 1935, Reel 10, #1090, Part I, Press Releases, CAB-NCSU; see also John Robinson to Claude Barnett, 3 June 1935, Box 170, Folder 9, CAB-ANP.

U.S., Julian was "going to run a racket" and tell others that he had been employed "to get people to bring back" to Ethiopia to work in various capacities, including piloting. Robinson also was afraid that Julian's malfeasance would bollix his own efforts "to get some jobs" in East Africa for U.S. Negroes, including "mechanical work." "I really believe the higher [elite] Abyssinian wants the American Negro," Robinson wrote, but he also believed that Julian was misleading "poor people about the schools he is going to give them free and teach 100 boys a week to fly in the 60 airplanes he is going to bring from America."[79]

When Julian left Ethiopia, Robinson gleefully berated his rival, reporting that Julian had quit "in disgust"—that he was envious of the high-level post the Chicago pilot had attained and angry at his apparent inability to "marry one of the royal princesses."[80] The sardonic ANP correspondent, Frank Marshall Davis, also derided Julian as a "publicity-hunting Harlemite," noting: "If the flyer should next be spotted in a fascist plane dropping bombs on the Imperial Palace in Addis," then "no Aframerican [sic] need be surprised."[81] Julian was later "given the proverbial "bum's rush" at a meeting of the left-leaning National Negro Congress, which convened stateside in February 1936.[82] By June, however, he had set sail for Italy, reportedly with an Italian passport and his "pockets well-lined." This left several ANP reporters with the impression that Julian's journey to Ethiopia may have been for purposes of subversion.[83] "Huberto Fauntleroyana Juliano" was the sardonic name accorded him thereafter in the Negro press.[84]

Of course, Julian claimed that the negative reports were all hogwash. He further claimed that Malaku Bayen had arranged his journey to

---

79 John Robinson to Claude Barnett, 3 June 1935, Box 170, Folder 9, CAB-ANP.
80 Press Release, November 1935, Reel 11, #813, Part I, Press Releases, CAB-NCSU.
81 Press Release, November 1935, Reel 11, #901, Part I, Press Releases, CAB-NCSU.
82 Press Release, February 1936, Reel 12, #119, Part I, Press Releases, CAB-NCSU.
83 Press Release, June 1936, Reel 13, #40, Part I, Press Releases, CAB-NCSU.
84 Press Release, June 1936, Reel 13, #182, Part I, Press Releases, CAB-NCSU.

Ethiopia and that he had been paid the "handsome salary of $1,000 a month." He also maintained that he had conferred with His Imperial Majesty directly upon his arrival, was slated to become Selassie's "personal pilot," and was learning Amharic to that end—that is, until his enemies sabotaged him. (Julian professed earlier to have toiled as the "personal pilot" of Father Divine at a princely $100 per day.) Julian also asserted that he was so popular that Ethiopian women—"we counted more than 500 ladies queuing up"—were willing to pay him $5 "for the pleasure of kissing [him]." Though he admitted travelling to Rome after leaving Ethiopia, he alleged that he had taken with him a "tiny revolver" with which he planned to assassinate Benito Mussolini. He pleaded that his scalding critique of Ethiopia and the solidarity movement was all part of a plot to convince Rome of his trustworthiness.[85]

To be fair, the critical Robinson was not only displeased by those who arrived—e.g., Julian—but also by those who did not. He cabled Chicago seeking to recruit other U.S. Negro pilots to come and join the fray but soon conceded bitterly that "every one of them have failed me so far, which means the last time I will ask the Emperor permission to send for anyone else." It "seems impossible to get colored Americans" to come to Ethiopia, Robinson lamented, but the U.S. government may have played a role in this reluctance. As Robinson noted, "[O]ne of the American consuls attached to the American legation has made it his business to call me to the legation and ask…many annoying questions" about his activity and recruitment attempts. He was convinced that this scrutiny had a discouraging impact on potential emigrants.

The ANP's Barnett likewise sought to recruit others to follow in Robinson's footsteps—or rather, in his airstream. He successfully enlisted the likes of Cornelius Coffey, one of Black Chicago's leading

---

85   Julian, *Black Eagle*, 87, 99, 101, 115. Washington confirmed that Bayen sought to arrange Julian's journey to Africa—but soon was charging the pilot with collecting funds under false pretenses. See Memorandum, 17 February 1932, Box 287, PI 157, E200 HM 1991, Record Group 59, Central Decimal File and Memorandum, 23 February 1935, 765.84/178, Record Group 59, National Archives and Records Administration, College Park, Maryland.

pilots, to the Ethiopian cause in late 1935, but ran into trouble trying to get passports and State Department clearance for his recruits.[86]

Robinson also had unkind things to say about his fellow Negro writer, J. A. Rogers, who also made it to Addis Ababa. Rogers "did not go so good with the people here," said the pilot, "as he is always talking about himself and what he has done and what he can do." Other factors may have exacerbated the personal conflicts affecting Robinson's and others' efforts to recruit foreign Blacks to Ethiopia. One observer noted a "definite schism between the West Indians and the Americans." The former, he noted, believed that they were being "jobbed" by an influential U.S. Negro, Willis Huggins.[87] This schism may shed some light on the terrible conflict between the Mississippi-born Robinson and the Trinidad-born Julian, who seemed to inflame the ire of the sarcastic Chicagoan the most.

By November 1935, Hubert Julian had departed East Africa. "I really think he is a little off in the head," recalled Robinson, noting that the erratic Julian had "laid down in front of the Emperor's automobile three or four times" and when the car would stop, "he would get up and beg for money."[88]

Reeling from blows inflicted by Italian invaders and acerbic conflicts with fellow Negroes, Robinson too was ready to depart East Africa by spring 1936, and Barnett was pressing him to do so. Barnett reminded Robinson that he had "promised Tuskegee [then-Institute] officials"— and Barnett himself—that he "would lay plans for the establishment of a school of aviation" at that Alabama institution.[89] Barnett believed the Tuskegee flight center "would be an effective publicity bit," and he was determined to capitalize on Robinson's air combat experience and

86 Claude Barnett to "Dear Johnny," 31 December 1935, Box 170, Folder 9, CAB-CHM.
87 Alvin White to "Dear Chief," 20 December 1936, Box 171, Folder 1, CAB-ANP.
88 John Robinson to Claude Barnett, 21 November 1935, Box 170, Folder 9, CAB-CHM.
89 Claude Barnett to John Robinson, 22 April 1936, Box 170, Folder 9, CAB-CHM.

"the tremendous interest" his return would engender.[90]

Barnett had convinced the Institute's leader, Frederick Douglass Patterson, that his "aviation venture" had "glamour" that would redound to the benefit of the school as a whole. In May 1936, he wrote: "I am having our Washington correspondent inquire [as to] why colored men are not permitted in the Army Air Corps." To punctuate his point, he arranged for Colonel Robinson to be interviewed upon his return by the highly popular radio host, Lowell Thomas.[91] Barnett also arranged a crowded and boisterous reception for Robinson when the latter arrived in New York City. This built momentum for his multiple goals of bringing attention to the conflict in East Africa while calling for the desegregation of the skies and bolstering his Tuskegee aviation experiment.

Given the tremendous welcome Robinson received, Barnett's trip to New York extended into ten days rather than the two or three he had planned.[92] Barnett, of course, was overjoyed, telling the legendary educator Mary McLeod Bethune that Robinson, who "performed so brilliantly" in Ethiopia, had been subjected to "one unending round of fetes and honors" since his return. He boasted that 4,000 people had welcomed Robinson at Harlem's Rockland Palace, where a memorial fund was proposed to raise funds "to promote aviation" among U.S. Negro youth." Barnett asked Bethune to "represent the women of the country" in this crusade, which was to be launched at Tuskegee.[93]

Barnett concluded that Robinson "gave a good account of himself" while in New York and that the "Tuskegee angle was worked out to perfection." "Every story carried the fact that the Colonel was going to [Tuskegee Institute] to teach aviation," he wrote. He urged President

---

90   Claude Barnett to Frederick D. Patterson, 7 May 1936, Reel 7, #33, Series B, Part III, Subject Files on Black Americans, CAB-NCSU.

91   Claude Barnett to Frederick D. Patterson, 12 May 1936, Box 170, Folder 9, CAB-CHM.

92   Claude Barnett to Haven Requa, 6 June 1936, Reel 4, #663, Series E, Medicine, 1927-1965, CAB-NCSU.

93   Claude Barnett to Mary McLeod Bethune, 5 June 1936, Reel 4, #629, Series G, Philanthropic and Social Organizations, CAB-NCSU.

Patterson to "get some aeroplane company to donate a plane to Tuskegee" to jumpstart the venture.[94]

Robinson, who had his own plans for his post-Ethiopia future, arranged to have funds for the purchase of a plane donated directly to him.[95] This divergence may have been only dimly understood by Barnett, who was too busy capitalizing upon Robinson's popularity to notice. Barnett instead encouraged Robinson to "write to the Emperor's financial men sounding him out on the idea" of making a movie about the Colonel's exploits in Ethiopia—with a burnished depiction of His Imperial Majesty as part of the bargain.[96]

Paul Williams, Hollywood's leading architect (who happened to be African American[97]), considered it a "capital idea to use [Robinson's] brilliant career to stimulate the youth in the possibilities of aviation."[98] Another Hollywood insider agreed that there "should be tremendous interest" in the proposed movie.[99] The proposed centerpiece of this ambitious venture—Colonel Robinson himself—was not as enthusiastic about Barnett's plans, and by July 1936, the two were enmeshed in a bitter dispute that was to lead to Robinson being excluded from the Tuskegee venture too.[100]

After New York, Robinson was greeted rapturously by a stunning 20,000 in Chicago, who hailed him as a conquering hero.[101] There, and in Pittsburgh, Washington, DC, and other stops, while Barnett was promoting his plans for the Tuskegee flight school, the films, and other

94 Claude Barnett to Frederick D. Patterson, 20 May 1936, Box 170, Folder 9, CAB-CHM.
95 P. M. H. Savory of United Aid for Ethiopia–Harlem to John Robinson, 25 May 1936, Box 170, Folder 9, CAB-CHM.
96 Claude Barnett to L. A. Wilkinson, Motion Picture Producer & Distributors of America, 4 June 1936, Box 171, Folder 1, CAB-ANP.
97 Karen E. Hudson, *Paul R. Williams, Architect: A Legacy of Style* (New York: Rizzoli, 1993).
98 Paul Williams to Claude Barnett, 9 June 1936, Box 171, Folder 1, CAB-CHM.
99 Arthur Silber to Claude Barnett, 23 June 1936, Box 171, Folder 1, CAB-CHM.
100 Claude Barnett to R. R. Moton, 8 July 1936, Box 171, Folder 1.
101 William R. Scott, "Colonel John C. Robinson: The Condor of Ethiopia," *Pan African Journal*, 5(1), (Spring 1972), 59-69, 65; Press Release, May 1936, Reel 12, #1080, Part I, Press Releases, CAB-NCSU.

ventures, Robinson was presenting his plan for the establishment of a Negro airline. His rationale was simple: "Negroes for the most part are prevented from traveling by air on Southern [air]lines."[102]

Despite the crowds, Robinson felt he was "grossly mistreated," most notably in Chicago. When he sought to buy a plane with the funds supposedly donated on his behalf, he claimed that Barnett "refused to sign" for the transaction. This "really hurt me very much," he told Barnett. He felt that Barnett's New York organizers had overreached by "organizing the Colonel John C. Robinson Aviation Committee" without his consent. Brusquely, he returned unsigned a contract Barnett offered him for his role in the "future development of aviation at Tuskegee." Dyspeptically, he added that Barnett and his partners must believe "that I am a fool or that I am [a] slave." Barnett, the unsung creator of the Tuskegee Airmen, may have been, in Robinson's view, "one of the leaders of the Negro race with much power," but Robinson deemed himself to be no cipher. Instead, he wrote: "I am drawing up a charter dedicated to the development of aviation among the colored race and to help make America supreme in the air."[103]

To that end, Robinson went to Fort Worth, Texas, in mid-1937 and there began serving as the personal pilot for the wealthy Negro entrepreneur, Annie Malone. He wore his Ethiopian military regalia in that role and fashioned his goatee and sideburns after those of His Imperial Majesty. He was the "lion of the hour," wrote one observer, noting that members of the Fort Worth NAACP were among those thrilled by his appearance.[104]

Meanwhile, Robinson's sometimes sparring partner—Hubert Julian—was reclining injured in a hospital bed in Paris, planning a journey to China and bent on deploying his fungible skills as a pilot on behalf of the beset there—or perhaps for the Japanese attackers—

---

102   Press Release, June 1936, Reel 13, #182, Part I, Press Releases, CAB-NCSU.
103   John Robinson to Claude Barnett, 1 July 1936, Box 171, Folder 1, CAB-CHM.
104   Press Release, July 1937, Reel 15, #258, Part I, Press Releases, CAB-NCSU.

given that, with Julian, one could never be certain.[105] By October 1937, Julian turned up in London, boasting: "I am a man who makes parachute jumps and plays a saxophone on the way down" —which was true—and "I am proud to be a Negro" —again, also true. Yet while ensconced there, Julian occupied an expensive suite at an exclusive hotel, and the source of his income was unclear.[106]

In Ethiopia, His Imperial Majesty was, by June 1936, receiving negative reviews from those with whom Robinson was jousting. ANP's London correspondent, Rudolph Dunbar, was attempting to make his employer "a power in Europe" by mobilizing a broad array of forces to buttress His Imperial Majesty's throne.[107] By July, however, Dunbar wrote that he was "thoroughly disgusted" with the exiled monarch, who had since abandoned Addis Ababa for London.[108] He termed Selassie a "sad spectacle," one of whose key aides told a "famous journalist at a dinner party that the Abyssinians will be frightfully annoyed if they are classed as Negroes."[109]

By late 1936, even the ambitious Barnett was souring on his ambitious plans. He observed that Ethiopia no longer was tugging at the "heartstrings nor purse strings" of African Americans.[110] Malaku Bayen, the Emperor's relative, had turned with a vengeance on Marcus Garvey, the man he previously viewed as the embodiment of the Pan-Africanism that had propelled Robinson to East Africa. Garvey himself was viewed by that time as either a "fool, hypocrite, idiot or traitor," Dunbar charged, accusing the Jamaican of collaborating with Rome. "By his confessions," Dunbar wrote of Garvey, "he is a devout Catholic," who referred to Selassie's beleaguered nation as "Abyssinia" instead

105 Press Release, September 1937, Reel 15, #694, Part I, Press Releases, CAB-NCSU.
106 Press Release, October 1937, Reel 15, #812, Part I, Press Releases, CAB-NCSU.
107 Rudolph Dunbar to Claude Barnett, 2 June 1936, Box 171, Folder 1, CAB-CHM.
108 Rudolph Dunbar to Claude Barnett, 20 July 1936, Box 171, Folder 1, CAB-CHM.
109 Rudolph Dunbar to Claude Barnett, 28 October 1936, Box 171, Folder 1, CAB-CHM.
110 Claude Barnett to Rudolph Barnett, 25 November 1936, Box 171, Folder 1, CAB-CHM.

of the upgraded term, "Ethiopia."[111] (It should be noted that Garvey was not alone in his purported distaste for the East African monarch. Reputed Communist Party journalist Frank Marshall Davis, who was to decamp to Honolulu in the following decade, then befriending a future U.S. president, asserted that he "tried with every atom" in his being yet could "register no more than skin deep concern over dark losses" in Ethiopia because of his abhorrence of Selassie's feudal rule.[112])

Bayen did not escape censure either. Dr. Willis Huggins, viewed widely as a leading Harlem intellectual, was reproachful of the expatriate Ethiopian, reminding him that "for forty years blacks tried time and again to get close enough to Ethiopians to warn them of impending danger which no white man would mention to them." "Such advances," Huggins maintained, "were met with a stony silence or actual scorn." Bayen in particular, Huggins charged hotly, "is the last and least fitted Ethiopian to ask Americans for money [since] he lived here from 1925 to 1935 almost completely ignoring the American people."[113]

Huggins went on to contend that, in 1935, Bayen and Prince Desta "refused to come to Harlem for an entertainment that had been prepared for them because they considered it 'inadvisable' to be openly identified with colored people."[114] This was in direct refutation of Colonel Robinson's earlier claim that "the Ethiopian does not attack or disparage Negroes of other nations."[115] Bayen responded by calling Dr. Huggins a "fascist," as the pro-Ethiopian solidarity movement was collapsing in a farrago of recriminations.[116]

In Addis Ababa, the advent of Italian rule meant the entrenchment of Jim Crow on buses, in housing and elsewhere, along with an unhealthy

---

111   "The Voice of Ethiopia," New York City, January 1937, Box 171, Folder 3, CAB-CHM.
112   Press Release, October 1935, Reel 11, #711, Part I, Press Releases, CAB-NCSU.
113   Press Release, January 1937, Reel 14, #05, Part I, Press Releases, CAB-NCSU.
114   Ibid.
115   Press Release, October 1935, Reel 11, #486, Part I, Press Releases, CAB-NCSU
116   Press Release, February 1937, Reel 14, #139, Part I, Press Releases, CAB-NCSU.

dose of misery in that nation.[117] Paradoxically, this admitted setback delivered a victory for Black aviation in the U.S. In 1936, the number of Negroes holding commercial pilot's licenses went from virtually zero to seven. Chicago—the vector for this leap forward—became the unofficial headquarters of Black aviation as an outgrowth, with about 30 Negro pilots reported in that city alone.[118]

Colonel Robinson's East African venture also served to propel Pan-Africanism beyond the realm of rhetoric. His heralded derring-do in the air reached readers of the Negro press, leading him to conclude, not wrongly, that he ranked with Marcus Garvey in raising African American interest in Africa. Robinson soon succeeded Bessie Coleman as the pilot who best expressed the importance of aeronautics to and for African Americans. His heavenward heroics served to ignite growing interest in aviation among African Americans, giving justification to the notion that he—and not Claude Barnett—was actually the "father" of the Tuskegee Airmen,soon to begin an ascent of their own.[119]

---

117   Press Release, July 1936, Reel 13, #303, Part I, Press Releases, CAB-NCSU.
118   Enoch P. Waters, *American Diary: A Personal History of the Black Press* (Chicago: Path Press, 1987), 199, 197.
119   Tucker, *Father of the Tuskegee Airmen*, 179.

Chicago was an early cradle of Black Aviation. Pictured here are pilots and enthusiasts. (Courtesy Chicago History Museum)

Pilot from the 332nd Fighter Group (Tuskegee Airmen) signing the Form One Book, indicating any discrepancies of aircraft, prior to take off. (Courtesy Library of Congress)

CHAPTER 3

FROM CHICAGO TO TUSKEGEE TO AFRICA

Claude Barnett, the entrepreneurial leader of the Associated Negro Press (ANP), had sponsored Colonel John Robinson's journey to Ethiopia, where the latter fought and filed stories on behalf of the ANP. Robinson also pursued a third angle. As he began his voyage home from Ethiopia in 1936, Barnett reminded him of a larger, "strategic" goal. "You had promised Tuskegee [Institute's] officials and me that you would lay plans for the establishment of a school of aviation there," he wrote. The time had arrived, in his view, for Robinson to fulfill that obligation.[1] The ensuing dispute between the two forbade the fulfillment of this evident agreement. By 1939, the embattled pilot was back in Chicago, leading the eponymous John C. Robinson National Air College and School of Automotive Engineering. The school was sited on the spacious grounds of Poro College on South Parkway and was headed by his sponsor, the beauty care magnate Annie Malone. Robinson was Ms. Malone's pilot.[2]

---

1 Claude Barnett to John Robinson, 22 April 1936, Box 170, Folder 9, CAB-CHM.
2 John Robinson to Claude Barnett, 20 February 1939, Reel 1, #460, Series C, Part III, Subject Files on Black Americans, CAB-NCSU. See also Press Release, October 1939, Reel 19, #795, Part I, Press Releases, CAB-NCSU: Robinson was selected by the National Youth Administration as an "aviation consultant"; he was slated to have "personal direction of the aviation school at Poro Institute, which he had operated for colored youths as a private nonprofit venture."

Despite Robinson's other commitments, Barnett, a member of Tuskegee's board continued to pursue his goal, which led directly to the formation of the now-celebrated Tuskegee Airmen. That someone as influential and energetic as Barnett was pushing this project served the Airmen well, for the Tuskegee project encountered potent headwinds—externally in the form of Jim Crow advocates—and internally in the project supporters' reluctance to engage the formidable talents of African American women pilots. Foremost in the overlooked talent category was Glasgow, Kentucky's Willa Brown, daughter of a pastor.[3] Born in 1906, Brown's family moved to Terre Haute, Indiana, where she graduated from Indiana State University in 1927 with a B.A. in commerce and a minor in French. She later moved to Gary, Indiana, where she taught at Roosevelt High School. There, she had a brief (one-and-a-half years) and stormy marriage to Wilbur J. Hardaway, Gary's first Black firefighter, who went on to become a leading politician and businessman in that city.

By 1932, Willa Brown was living in Chicago, where she was matriculating at Northwestern University. There, in 1933, she met Robinson and Cornelius Coffey, the two avatars of Black Aviation. She married the taciturn Coffey in 1939.[4] Apparently, the connection between the two was dialectical because Brown was talkative and Coffey was not. She once wrote that one could spend eight hours with him, and unless he was spoken to, he would not say a word.[5] Coffey nonetheless taught her the basics of piloting, a field in which she had expressed interest long before their betrothal. Soon the talented student sought to enter the Afro-American Texas-to-New York Air Derby, an aerial race from Galveston to the World's Fair.[6]

---

3 Pamphlet on Willa Brown, circa 1941, Box II: A89, NAACP Papers.
4 Undated Material on Willa Brown, Box 1, Gubert Papers.
5 Undated memorandum, Box 3, Gubert Papers.
6 Press Release, March 1940, Reel 20, #541, Part I, Press Releases, CAB-NCSU.

Brown found in Coffey a willing partner for her aviation dreams. By 1940, he controlled a fleet of six planes: two 50-horsepower Continental Cubs; two 220-horsepower, open-cockpit Waco trainers; a four-seater Travelair cabin plane; and a 100-horsepower Lincoln-Paige biplane trainer. At the time, he was reportedly training 25 young men and "one girl"—presumably his wife, Willa.[7]Brown's interest in aviation peaked in 1941, when the prominent *Chicago Defender* journalist Enoch (a.k.a. Enoc) P. Waters nominated her for the Spingarn Medal, the NAACP's most prestigious prize. "More than any other single individual," Waters wrote in his nomination proposal, Brown was "responsible for the present interest of Negroes in aviation."[8] Waters further boasted that Brown was "the first and only Negro woman to earn a commercial pilot's license." She "personally did all the manual work connected with the successful campaign to insert guarantees into the Civilian Pilot Training Act which made possible the participation of Negro colleges in the program," Waters continued. Moreover, "she has developed the largest privately owned Negro aviation school in the country."[9]

Waters further highlighted Brown's tenaciousness, recalling that while she was working with the New Deal's Works Progress Administration, she found time and resources to type and send letters to every member of Congress. In those letters, she asked the legislators to support the Civilian Pilot Training Act and to assure the participation of Negroes therein.[10] This was hardly a minor request. The National Urban League boasted that the Civilian Pilot Training Act, enacted in 1940, was "probably the largest mass-flight training program ever undertaken in the world." In its inaugural year, it resulted in 25,168

---

7 Press Release, December 1940, Reel 21, #1023, Part I, Press Releases, CAB-NCSU.

8 Enoc Waters of National Airmen's Association of America to Claude Barnett, 7 November 1941, Box 2, Gubert Papers.

9 Enoc Waters to Claude Barnett, 7 November 1941, Reel 1, #612, Series C, Part III, Economic Conditions, CAB-NCSU.

10 Enoc Waters to Spingarn Committee, 5 November 1941, Box II: A89, NAACP Papers.

youths receiving their private pilots' certificates and in appropriations of $40 million for the construction and improvement of the nation's airports.[11]

Popular bandleader Jimmie Lunceford[12] and the budding anthropologist St. Clair Drake were among those endorsing Brown's nomination for the Spingarn Medal. Drake noted proudly that the aviation students at Chanute Field, a U.S. Air Force training base located about 130 miles south of Chicago, viewed Brown "as the symbol of Negro activities in aviation." He further marveled that she had "turned down several lucrative offers from persons who wished her to compromise and remain silent on the question of Jim Crowism in the air force."[13]

Waters also noted that in 1940, Brown attended a meeting in Chicago with officials of the nation's air corps. The minutes of that meeting reveal what had become increasingly evident by that date—that there were "two Negro factions, one of which [led by Colonel Robinson] advocated the training of a college group [at Tuskegee Institute]" while the "other [represented by Brown and Coffey]... insisted upon the establishment of a non-college unit for Negroes at Chicago."[14] The latter faction, the minutes reported, with delicacy, adopted an "argumentative stand," but the air corps officials apparently were swayed toward the Tuskegee option, given Robinson's support. One of those officials, Major General B. K. Yount maintained that "disturbance and possibly riots" would probably ensue at Chanute Field and the nearby Illinois communities if Negro pilots were trained in the Chicago vicinity. As for establishing a school to train colored aviation

---

11 Press Release, 29 December 1940, Box I: F10, National Urban League Papers, Library of Congress.

12 Jimmie Lunceford to National Airmen's Association of America, 11 December 1941, Box II: A89, CAB-CHM.

13 St. Clair Drake to Walter White, 3 December 1941, Box II: A89, NAACP Papers.

14 Minutes of Meeting, 18 January 1940, 220.765-2, 220.8635.1, 1943 Volume 4, Volume 2, Air Force Historical Research Agency, Maxwell Air Force Base, Montgomery, Alabama [hereafter denoted as AFHRA].

mechanics, he concluded that such programs should be consolidated at Tuskegee Institute.[15] It was a short step from there to consolidate all training of Negroes there.

Subsequently, Waters illuminated the uphill climb Brown encountered as she sought to make her mark in aviation. Women pilots, he posited, "apparently believed that the more attractive they were, the better the chances of getting their items or pictures in the paper. And they were right." He recalled the stir Brown created when she first visited him in his cubbyhole of an office at the *Chicago Defender* in 1936. Brown, he recalled, was a "shapely brown-skin woman wearing white jodhpurs, a form fitting white jacket and white boots." She "made such a stunning appearance that all the typewriters suddenly went silent" as she strode steadily, with an "undercurrent of determination" and a "confident bearing" while speaking in a "husky voice."[16]

Either coincidentally or as a result of Brown's influence, it was Waters who later applied for a state charter to form the National Negro Airmen's Association of America in 1939. He, Brown, and pilot Chauncey Spencer wrote the charter at the Wabash Avenue "Y," and *Chicago Defender* founder Robert Sengstacke Abbott allowed the organization to use the newspaper's 3435 South Indiana Avenue headquarters as its mailing address. Its founders later chose to remove the word "Negro" from the name of the organization since they believed its inclusion would be antithetical to the rising anti-Jim Crow sentiment.

---

15   Memorandum by Major General B. K. Yount, 5 October 1940, 145.93-80, 145.93-92, January 1936-April 1936, June 1941-September 1941, AFHRA.

16   Waters, *American Diary*, 201. Unfortunately, Brown's encounter with Waters' sexism was not unusual. Her attempts to make her way in an environment dominated by men were legion. Leon Jennings of Chicago, who once worked for Brown at Chicago's Harlem Airport, described her as a "horrible" employer. He claimed to have lost his temper once after a "blowup" with Brown. "I do remember trying to hit her with the wall telephone," he admitted; however, "The cord was not long enough, so the phone did not actually hit her." Despite their near-violent differences, Jennings added that, he did not think of Brown as a "bad" or "evil" person; rather, he viewed her as "selfish" and "self-centered." See Leon Jennings to Betty Gubert, 12 September 1995, Box 3, Gubert Papers. Additionally, in 1934, Brown was seriously injured in an auto crash that killed a man described as her "companion" (*Chicago Defender*, May 19, 1934).

Thus, not coincidentally, Chicago—the home of Robinson (who earlier formed the Challenger Air Pilots Association in 1931), Waters, Coffey, and Brown—became the citadel of aviation initiatives spearheaded by African Americans. However, the fact that the Windy City soon was supplanted by Alabama as the byword of Negro aviation was not simply due to the lobbying of Claude Barnett—yet another Chicagoan. According to Chauncey Spencer, Tuskegee won out over Chicago as the primary site for the training of Negro pilots simply because of one factor: less inclement weather.[17]

But why did Chicago rise to such early prominence for Negro aviation? The answer: It was partly due to happenstance and partly to the result of a coming together of a uniquely constituted and populous community. With more than a hint of exaggeration, Duke Ellington, the famed composer, hailed Chicago's South Side as "a community of men and women who were respected, people of great dignity—doctors, lawyers, policy operators, bootblacks, barbers, beauticians, bartenders, saloon keepers, night clerks, cab owners and cab drivers, stockyard workers, owners of after-hour joint, bootleggers—everything and everybody."[18] This phalanx of Negro rectitude was confronted with a firm Jim Crow that helped to spawn a firmer still Negro creativity, a good deal of which was poured into aviation. Ironically, racist efforts to undermine Black initiative served only to reinforce Black Chicagoans' desire to overcome.

During this era, according to Waters, "it was not uncommon for a [Chicago] Negro to find the tires of his new car slashed or the windshield shattered." With a lingering bitterness, he recalled: "Some whites even resented being passed on the highway by a more powerful car driven by a Negro," leaving to his readers' imaginations how those whites felt when espying Negroes climbing through the skies. "Even the pets of

---

17 Interview with Chauncey Spencer, 3 June 1995, Box 3, Gubert Papers.
18 Waters, *American Diary*, 69, 79, 84 (Ellington quoted in these pages).

Robert Abbott. Founder of the Chicago Defender newspaper. (Courtesy Moorland-Spingarn Research Center, Howard University)

Negroes were regularly denied treatment at white-owned vet hospitals and deprived of a burial plot by some white pet cemeteries," he added, sardonically asserting that those whites apparently believed the animals had "acquired during life the racial identities of their masters."[19]

Thus, when the owner of Chicago's Harlem Airport decided that he had seen enough of the likes of Coffey and Brown out of fear that their presence was persuading some to conclude that his was a "Negro"

---

19 Ibid.

facility, he explicitly told them to stay away.[20] This, of course, mightily complicated their efforts to train more Black pilots. It was especially unfortunate because a number of Negroes were receiving their early training there, including Grover C. Nash, the first Negro to deliver the U.S. mail by air. Nash had begun flying at Harlem Airport in 1931 under the tutelage of Colonel John Robinson.[21]

African American pilots and enthusiasts meet at Harlem Airport, Chicago, 1937. (Courtesy Chicago History Museum)

Marie St. Clair Thompson was another of the many Black pilots who got their first training at the Chicago airfield. Thompson, however, maintained that it was Willa Brown, not her taciturn spouse Cornelius Coffey, who was the brains behind the Negro aviation operation at Harlem. Perhaps that helps explain why Thompson, reflecting years

20   Undated memorandum, Box 3, Gubert Papers.
21   Press Release, April 1941, Reel 22, #372, Part I, Press Releases, CAB-NCSU.

later, insisted that she never detected any harassment against women in those early days. "We were just one big family," she recalled, "there was [no] resentment toward women—nothing like that"[22]

In other words, the non-sexist nature of the Harlem Airport training experience was due in no small part to the influence of Willa Brown. Yet, as Brown was reaching her peak at Harlem Airport, news accounts were reporting that

> ...female students interested in aviation have not been accepted in some of the Negro institutions authorized by the government to teach aeronautics to colored, largely because there have been no facilities for their accommodation and instruction of the fields. In one large university, the girls flocked to the class seeking admission [but] they were gently turned away.[23]

Brown, by way of contrast, was instrumental in introducing an aviation curriculum at the Wendell Phillips Evening School in Chicago in January 1940. For that, she brought together as collaborators the NAAA, the local Board of Education, and what would later became the U.S. Civil Aeronautics Board, a federal agency. Not only did the Wendell Phillips program teach students how to fly, it also trained aircraft woodworkers, sheet metal workers, and engine mechanics. Its centerpiece, however, was the air pilots' program, which enrolled more than 150 students and offered such courses as History of Aviation, Theory of Flight and Aircraft, Civil Air Regulations, Practical Air Navigation, Meteorology, Parachuting, Aircraft Instruments, and Radio Uses and Terms. Most students trained in Piper Cub planes, with Coffey and Brown serving as their principal instructors. More advanced students trained in the two 220-horsepower Army Waco open planes provided to the program by the U.S. Army Air Corps or engaged in "observation study" in the program's Boeing P-12 pursuit plane.

---

22 Interview with Marie St. Clair Thompson, 9 September 1996, Box 3, Gubert Papers.
23 Press Release, January 1940, Reel 20, #212, Part I, Press Releases, CAB-NCSU.

The versatile Brown was also the program's principal instructor in aviation mechanics. Reportedly, she was the only woman in the nation employed in such a capacity at the time. Mounted in her shop were two late-model Pratt and Whitney radial engines as well as two Curtiss Conqueror water-cooled engines. Scattered about were various carburetors, magnetos, generators, starters, and aircraft instruments. Her shop was equipped to provide instruction in various aviation-related operations such as rigging, top overhauls, carburetion, fabrication, covering, and doping.

Tellingly, the program's students were not just Negroes but included various U.S. nationals of Polish, Italian, Mexican, and Bohemian descent. That students of various ancestries chose to study under the tutelage of African Americans is suggestive of the high level of dedication and interest in aviation demonstrated by the program instructors. It may also suggest, as happens so often in the U.S., that the white students, in particular, may have been amenable to Black trainers only so long as they (whites) were being prepared to replace those instructors pursuant to Jim Crow rules.[24]

Although Brown was an instructor with the Wendell Phillips program, when advertising was done to solicit students for the program those ads explicitly targeted men between the ages of 18 and 28.[25] This was unlike what she had experienced at Harlem Airport. Rachel Carter Ellis, one of the few women who somehow managed to get into the Phillips program and who was trained by Brown, confirmed years later that the "federal rule" at the time was that "one woman was to be taught for every ten men."[26] As Waters suggests, however, Brown may have been moved to open the doors of Harlem Airport to women based on her own unfortunate experiences. In his view, her

24 Clifford J. Campbell, "They're Learning to Fly in Chicago," *Opportunity*, 5, (March 1941), 132-134.
25 Press Release, March 1940, Reel 20, #561, Part I, Press Releases, CAB-NCSU.
26 Interview with Rachel Carter Ellis, 22 July 1995, Box 3, Gubert Papers.

soaring skyward was a metaphor for the sexism she sought vainly to transcend.

James L. H. Peck, a storied Negro pilot, earlier had traveled to Spain to fight fascism and had encountered the worst that Jim Crow had to offer, yet those experiences did not necessarily mean that he was able to overcome the manacles of gender bias. Peck reflected without irony on the "Winsome Willa Brown, our First Lady of the sky." Before she wed Coffey, he gushed effusively about her status:

> What we don't know [is] how she has managed to escape Cupid thus far! Brains and beauty in the same girl is NEWS, people! Happy landings, lovely ladybird!…[Who] wants to be all alone in the vast, thought inspiring skyland when the company of Wonder Girl Willa is to be had to point out the pretty clouds and such…?

Understandably, this "pretty lady" often opted to escape to the "vast thought-inspiring skyland" to escape the prying—and leering—eyes of her peers. Still, even the limited Peck noticed that while "many women fly, few indeed know how to diagnose the ills of a sick meter" or had "nearly 400 hours solo flying time," both of which summed up Brown's experience at that juncture. "People like to fly with Willa," he commented, for "she's carried almost 500 passengers from Harlem Airport" alone. Still, he could not refrain from adding that the woman who was billed as the "Queen of Aviation" and the "highest-ranking colored woman in the field"—and who was "part owner of the largest privately owned Negro aviation school in the country [the Coffey School of Aviation]"[27]–was also a "boss of the airport restaurant on the side."[28]

Undeterred by the obvious sexism of her day, Brown continued to train pilots, including Rose Agnes Rolls, who, at 21 and in the spring

---

27   Press Release, August 1941, Reel 22, #1003, Press Releases, CAB-NCSU.
28   Press Release, April 1940, Reel 20, #698, Part I, Press Releases, CAB-NCSU.

of 1941, was reportedly the "youngest Negro woman licensed pilot in the country."[29] Rolls—also known as Rose Agnes Rolls Cousins—once observed that her interest in piloting stemmed from the fact that she "always [did] 'boy' things." She also maintained that her attempt to continue in the aviation field at Tuskegee was blocked because of her gender. "I would definitely have been accepted if I had been a man," she insisted. The same could have been said for Dorothy Arline Layne McIntyre, the mother of contemporary choreographer Dianne McIntyre. The elder McIntyre earned her pilot's license in 1940.[30]

As one scholar argues, women, "as pilots…experienced feelings of strength, mastery and confidence." Though the same could be said of male Negro pilots, it applies doubly or triply perforce to Negro women pilots. Ironically, this conclusion is reinforced by the strenuousness with which force was exerted to keep women out of airplanes. It was not unusual, for example, for women to be expelled forcibly from the cockpit,[31] but this often served only to reinforce their determination to fly—this was especially so, *a fortiori*, for Negro women.

* * *

The Brown–Coffey model of pilot training was not necessarily congruent with the model that developed later at Tuskegee. That is, the former—though led by Negroes—was integrated, both in terms of race and gender, while the latter (led by Euro-Americans) was segregated. In early 1941, after a meeting with Brown—one that she left, displeased—Barnett acknowledged that Brown wanted an "integration" that his *alma mater*, Tuskegee Institute, was simply unable to deliver in Alabama.[32] Illiberal Jim Crow did not lend itself

---

29 Press Release, May 1941, Reel 22, #541, Press Releases, CAB-NCSU.

30 Article from *American Visions*, August-September 1998, Box 7, Gubert Papers. See *New York Times*, June 17, 1984: The choreographed performance, "Takeoff from a Forced Landing," was grounded in her mother's experience.

31 Corn, *Winged Gospel*, 73, 130.

32 Press Release, January 1941, Reel 11, #355, Series B, Part III, Subject Files on Black

to progressivism, particularly in Alabama. Ambrose Andrews, who was trained at Tuskegee, later admitted that Negroes were subjected to "abusive" maltreatment there.[33]

Barnett believed that Brown and her cohorts were being unduly influenced by an "intellectual"—Howard Gould of the National Urban League—who was "near the fringe of radicalism, a highly emotional person." He further claimed that, in their stormy encounter, he had "punctured" Brown and company's "dream of personal benefit" and, by doing so, had "hurt their pride to think they could not stop the Tuskegee program." Though he admitted that Chicago was "the center of Negro aviation among Negroes in America" Barnett argued that the recruitment of pilots in the Second City had fallen off to "practically nil" at a time when war clouds were developing ominously in Europe.[34] He neglected to note that his own news agency had reported in March 1940 that 20 young men received scholarships to attend the Brown-Coffey aviation school. What Barnett could not obscure, however, was that if the Chicago Training Center of the Civil Aeronautics Authority had prevailed, newly minted Negro aviators would have been trained by a corps led by a woman—namely, Willa Brown. [35]

In early 1941, in a "confidential" missive, Barnett dismissively referred, with disgust, to "some misguided people" whom he felt were "preparing to attack the aviation program at Tuskegee on the basis of it being segregated." He wrote that he was aghast at that assertion, observing that "any program which Negroes develop will be segregated." He also noted that Harlem Airport in Chicago—where Brown, Waters, and Gould wanted pilots to be trained—had its own Jim Crow problems. "It is entirely segregated in the north when it

Americans, CAB-NCSU.

33 *Hartford Courant*, September 28, 1992.

34 Memorandum, circa 1941, Reel 11, $411, Series B, Part III, Subject Files on Black Americans, CAB-NCSU.

35 Press Release, March 1940, Reel 20, #563, Part I, Press Releases, CAB-NCSU.

need not be," he charged while acknowledging that the three could "do some harm if they start a lot of mud slinging."[36] Waters would not yield, however, and after speaking with him, Barnett concluded that Waters believed "that if ever there was a time for Negroes to strike for integration it is now" while a "separate unit," as proposed for Alabama, was little more than a "sop"—and an ineffective one at that.[37]

In its favor, Tuskegee had Barnett in its corner. His presence in Chicago and his influence there was a demerit for the Brown–Coffey initiative in that it suggested something less than monolithic backing in that metropolis. Barnett was just one of a corps of active Tuskegee Institute alumni in Chicago who, according to Daniel Faulkner, chair of the Aviation Committee of the Chicago Tuskegee Club, were trying to raise $5,000 for "the construction of an airport on the campus." At the time, Tuskegee was leasing an airfield from an entity Faulkner described as the "White Estate Co.," but it planned to void that lease soon. "The Negro Youth of 17 states whose applications are on file at Tuskegee would get the opportunity which has been denied to the[m] in other places," Faulkner boasted, bemoaning a recent report that the government was "training more White Women to fly than Negro Men."[38]

What even influential Tuskegee alumni found hard to deny was the opposition in Alabama to the idea of training Negro aviators. "Airport hysteria reached new heights" was one headline describing the reaction there. Supporters wheeled out Barnett to address these concerns. He was joined by Janet Harmon Waterford, the veteran aviatrix, who later was disappointed when she was not asked to play a role in the headline-grabbing venture.[39] Barnett, of course, frequently expressed his ire,

---

36 Claude Barnett to F. D. Patterson, 18 January 1941, Reel 7, #559, Series B, Part III, Subject Files on Black Americans, CAB-NCSU.

37 Claude Barnett to F. D. Patterson, 26 January 1941, Reel 7, #568, Series B, Part III, Subject Files on Black Americans, CAB-NCSU.

38 Daniel Faulkner to Roscoe Giles, 8 July 1940, Reel 11, #339, Series B, Part III, Subject Files on Black Americans, CAB-NCSU.

39 Press Release, November 1940, Reel 21, #867, Part I, Press Releases, CAB-NCSU.

Janet Harmon Waterford Bragg. This Chicagoan, pictured in the 1930s, was the first African American woman to hold a full commercial pilot license.
(Courtesy Chicago History Museum)

complaining to Ohio Congresswoman and desegregation proponent Frances Bolton that the process of allocating the contract for the airfield in Tuskegee was "rigged." Tuskegee, he demanded, wanted a "colored man" to head the project but the Institute's choice, engineer/ mathematician Archie Alexander of Des Moines, was being "blocked."[40]

---

40 Claude Barnett to Congresswoman Frances Bolton, 4 December 1941, Reel 1, #88, Series

Apparently, Barnett and Colonel Robinson had reconciled their earlier differences by 1941, for the acclaimed defender of Ethiopia told a Tuskegee official that year that although he had "plenty of financial obligations on returning to Chicago," he was eager to head to Alabama to work with the college's nascent program. Robinson, who by then had his own Chicago-based aviation school and owned three planes (housing one of them at Glenview Field in the Chicago suburbs),[41] was enthusiastic about the Tuskegee flight training initiative. After visiting the Institute, he professed, he was "very much impressed" with its program. "[I] want to do everything in [my] power," he proclaimed, "to assist you in any way that I can." Robinson went a step further, reproving the Brown-Coffey effort as being "set up to save the face of the Army and as an excuse not to admit Negroes into the Army Air Corps."[42]

Having Robinson on board was a coup for Tuskegee. To add luster to its application, the Institute listed Robinson as "President" of the Chicago Tuskegee Club, which busily lobbied on behalf of the school's proposed aviation training program.[43] For his part, he seemed hell-bent on going to Alabama to teach, adding the following qualifications to the application:

> I have over two thousand solo hours of flying, which includes two motor airplanes as well as three motor aircraft [although] most of my flying has been in heavy aircraft....I [had] a considerable amount of actual blind flying [that is, flying without radio contact or adequate instrumentation] before going to Ethiopia. I taught over one hundred and fifty students, white and colored, to fly and also taught airplane mechanics.[44]

C, Economic Conditions, Part III, CAB-NCSU.

41 Memorandum, circa 1941, Reel 7, #716, Series B, Part III, Subject Files on Black Americans, CAB-NCSU.

42 John Robinson to G. L. Washington, 20 May 1941, Reel 7, #632, Series B, Part III, Subject Files on Black Americans, CAB-NCSU.

43 Alvin Neely to J. W. Dunn, 4 March 1941, Reel 11, #389, Series B, Part III, Subject Files on Black Americans, CAB-NCSU.

44 John Robinson to F. D. Patterson, 3 April 1942, Reel 7, #761, Series B, Part III, Subject

Barnett did not stop there. By 1941, he had on his side the other "star" of Black aviation: James Peck, now returned from combat on the frontlines in Europe. Peck, Barnett claimed, was a "real aviator" with "war experience in Spain" and a "most intelligent chap" besides. In an effort to deliver a "tremendous lot of publicity,"[45] he maneuvered to have both Peck and Robinson visit Tuskegee simultaneously.

This fervent interest by Negroes in aviation was duly noted by the senator from Missouri, Harry S Truman. Upon learning of a 1939 biplane flight from Chicago to Washington, DC, executed by Chauncey Spencer and Dale White, Truman expressed surprise that the Army Air Corps would not accept Negroes. This set in motion a chain of events that led to the formation of the Tuskegee Airmen, although it just as easily could have meant the creation of the Brown-Coffey Airmen (and women).[46] The National Urban League posited in January 1941 that it was "quite obvious that the facilities for training a Negro Air Corps group at Tuskegee will be inferior to those existing at other government training fields, such as Kelly Field in Texas and McChord Field in the state of Washington."[47] The latter sites did indeed come up short and as things turned out, so did Robinson. Though Robinson's endorsement of the Tuskegee site was important, by the time the program took off there a Tuskegee official conceded that working with the Colonel, whose reputation for prickliness evidently had preceded him, was a disdainful exercise: "I do not feel our staff would be too well disposed towards this young man."[48]

Apparently, Barnett was more inclined to aid his *alma mater* than his hometown, particularly given that he had more influence over the

---

Files on Black Americans, CAB-NCSU.

45   Claude Barnett to F. D. Patterson, 27 February 1941, Reel 7, #588, Series B, Part III, Subject Files on Black Americans, CAB-NCSU.

46   *Lynchburg News and Advance*, 5 March 1995, Box 8, Gubert Papers.

47   Edward Lawson to Lester Granger, 18 January 1941, Box I: F11, National Urban League Papers.

48   G. L. Williams to F. D. Patterson, 8 April 1942, Reel 7, #777, Series B, Part III, Subject Files on Black Americans, CAB-NCSU.

former than the latter. "I talked with Willa Brown," he commented in January 1941, "and sought to show [her] the value of confining their efforts to fighting for Negro integration into the air corps and to avoid their threatened attacks upon Tuskegee." He found her attitude," in response, "not altogether satisfactory." Barnett also treated the National Urban League's Howard Gould, Brown's partner in the Chicago effort, dismissively, asserting to Tuskegee President Frederick Douglass Patterson that Gould "seems to think that it was his herculean efforts which got [the federal government] to start colored schools in the first place." He added that Gould accused Patterson of "throwing off" the Chicago initiative; and that he had similarly accused William Hastie, the eminent lawyer, and Truman Gibson, a member of President Franklin Roosevelt's "Black Cabinet," of "laying down on the issue of integration" by pushing for Tuskegee as the site for training of Negro pilots.[49]

Barnett's position was in line with that of a number of influential activists of the time, who thought the siting of Tuskegee as the prime place for Black aviators was a victory for Jim Crow. To drive home their point, he chastised Waters and Brown, whom he felt "assume[d] that it is possible to break the tradition of no mixed units in the air corps since there has been no segregation within that corps,"[50] Additionally, he did not hesitate to assail "the Coffey School with the attractive Miss Brown" at the helm, even though Brown had the "[*Chicago Defender*] for a personal publicity organ until they transferred her great and good friend [Waters],"[51] whom Barnett was to hire eventually.

It is not that Barnett and his ilk were pro-Jim Crow, it was more that they were bent determinedly on securing a plum assignment for Tuskegee. They also were aware that establishing a "mixed unit" in

---

49   Claude Barnett to F. D. Patterson, 20 January 1941, Reel 1, #610, Series C, Part III, Economic Conditions, CAB-NCSU.
50   Press Release, January 1941, Reel 15, #292, Part II, Organizational Files, CAB-NCSU.
51   Claude Barnett to Ernest Johnson, 20 March 1943, Reel 1, #614, Part III, Economic Conditions, CAB-NCSU.

apartheid Alabama would be neither easy nor simple—or even probable. Feeling the heat, the NAACP, in February 1941, denounced the formation of a "Jim Crow Air Squadron" at Tuskegee.[52] This view was consistent with the previously enunciated stances of that organization, whose leader, Walter White, had been told by the Secretary of War in 1938 that the "exclusion of Negro citizens from the flying service of the Army" was perfectly acceptable. White, of course, was outraged by this assertion, which, according to the Secretary, followed the "well established principle that the races should not be mixed within organizations, a principle which is endorsed by your own people." The Secretary's latter reference was left unexplained, but he also added: "Since no colored units of the Air Corps are provided for in the Army of the United States, it is impossible for the War Department to accept colored applicants at Air Corps schools."

Tuskegee thus became a kind of work around Washington, allowing for the training of Negro pilots while maintaining the apparently sacrosanct principle of Jim Crow—a principle much of the Negro leadership of that time felt compelled to accept.[53] That consensus did not include Walter White, who responded to the Secretary accordingly: "How hypocritical it is that the United States is denouncing the action of Germany and Italy for discriminating against citizens because of race and creed while the War Department is doing precisely the same."[54]

By spring 1941, Hastie—known to be close to the NAACP leadership—was said to have "requested no segregation of Negroes and Whites in the Aviation Units." Robert Lovett, an eventual Secretary of Defense and then well connected in U.S. war councils, was said to have answered Hastie's request resoundingly: "[D]efinitely no—

---

52 Press Release, 14 February 1941, Box II: B194, NAACP Papers.
53 Harry Woodring, Secretary of War to Walter White, 12 December 1938, Box II: L31, NAACP Papers.
54 Walter White to Harry Woodring, 2 December 1938, Box II: L31, NAACP Papers

there must and will be segregation."[55] Lovett may have been aware of the 1939 opinion from the Air Corps, which concluded, in effect, that desegregation was hardly mandated:

> ...the law does not specifically require that Negro pilots be trained, although it does provide that one or more schools...be designated...for the training of any Negro air pilot. Therefore, the law is complied with when the school has been designated.[56]

Upon learning of Lovett's position, Barnett did not say what a later historian acknowledged, which was that the region surrounding Tuskegee not only was hostile to "integration" at that juncture but also that the renowned Tuskegee Institute had no flight equipment, no flight personnel, and no suitable airfield for advanced training.[57] The Institute seemed to be in a steep decline in any case. By early 1939, Jesse Thomas of the National Urban League told Barnett that he was "very much distressed at the plan afoot to "discontinue the Nurses' Training School at Tuskegee."[58] Barnett conceded, noting that that Hampton Institute in Virginia had also recently closed its nursing school and, with regard to Tuskegee: "[T]here is a $75, 000 deficit in the budget and you can't sneeze that off, neither can you raise it from rich folk," he added.[59] This decline seemed not to discourage Barnett but rather to encourage him to press even harder for pilots to be trained at Tuskegee to compensate for that loss. The Brown–Coffey initiative, on the other hand, was well equipped to soar but instead was to be grounded.

---

55 Major Ralph F. Stearley, Air Corps to Commanding General of Air Corps Training Center, Maxwell Field, 8 May 1941, 220.740, 220.765-2, 1940-1945, 1942, Volume 2, Volume 3, AFHRA.

56 Memorandum from "C. S., Chief, Plans Division," 3 April 1939, 145.93-80, 145.93-92, January 1936-April 1936, June 1941-September 1941, AFHRA.

57 Broadnax, *Blue Skies, Black Wings*, 27, 30.

58 Jesse O. Thomas to Claude Barnett, 28 February 1939, Box VI: A60, National Urban League Papers.

59 Claude Barnett to Jesse O. Thomas, 2 March 1939, Box VI: A60, National Urban League Papers.

Pressures were building to incorporate Negro aviators into the armed forces nonetheless. Part of this accumulated pressure was generated by Negro aviators themselves, but the Selective Service Act also began to assert itself on the issue. Analysts predicted that a growing number of Black inductees would be drafted into military service, at least in proportion to the overall population, and those inductees would have to be absorbed by some branch of the armed forces. The Army seemed the most logical landing place; but when the influx of Negro servicemen actually occurred, the Army began to pressure the Air Corps to take its share, and the latter was compelled to accede.[60]

Another source of this building pressure was the alteration of military strategy brought by the growth of aviation. The pilot James Peck, whom Barnett employed to write a regular column entitled "Plane Talk"—which was, in itself, yet another indicator of rising Negro interest in aviation—told his audience that airpower had changed fundamentally how wars would be fought, as aviation bolstered reconnaissance and amplified bombing. Peck was not alone in sensing that African Americans would be forced once again to make the ultimate sacrifice on behalf of freedoms they did not enjoy. Yet even Peck realized that aviators were being trained disproportionately in Dixie—not just Alabama, but Texas (San Antonio) and Florida (Pensacola) too. The Jim Crow circumstances of the South, in his view, presented "multifold difficulties for colored flying cadets."[61] By September 1940, he noted, aviation training had commenced at the historically Black Lincoln University in Missouri, but it too was located in a Jim Crow region and did not promise surcease from harassment.[62]

---

60 Claude Barnett to [Tuskegee Institute] President F. D. Patterson, 20 January 1941, Reel 1, #610, Series C, Part III, Economic Conditions, CAB-NCSU.
61 Press Release, April 1940, Reel 20, #743, Part I, Press Releases, CAB-NCSU.
62 Press Release, September 1940, Reel 21, #521, Part I, Press Releases, CAB-NCSU.

The press of war by early 1941 most likely led to the enlistment of the first Nigerian pilot in the British Royal Air Force (RAF).[63] Soon thereafter, three Bahamians of African descent were accepted into the British air corps.[64] Negro aviators barred from upward mobility in the U.S. also moved to join the RAF. This list included Fred Hutcherson of Evanston, Illinois, who trained with Brown and Coffey and also managed a local airport in the 1930s.[65] After being rejected by the U.S. Air Corps, he left the country for England, where he became an RAF pilot.[66] Yet even the heralded RAF was inconsistent in its call for diversity among its flight corps. In Montreal, Canada, RAF recruitment advertisements calling for pilots for a ferry service explicitly stated that "no colored" applicants would be considered.[67]

The press of war had impact beyond the North Atlantic. Perhaps realizing the value displayed by Colonel Robinson, Ras Kassa, a chief advisor to His Imperial Majesty, then learned to fly too.[68] Hence, by 1940, Peck was excited about the possibilities for Black aviation. As he wrote, "[W]ithin the last five years more than a few Negroes have had occasion to travel by air," including the reigning celebrity of them all—heavyweight boxing champion Joe Louis—a "constant air traveler" whom Peck claimed was "crazy for airplanes and would like to have a small one of his own."

Although flying primarily with foreign carriers may have influenced his opinion unduly, Peck found the airline personnel of the day to be "extremely courteous and efficient." He reported having flown "some 15, 000 miles as an airline passenger—in the U.S. and with British Airways and Air France"—and professed to have had

---

63 Press Release, January 1941, Reel 21, #1236, Part I, Press Releases, CAB-NCSU.
64 Press Release, August 1941, Reel 22, #975, Part I, Press Releases, CAB-NCSU.
65 Clipping, circa July 1950, Box 6, Gubert Papers.
66 Press Release, October 1943, Reel 26, #1158, Part I, Press Releases, CAB-NCSU.
67 Press Release, September 1941, Reel 23, #38, Part I, Press Releases, CAB-NCSU.
68 Press Release, February 1941, Reel 21, #12, Part I, Press Releases, CAB-NCSU.

"the same pleasant experience" on all carriers. Peck also maintained that the Civil Aeronautics Authority, the federal agency charged with regulating aviation services, dealt "fairly with colored airmen," but even he had to ask: "will these airlines hire Negro pilots, stewardesses, radiomen, mechanics?" His answer: "unfortunately not."[69]

Joe Louis was not the only Negro celebrity of his day who was being bedazzled by aviation. The popular Negro musician Jimmie Lunceford began taking flying lessons in 1939. By 1940, he had a license to fly; and by 1941, he had purchased a fast three-seater, a Bellanca Model 19-9 Junior, for a hefty $20,000. Lunceford then began flying to his many engagements along with his spouse, who would soon obtain her own license. Although he crashed once, he was undeterred and, thumbing his nose at peril, promptly bought two more planes.[70]

Peck's, and presumably Lunceford's, somewhat rosy view of aviation was echoed by J. E. Taylor Jr., a graduate of and teacher at Langston University in the Sooner State. Taylor argued: "aviation is the only field wherein I have not encountered any prejudice against the Negro in Oklahoma."[71] Yet, if he had spoken then to NAACP attorney Thurgood Marshall about that issue, Taylor would have received an earful about what the future Supreme Court justice described as a "case involving the refusal to accept the application of a Negro for enlistment in the Air Corps."[72] He might also have been informed about the circumstances surrounding Carl Hurd's grievances. In that case, Hurd directly informed President Roosevelt that he had been "barred from the Air Corps...because [he was] a Negro."[73]

The opportunistic Hubert Julian did not await an answer to Peck's inquiry about opportunities for Negroes in aviation. After the debacle

---

69 Press Release, May 1940, Reel 20, #876, Part I, Press Releases, CAB-NCSU.
70 Eddy Determeyer, *Rhythm is Our Business: Jimmie Lunceford and the Harlem Express* (Ann Arbor: The University of Michigan Press, 2009), 183.
71 Press Release, January 1941, Reel 21, #1210, Part I, Press Releases, CAB-NCSU.
72 Thurgood Marshall to Dr. L.A. Ransom, 9 October 1940, Box II: B194, NAACP Papers.
73 Carl Hurd to President Roosevelt, 28 November 1940, Box II: B194, CAB-CHM.

of his East African escapade, he promptly turned to other ventures. By early 1940 he was working with the pioneering Black filmmaker Oscar Micheaux in the production of movies.[74] Finding moviemaking insufficiently captivating, he soon decamped to France, but quickly fled that nation after being accused of fraud.[75] A few months later, he was in Finland, fighting against the Soviet Union as a "captain in the Finnish Air Force" with a commission from the fabled Baron Mannerheim himself. He returned to the U.S. briefly, purportedly to obtain 10 ambulances for the harried Finnish forces.[76]

Julian also met in the U.S. with William Pickens of the NAACP and British activist Sylvia Pankhurst to discuss the creation of a Red Cross unit of U.S. Negroes to be sent to Ethiopia under London's sponsorship.[77] Weeks later, the peripatetic Julian was in Montreal, planning a flight to London to engage the Nazi chief Herman Goering in an air duel to the death.[78] He was next sighted in Ottawa, where he failed a flight test to join the Royal Canadian Air Force, almost crashing his plane.[79] He survived, as did his colorful career.

As Peck mused about the new vistas opening for Negroes in aviation and Julian awkwardly sought to take advantage of this new scenario, a predictable and especially pointed counter-reaction was mounting. Likewise predictable, the man at the tip of the spear was one who knew more than most of the strategic value of aviation in warfare: Charles "Lucky Lindy" Lindbergh. Since his trendsetting 1927 trans-Atlantic journey, Lindbergh had moved steadily to the political right— so much so that he was viewed widely as the face of U.S. fascism. Gordon Hancock, a moderate Negro leader in Dixie,[80] was among

74 Press Release, January 1940, Reel 20, #323, Part I, Press Releases, CAB-NCSU.
75 Memorandum, 31 January 1940, Box 620, PI 57 Epp HM 1992, Decimal files, NARA-CP.
76 Press Release, July 1940, Reel 21, #99, Part I, Press Releases, CAB-NCSU.
77 Press Release, August 1940, Reel 21, #278, Part I, Press Releases, CAB-NCSU.
78 Press Release, October 1940, Reel 21, #691, Part I, Press Releases, CAB-NCSU.
79 Press Release, December 1940, Reel 21, #1017, Part I, Press Releases, CAB-NCSU.
80 Raymond Gavins, *The Perils and Prospects of Southern Black Leadership: Gordon Blaine*

those appalled when the famous aviator announced, after the German military invaded Poland in 1939, that "if the white race is ever seriously threatened, it then may be time for us to take our part in its [Europe] protection, to fight side by side…but not with one against the other for our mutual destruction."[81] Lindbergh "knows how to fly but knows very little else," cracked the NAACP's William Pickens. "We can forgive him for scorning and harassing the Negro who found his dead baby's body," said Pickens, referring to the infamous kidnapping and murder that only recently had gripped the nation, "but we will not forgive his [support]" of Nazis.[82]

It was not just Lindbergh who attracted the acerbic Pickens' ire. "There are no angels in this affair," he wrote, observing as world war unfolded that African Americans found it difficult to back London, Africa's tormentor, even against Berlin. "[B]ut we do not have to choose the worst of the devils," he added, referring to those backed by the "pro-fascist" Lindbergh.[83] Pickens further disparaged as having a "pitiable mentality" any Negroes, even presumably "intelligent" Negroes, who alluded to being "happy and hopeful, because those white folk are killing each other off."[84] Outraged by this maundering, he maintained that such alienated Negroes were "idiots" for proclaiming "it won't hurt colored people if the Germans win" or "if Hitler wins this war, it will help the Negro."[85]

Arguably, the emergence of Charles Lindbergh, a famed aviator, as fascism's most notorious defender turbo-charged already accelerating Negro interest in the strategically important field that was aviation. Linking Lindbergh, fascism, and the bedevilment of Ethiopia—

Hancock (Durham, NC: Duke University Press, 1993).

81 Press Release, October 1939, Reel 19, #799, Part I, Press Release, CAB-NCSU.

82 Press Release, October 1939, Reel 19, #876, Part I, Press Releases, CAB-NCSU.

83 Press Release, May 1941, Reel 22, #523, Part I, Press Releases, CAB-NCSU.

84 Press Release, June 1940, Reel 20, #1136, Part I, Press Releases, CAB-NCSU.

85 Press Release, March 1941, Reel 22, #164, Part I, Press Releases, CAB-NCSU.

and, by inference, the intensified bedevilment of African Americans themselves—was not a difficult task. Lindbergh, scoffed Gordon Hancock, was one of "Hitler's stooges."[86] Lindbergh's "anti-Negro attitude is so generally acknowledged by Negroes themselves," he continued, "that on general principles we oppose him." The aviator's backing of the "America First" movement, which sought to keep the U.S. out of the impending world war, was reason enough for Hancock—and other Negroes—to look askance at that Lindbergh-influenced crusade.[87] Lindbergh's popularity was doubtlessly a factor when leading Negro intellectuals began predicting the eminent rise of a peculiar brand of U.S. fascism.[88]

* * *

By 1941, the pressure of a changing world was compelling colonial and Jim Crow regimes alike to reconsider segregationist aviation policies thought to be sacrosanct. Pan American Airlines' service from Cape Town to New York was inaugurated that year, with the city then known as Leopoldville being the first leg heading north on that 9,235 mile journey. The U.S. airliner crowed that its intercontinental service could "bring the Dark Continent within five days of New York City."[89] As the world shrank and became more interconnected, and as war and grievous loss loomed, the major powers found it increasingly necessary to employ their darker citizenry. Thus, subjects theretofore ignored moved more and more to the forefront.

Advances in aviation also brought the Western Hemisphere's rising power—the United States of America—into the colonial backyards of the European colonial powers, leading Washington to develop a pragmatic interest in anti-colonialism. This shift would

86 Press Release, June 1941, Reel 22, #552, Part I, Press Releases, CAB-NCSU.
87 Press Release, July 1941, Reel 22, #933, Part I, Press Releases, CAB-NCSU.
88 Press Release, August 1940, Reel 21, #400, Part I, Press Releases, CAB-NCSU.
89 "New Horizons" newsletter, December 1943, Box 200, Folder 19, Pan Am Papers.

contribute to the erosion of longstanding preferential trade agreements that often excluded or discriminated against U.S. corporations, including its airlines, and give the U.S. a vested interest in the decline of colonialism. By 1941, Pan-Am was offering flights to and from Ghana, West Africa, and rapidly becoming a serious competitor to its British counterpart, the British Overseas Airways Corporation (BOAC).[90] Pan Am executives deftly disarmed the competition, creating the possibility that these colonialists would be less prone to resist usurpation. That was the implication when a Pan Am executive queried, noting that "some of the British are very anxious to buy some polo bulls, a dozen, if they are available in the States": "Again, could you oblige?"[91]

Naturally, the upstart U.S. thought they could do a better job in colonial West Africa than the U.K. "The European district [in Accra] is extremely lovely," wrote the appropriately named Harold Whiteman, one of Pan Am's top Africa executives, but "the native quarters are foul and repulsive." "The natives here," the North American continued, "are small, comparatively innocuous, but very bothersome."[92] Ineluctably, clashes erupted between Pan Am and BOAC. Such was the case, for example, when Pan Am asserted that it had the right to use not only the buildings at the airport in Kano, Nigeria—buildings erected by BOAC for its air services—but also all the land, ground equipment, and structures—likewise improved upon by the British for air travel—on the route stretching from the Gambia to Khartoum.[93] When the two major air powers clashed over such issues, arbitrage and leverage opportunities were created for the colonial subjects who were victimized routinely by those powers.

---

90 Harold Whiteman to William Van Dusen, 14 November 1941, Box 54, Folder 5, Pan Am Papers.

91 Ibid., 4 December 1941, Box 54, Folder 5, Pan Am Papers.

92 Ibid., 6 November 1941, Box 54, Folder 5. Pan Am Papers.

93 J. H. Smith Jr., Assistant Manager of Pan Am Africa to Brigadier General J. F. C. Hyde, 19 October 1942, Box 74, Folder 6, Pan Am Papers.

Whiteman also may not have considered bothersome the fact that African locales that once were hard to reach became more accessible at a time when the U.S. was not adverse to the erosion of their European rivals' influence and markets. The momentum for anti-colonial advance was gaining strength. As the African nations began to strain against the European chains that had bound and colonized them, many of their leaders cast a hopeful, yet skeptical, eye toward the U.S.—Jim Crow, notwithstanding—thus creating a momentum favorable to both Africans and African Americans alike.

Understandably, airlines like Pan Am, were powerful players in Washington. The U.S. aviation industry was regulated tightly, and the government often intervened to enable domestic carriers to reach far-flung sites. Juan Trippe, the founder of Pan American Airlines, was married to the daughter of Edward Stettinius, who later became—quite conveniently for the airline—the U.S. Secretary of State.[94] Then there were the government subsidies to plane manufacturers, direct and indirect, which made that industry even more susceptible to prodding by Washington, which in turn was prodded by increasingly well-organized Negro voters.[95] This forced airlines like Pan Am and, by inference, those who supplied them with planes to pay attention to both national and global trends. The growing movement toward socialism, which had sunk deep roots among the African American population by the 1930s and 1940s, was likewise globally minded, extending to Africa, Brazil, and other lush markets deemed important by U.S. carriers.[96]

---

94 Matthew Josephson, *Empire of the Air: Juan Trippe and the Struggle for World Airways* (New York: Harcourt Brace, 1944), 61.

95 See, e.g., Peter M. Bowers, *Boeing Aircraft Since 1916* (London: Putnam, 1966); Walter J. Boyne, ed., *Boeing B-52: A Documentary History* (London: Jane's, 1981).

96 See, e.g., Gerald Horne, *Black Revolutionary: William Patterson and the Globalization of the African American Freedom Struggle* (Urbana: University of Illinois Press, 2013); Gerald Horne, *Black Liberation/Red Scare: Ben Davis and the Communist Party* (Newark: University of Delaware Press, 1994); Gerald Horne, *Race Woman: The Lives of Shirley Graham Du Bois* (New York: New York University Press, 2000).

Surely, U.S. airline executives, who were in the vanguard of their nation's advance into Africa, were aware more than most of the transformative dynamics at play. This explains why Pan Am was mulling the Brazilian constitution in 1934 and concluding: "[T]aken as a whole, is not bad…considering the present socialistic wave that is menacing the peace of the world."[97] As a writer for Barnett's Associated Negro Press chortled in 1940, "[E]ven two hours in Brazil will show how….this must be the best country of all for people of color!"[98]

The war and the concomitant presence of more U.S. nationals globally also created a need for more passenger and cargo plane service in Africa. This led Pan American Airways to establish a local route initially within Liberia, a U.S. neo-colony.[99] It also created a supply line linking Miami to Karachi via Georgetown [British Guiana], Natal [Brazil], and Liberia, with other stops before reaching what is now Pakistan.[100] Pan Am had even more ambitious plans that implicated the African continent.[101] When Miami was linked to West Africa, ostensibly this also linked Jim Crow directly with colonialism and *neo*-colonialism. This worked to the detriment of these systems of scabrous wickedness in that Pan Am simultaneously had an interest in undermining the influence of the colonizing power and U.S. Negroes were brought closer to foreign allies.

With a foothold in Liberia, Pan Am began spreading its tentacles outward. William Van Dusen, a Pan Am official in the city that he referred to as "Leopoldville-Kinshasa" in the Belgian-colonized Congo, noted with surprise: "Few of us back home realize it, but the U.S. really means something down here." Van Dusen recalled the

---

97 Cauby Aruaujo to Vice President, Pan Am, 5 October 1934, Box 252, Folder 7, Pan Am Papers.
98 Press Release, March 1940, Reel 20, #565, Part I, Press Releases, CAB-NCSU.
99 Undated History of Pan Am Service in Africa, Box 258, Folder 3, Pan Am Papers.
100 Memorandum, 25 August 1942, Box 70, Folder 1, Accession II, Pan Am Papers.
101 "Agenda for Organization of African Operations," "Secret," 17 August 1941, Box 74, Folder 4, Accession II, Pan Am Papers.

United States' early recognition of the "Independent State of the Congo way back in 1884," noting that this contact was also an early indication that pro-Brussels and pro-colonial sentiments would soon become a hindrance as Washington began to exert more influence in the heart of Africa. He concluded nonetheless that "things have been doing pretty well" ever since tiny Belgium—"90 times" smaller than the Congo—"annexed'" that African nation. He reported that, as of 1941, his airline was offering "regularly scheduled Clipper service providing five-day schedules to the North American continent and direct connecting lines with practically every other section of the globe." Thus, Pan Am's flights made it possible for both the curious and the hostile to reach a city in a besieged colony previously shrouded from public view-—a city Van Dusen described as "probably the most modern town on the continent" with "modern sewers, electric lights, good water supply, paved streets." He thus recommended further U.S. penetration of the region, boasting that "half of the Congo's trade used to be with the British, the rest of it with Europe. Now practically all goes to the U.S." With the war and the reduction of "direct communication with Europe," Van Dusen saw wider opportunities in Africa for his airline and nation.[102]

By 1939, the tumult brought by Germany's war in Europe was also of consequence for Africa. It also allowed the United States to introduce itself more forcefully to the continent in a manner not seen since the bad old days of the African slave trade. This created favorable conditions for Washington to challenge "imperial preference" and other market barriers that sustained colonialism, which in turn created arbitrage opportunities for Africans. At the same time, a pre-existing interest in aviation combined with surging anti-fascist trends to propel African Americans to the forefront of what became World War II.

---

102   William Van Dusen to "Alo Mistah!" 12 December 1941, Box 260, Folder 2, Pan Am Papers.

Their mounting enthusiasm for and participation in aviation, as pilots in particular, served to challenge Jim Crow and colonialism frontally—thus creating a downward spiral for these dual systems of structural inequality that was difficult to reverse.

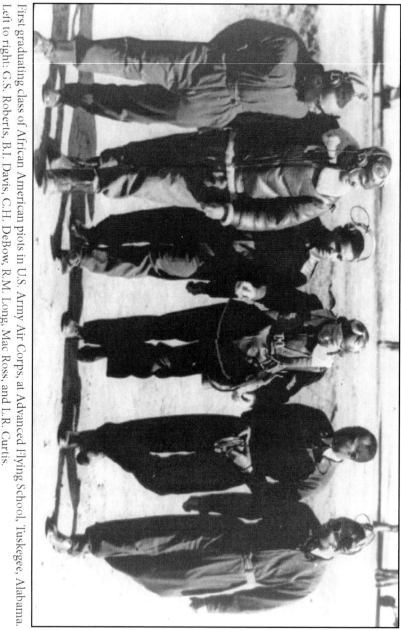

First graduating class of African American piots in U.S. Army Air Corps, at Advanced Flying School, Tuskegee, Alabama. Left to right: G.S. Roberts, B.I. Davis, C.H. DeBow, R.M. Long, Mac Ross, and L.R. Curtis. (Courtesy Library of Congress, Prints and Photographs)

CHAPTER 4

JIM CROW AND COLONIALISM: UP IN THE AIR?

Jim Crow not only meant that African Americans faced difficulty climbing into cockpits, it also meant that barriers were strewn in their path when they sought to build cockpits. As aviation took off as a major force in transportation and combat, often buoyed by lush government subsidies, the business of building planes quickly became Big Business. By late 1940, the Civil Aeronautics Administration (CAA) announced that "American civil airplane production for the first three quarters of 1940 shows an increase of 69.7 percent over the same period in 1939....4,453 airplanes were constructed at the various factories during these months as against 2,698 last year." Moreover, "[D]uring the January-September period, 93 large transport planes were turned out, 178.3% more than in the same period in 1939, when 46 were produced."[1]

By spring 1941, President Franklin D. Roosevelt authorized a schedule of U.S. airplane production that included 500 heavy, four-engine bombers per month.[2] Additionally, 20 of the federal government's 100 largest contractors were engaged primarily in

---

1 Press Release, 11 November 1940, Box I: F10, National Urban League Papers-Library of Congress.
2 Richard Overy, *The Bombers and the Bombed: Allied War Over Europe, 1940-1945* (New York: Penguin, 2014), 85.

manufacturing products for the nation's air arsenal. Their goal was to produce 50,000 planes in a short period of time. To that end, the giant firm, North American Aviation, Inc. (NAA), emerged. The main floor of that behemoth, which featured 855,000 square feet of floor space, was at the time the largest industrial room in the world. By 1945, NAA employed a hefty 39,000 workers.[3]

In Texas, aircraft factories gained a reputation as some of the most heavily organized—and most union-dominated—workplaces in the state. Boeing's closed shop facility in Seattle was typical of many of the newer factories. According to one source, Boeing, with a workforce of 41,000 in 1941, had not even a single Black employee—even as the threat of world war was leading to increased spending and hiring in its rarified realm. As late as October 1944, a major aircraft plant in Fort Worth, Texas, only employed about 600 African Americans out of a total workforce of some 20,000. The Convair plant in San Diego, California, employed only 300 Negroes among the plant's 23,000 workers while its neighbor, Bell Helicopter, counted only 100 Negroes on its payroll of 3,100.

Those Negroes who did find work in aviation often found quotidian restrictions. Others found draconian working conditions such as having to walk a mile just to use a separate toilet. Although Lockheed Aircraft in Marietta, Georgia—billed as the single largest private employer in the Southeast—conducted its manufacturing in a facility owned by the federal government, almost all its Negro workers were concentrated in the single euphemistically titled classification of "structural assembly helpers," a finding that led to a major campaign against the company's hiring practices by the NAACP.[4] By that criterion, Birmingham's Vultee Aircraft qualified as "progressive" in that it deigned to hire

---

3   Ethelberg Courtland Barksdale, *The Genesis of the Aviation Industry in North Texas*, (Austin: Bureau of Business Research, University of Texas, 1958).
4   Joseph A. Abel, "Sunbelt Civil Rights: Race, Labor and Politics in the Fort Worth Aircraft Industry, 1940-1980," (PhD diss., Rice University, Houston, TX), 2011, 5, 90, 117, 165, 169.

Negroes, but only as janitors.[5] By comparison, however, the Blacks with paltry posts in Dixie's airplane factories were lucky. At least three aircraft firms in the northern state of New York—Republic, Grumman, and Brewster—refused to hire Negroes at all.[6]

Seemingly concerted effort was being made to bar U.S. Negroes from what many deemed to be the future–namely, aeronautics.[7] Yet, as U.S. aviation was taking off, the drums of world war were beating ever more loudly in the United States. Increasingly, the odiousness of Jim Crow, as it manifested itself in the emerging aviation industry, was being seen by wider sectors of the body politic as jeopardizing national security. This realization helped create additional leverage for the desegregation efforts that were gaining strength in this crucial economic sector, which had reverberating effects throughout the nation.

As aircraft production spiked upward, so too did the complaints from Negro workers about employment discrimination in the aviation field. The experiences of Freddie Peale and Joel Black, Negro workers in Buffalo, New York, were typical. In early 1941, the two men were studying aircraft fabrication along with 26 white students. All the latter were employed post-training at Curtiss Airplane and Bell Aircraft. The two non-white workers submitted applications to both but, according to Peale, they were "refused employment simply because [we] were Negroes." As he lamented, "The [New York] State Employment Office even refused to send [us] out there" to the two airline firms for an interview. "They need skilled men [at the Bell and the Curtiss plants] and are taking white men with 3 and 4 [weeks] training," he said, "but refuse to hire me with 608 hours of fabrication and 34 [hours of]

---

5 Press Release, June 1942, Reel 1, #675, Series C, Economic Conditions, Part III, CAB-NCSU.

6 Press Release, February 1941, Reel 22, #8, Part I, Press Releases, CAB-NCSU.

7 Sarah Jo Peterson, *Planning the Home Front: Building Bombers and Communities at Willow Run* (Chicago: The University of Chicago Press, 2013). Cf. Herrick Chapman, *State Capitalism and Working Class Radicalism in the French Aircraft Industry* (Berkeley: University of California Press, 1991).

blueprint reading."[8] What Peale did not state was the impact on national security of such myopic policies. Ultimately, however, this factor was to weigh heavily on what had become commonplace bias. Weeks after Peale's anguished plea, Bell Aircraft surrendered and pledged to hire more Negroes.[9]

Bell's surrender was not necessarily a trend, at least not in the view of Bronx, New York, resident Joseph Woods. Woods was 22 years old in 1941, a graduate of Evander Childs High School, who attended Saunders Training School Annex for Aviation in Yonkers. Although he had "400 hours [of experience] in aircraft riveting," his instructors, all of whom were employed by Brewster Aeronautical Company, refused to offer him a job at their firm.[10] Brewster seemed to be imperviously immune to reform. In 1941, Leroy Jeffries of the National Urban League sent a group of Black workers to solicit employment at the company. As he explained:

> [In the] average bomber, there are 450,000 rivets and that is why it takes so long to complete a plane. The riveters do the production work. Sheet-metal workers straighten out sheets, which are tacked on until the riveters come…strictly production work. The work is laid out from blueprints in the instrumental department. It is shunned by most good sheet-metal workers. It is cheap work.[11]

Apparently, however, the work was too elevated—and too pricey—to consider Negro workers for the jobs. All the Black candidates Jeffries sent to Brewster were qualified, he insisted, but all were rejected.

Jeffries' despair was echoed by that of yet another NAACP interlocutor who charged that Brewster was "refusing to hire qualified Negroes in other than menial capacities [while] holding millions of

8 Freddie Peale to Walter White, 2 March 1941, Box II: A332, NAACP Papers.
9 Press Release, 23 May 1941, Box II: A332, NAACP Papers.
10 Affidavit by Joseph Woods, July 1941, Box II: A332, NAACP Papers.
11 Statement by Leroy Jeffries, 6 August 1941, Box II: A332, NAACP Papers.

dollars in defense contracts"—contracts funded by taxpayers, including countless numbers of Negro taxpayers. "In every case without exception," the NAACP official reported, the Negroes referred to Brewster were rejected.[12] Like Bell Helicopter, Brewster Aeronautical could not withstand the pressure unleashed by clamorous protest, impending war, and grave concerns about national security. By mid-August 1941, the NAACP declared proudly, "for the first time in its history, Brewster took on a Negro employee in the regular course of hiring."[13]

Fairchild Aircraft was an aviation company that proved harder to change. The NAACP found in 1941 that Fairchild's plants in ostensibly progressive New York refused to employ minority-group employees despite President's Roosevelt's June 25, 1941, Executive Order 8802 barring discrimination in the defense industry. "[O]f all the concerns in New York," the anti-Jim Crow organization noted, "[this company] had been most adamant and had bluntly refused even to consider employment of Negroes."[14] A similarly discouraging situation was developing due west in Seattle. There, Le Etta King of the NAACP's branch in that city, griped:

> For a long time Negroes locally [had] been trying to get work at Boeing but were barred by the fact that the Aeronautical Union Local 751 would not admit them to membership. That at least is the reason the Boeing officials give, although the plant had been operating here for more than twenty years and has never employed Negroes and the contract with the Union has been for only three years.

Yes, King wrote, African Americans had "made applications for work at Boeing," but she was unaware of "any who [were] employed there in any capacity."[15]

---

12 Mr. Reeves to Walter White, 8 August 1941, Box II: A332, NAACP Papers.
13 Press Release, 15 August 1941, Box II: A332, NAACP Papers.
14 Memorandum, 10 September 1941, Box II: A334, NAACP Papers.
15 Le Etta King to Walter White, 6 September 1940, Box II: A332, NAACP Papers.

King and the NAACP were condemnatory of Boeing, but they also cited as problematic "discrimination" by the Machinists Union of the American Federation of Labor.[16] This discriminatory pattern was also uncovered in the Midwest, where a bomber plane plant operated by Henry Ford was alleged to have hired white women while showing Negro women the door.[17] Even after the bombing of Pearl Harbor, the NAACP continued to be deluged with complaints about the maltreatment of Negro workers in the aviation industry. Without any warning, for example, 16 Negro cafeteria employees of the Cessna Aircraft Company were dropped from the payroll in January 1942.[18] Then, in late April 1942, the government seized a U.S. aircraft plant after the NAACP complained that the plant continued to bar Negro workers while hiring instead, in key positions, workers described as "enemy aliens."[19]

* * *

Jim Crow, a policy deeply inured in U.S. society, proved difficult to erode even when national security was at stake. The growing role of Africa in U.S. war calculations complicated matters even further. On the one hand, the underdevelopment of Africa reinforced Jim Crow postulates about the alleged inherent underdevelopment of African Americans. On the other hand, U.S. government and business officials believed Washington would benefit from the erosion of the European colonial powers' influence in Africa. If European colonialism retreated, this could empower sovereign African nations that could then exert influence on behalf of African Americans.

"Africa is being rapidly militarized" was the view of Pan American Airlines' Jesse Boynton writing in a "secret" report in early 1942.

16 Memorandum, 10 September 1941, Box II: A334, NAACP Papers.
17 Release, circa 1940s, Reel 1, #695, Series C, Economic Conditions, Part III, CAB-NCSU.
18 Press Release, January 1942, Reel 23, #764, Part I, Press Releases, CAB-NCSU.
19 Press Release, 24 April 1942, Box II: A332, NAACP Papers.

Boynton's conclusion was a reflection of the reach and impact of the world war.[20] Around the same time, Pan Am executive Harold Whiteman, after meeting a visiting delegation of the "native paramount chiefs" in Accra, Ghana, noted that he detected "an underlying motive" on the chiefs' part—"namely, a desire to settle in their own minds whether the Americans were here to take over the colony."[21] The presence of another power in the colonial neighborhood provided Africans with additional leverage, even though Washington and London (as well as other colonizing powers) ostensibly were on the same side.

The onset of World War II brought an influx of Euro-Americans to West Africa at a level not seen since the heyday of the transatlantic slave trade. In 1937, according to a Pan Am analysis, there were only three scheduled vessels sailing between the U.S. and South Africa—the latter of which then, as now, had one of the more sophisticated economies on the African continent, a factor that seemingly would have dictated more frequent voyages. In 1938, there was no direct service between the U.S. and Liberia by vessels with passenger accommodations, yet Liberia too was one of the few African territories dominated by Washington. Subsequently, due to the perceived weaknesses in the African travel market, Pan Am sought to initiate more air service to and from that continent, even though its analysis noted the absence of "a heavy flow of passengers between the [U.S.] and Africa" up to that point.[22]

By 1939, as war swept through Europe, Pan Am was gearing up to descend upon Africa.[23] With the European powers reeling from the sledgehammer blows inflicted by their opponents in Berlin, Washington

---

20 "Secret" Memorandum of Jesse Boynton, Box 54, Folder 5, Pan Am Papers.
21 Harold Whiteman to William Van Dusen, 5 March 1942, Box 54, Folder 5, Pan Am Papers.
22 "Before the Civil Aeronautics Board, Docket No. 1171, Brief: In the Matter of the Application for Certification of Public Convenience and Necessity Between the United States and Africa," 8 March 1945, Box 344, Folder 1, Pan Am Papers.
23 "Early History of Pan American's Service to Africa," January 1954, Civil Aeronautics Board, #5818, Box 200, Folder 19, Pan-Am Papers.

too was poised to take advantage. In August 1941, President Roosevelt asked the politically connected air carrier to accept an assignment of an "importance [that] cannot be overestimated." He wanted Pan Am's assistance in ferrying to Africa military aircraft that could be deployed against the Italian forces in Ethiopia, perhaps used against German forces in North Africa, or enlisted to bolster the "Free French" regime in Brazzaville, Congo. Roosevelt also asked Pan Am to consider launching common carrier service between the U.S. and Africa.[24]

By April 1942, Pan Am's Whiteman was exulting in the fact that his airlines' Accra division was a profitable component of "one of the biggest commercial airlines operating today":

> [O]ur route from Bathurst [Gambia] to Calcutta spans one continent and half the other—and these [are] the two largest continents! The Accra airport is probably the busiest of all [as] planes land and take off about every fifteen minutes….the Accra and Khartoum stations operate on a 24-hour basis.[25]

At that point, Accra was part of a long supply line that not only reached Calcutta but also New Delhi, Karachi, Teheran, Aden, and Asmara. "At Cairo we deliver to the British," wrote Whiteman, "at Teheran to the Russians and at New Delhi and occasionally Calcutta our own Air Corps." He added, "[W]e have as many as four or five departures within an hour or two each morning." Whiteman was aware, however, that Pan Am's deeper penetration into markets that previously had been considered colonial bulwarks was raising tensions. As he concluded, with regard to "the general tenor of our relations with the British": "I have heard more and more complaints from different sources lately."[26]

---

24 "Brief History of Pan American Airways Service to Africa," 24 August 1964, Exhibit No. PA-1, CAB Docket #1171, Box 54, Folder 3, Pan Am Papers.
25 Harold Whiteman to William Van Dusen, 16 April 1942, Box 54, Folder 5, Pan Am Papers.
26 Harold Whiteman to William Van Dusen, 19 June 1942, Box 54, Folder 5, Pan Am Papers.

After traveling to Nigeria, Pan Am's W. L. Morrison complained of "a wariness and lack of cordiality" in his encounters with the airlines' British competitors. The British, he claimed, were "keenly interested in post-war aviation developments," even as the war grinded on mercilessly. "Jokingly, they asked me," said an ostensibly bemused Morrison, "'Well, what's it to be, war or peace between us?'"[27]

Numerous opportunities arose for this friction to flare between the U.S. and its erstwhile ally as U.S. incursions into Africa accelerated. Airmail service between Miami and the Belgian Congo was established by December 1941, with the British colony of Trinidad, along with Brazil, included in the long journey.[28] According to Morrison, a "tremendous percentage of the Belgian Congo['s] commercial relations, [notably] importation and exportation, have been carried on with the United States." He wondered, however, about the downstream effects of this on the British colony of Nigeria.[29] He was also aware that the U.S. was seeking the right to establish air bases and build airfields in the Congo, which had the additional benefit of containing a vast storehouse of uranium, already recognized as being essential for atomic bombs—the presumed "winning weapon" [30]

Indeed, Pan Am led the charge of U.S. airlines into Africa. Its success in building an aerial highway from west to east—crisscrossing the Atlantic and into the heart of Africa—dwarfed its previous feat of developing airports and airfields in the South American jungles and on desolate Pacific islands. Pan Am also was one of the few airlines that carried the U.S. flag abroad, a gesture made all the more unusual since the carrier's founder, Juan Trippe, had an unsavory

27 W. L. Morrison to V. P. Young, "Confidential," 17 April 1944, Box 41, Folder 8, Pan Am Papers.

28 Undated memorandum, Box 41, Folder 8, Pan Am Papers.

29 W. L. Morrison, Vice President for Latin America to Executive Assistant, 17 April 1944, Box 41, Folder 8, Pan Am Papers.

30 Press Release, November 1944, Reel 29, Part I, Press Releases, CAB-NCSU. See also Susan Williams, *Spies in the Congo: America's Atomic Mission in World War II* (New York: Public Affairs, 2016).

reputation in the White House. Nonetheless, Pan Am was able to gather essential intelligence, at least informally, and thus often was seen as an extension of Washington abroad—which eased Trippe's acceptance into elevated circles in the U.S. and abroad. It was Trippe who early targeted the Congo as the vector of a strategic route to the vast riches of Africa.[31]

* * *

When U.S. corporations and personnel arrived in Africa during World War II, African Americans were not far behind. By 1943, as Bishop W. Y. Bell of the "Colored Methodist Church" noticed "American Negro troops in vast numbers are serving in Africa," and he submitted that "many of them will want to settle there after the war is won." His latter point may have been true, but by the mid-1940s, African Americans undoubtedly were traveling to Africa at a time when anti-colonial sentiments were on the rise. This did not bode well for colonialism and, as the anti-colonialism movement gained strength, Washington had to be concerned about how Africans viewed the peculiar U.S. institution that was Jim Crow.[32]

Complaints of another type were emerging as a result of the U.S.'s foray into Africa. "Significantly," a Pan Am analyst wrote, "Americans from the North and the South could not be distinguished by their treatment of the African Negro." If the U.S. wanted to dislodge the European powers in Africa or even erode their influence, this analysis posited, its prospects would be improved greatly if that trend were to change. An added bonus of such a change, the report concluded, would be the creation of a predicate or model for improving the treatment of African Americans.

---

31 Marilyn Bender and Selig Altschul, *The Chosen Instrument: Pan Am, Juan Trippe, the Rise and Fall of an American Entrepreneur* (New York: Simon & Schuster, 1982), 14, 477, 352, 353.
32 Press Release, August 1943, Reel 26, #548, Part I, Press Releases, CAB-NCSU.

By early 1943, Pan Am executive Voit Gilmore noted that the airline's flight crews had become "familiar with the swampy thickets of the Cameroons and the rolling green hills of the Congo and Rhodesia."[33] They were noticeably more alert, however, when traversing the Liberian coast around Cape Palmas. That area, Gilmore claimed, was a favorite hunting ground for German submarines. Certainly, Berlin's—and Tokyo's—interest in Africa was well known by then,[34] but Gilmore asserted that the U.S. would find it more difficult to prevail in Africa as long as Washington's maltreatment of Africans and African-Americans proceeded.

Tellingly, as reports of the abuse and exploitation of Africans filtered out of the beleaguered continent, a group of pro-Tokyo U.S. Negroes was standing trial in Chicago on various charges involving allegations of sedition. Most of the Black defendants could be described as "Black Nationalists," sworn as they were to the defeat of their ostensible homeland, not least of all because of the historic and contemporary depredations visited upon Africa and Africans by Europeans and Euro-Americans. The prosecutors in the case asserted that the accused sought aid from Tokyo to construct planes that would allow them to "fight all white people like hell."[35] Punctuating this point was the fact that Paul Gilchrist, the grandson of the leader of these forces—Mittie Maud Lena Gordon—was intensely engaged in the study of aviation.[36]

---

33 "African Report....an Account of PAA-Africa Personnel Abroad by Voit Gilmore," January 1943, Box 54, Folder 5, Pan Am Papers.

34 Gerald Horne, *Race War! White Supremacy and the Japanese Attack on the British Empire* (New York: New York University Press, 2003). See also Gerald Horne, *Facing the Rising Sun: African-Americans, Japan and the Roots of Afro-Asian Solidarity* (New York: New York University Press), forthcoming.

35 *U.S. v. William Green Gordon, et.al.* (October Term 1942), 33646, Record Group 21, U.S. District Court, Northern District of Illinois, Eastern Division of Chicago, Criminal Case Files, Box 1152, National Archives and Records Administration-Chicago.

36 Brief and Argument for the Appellants, 8 June 1942, #8256, In the U.S. Circuit Court of Appeals for the 7th Circuit, *U.S. v. Mittie Maud Lena Gordon, et.al.*, National Archives and Records Administration-Chicago.

* * *

The exploitation of the African continent and Africans' anti-colonial awakening were reflected in the pages of the aptly named *West African Pilot*, a Nigerian newspaper. The *Pilot* frequently featured articles depicting African American progress in aviation as an indication of what was also in store for continental Africans. It further spoke to the emerging trends that were hastening the arrival of anti-colonialism and the anti-Jim Crow movement.[37]

As soon became apparent, West Africans were intensely interested in the study of aviation. In 1941, for example, Nigeria's Babatunde Alakija was on the verge of joining Britain's Royal Air Force (RAF), an appointment the British Press Service was quick to publicize.[38] The London press blared continually about the new reality of Black pilots in the RAF.[39] It likewise jumped on reports of a Jamaican tail gunner who won a trophy during his Canadian air corps training, promptly sharing the story with the U.S. Negro press.[40]

The momentum generated by the increasing numbers of Black pilots crashing the skyward ceilings over Britain propelled the same to occur in the skies above His Majesty's principal ally: the United States of America. The same forces that made it increasingly more difficult to maintain the segregationist policies that undergirded colonialism served in turn to undermine Jim Crow. Those forces were accompanied by a reawakening of sorts in the U.S., as those accustomed to Jim Crow came to realize that the cut and thrust of war was challenging their cherished system of oppression.

In 1942, for example, members of Congress and residents of various cities protested the stationing of "colored" military personnel in their

---

37 Vleck, *Empire of the Air*, 138.
38 David Ritchie, British Press Service to Claude Barnett, 20 October 1941, Box 201, Folder 4, CAB-CHM.
39 Joyce Leigh of BIS to Claude Barnett, 15 June 1944, Box 201, Folder 4, CAB-CHM.
40 Patricia Danby, British Information Service to Claude Barnett, 20 April 1944, Box 201, Folder 4, CAB-CHM.

community.[41] Yet, whether the issue pertained to staffing cockpits or constructing them, Washington generally took exception—and even recalcitrant objection—to Negroes' participation in flight and the U.S. aviation industry. Surely, this complicated the government's efforts to train a diverse cadre of personnel to engage its adversaries in air combat during the war.

By mid-1942, John Duff, president of the Miami Beach Hotel Association, was complaining about "rumors of possible colored squadrons" being sent to that resort town. "This naturally disturbed them [the city's whites]," Duff claimed, because "colored people have never been permitted to sleep on the Beach." Changing that policy, he declared, "would almost mean the end of those hotels when the war is over." Duff was placated only partly when a U.S. official, John McCloy, assured him that "he would do everything possible to see that colored [personnel] were not sent there."[42]

Sentiments such as these culminated in the policies that eventually contributed to the selection of Tuskegee Institute as the ultimate site for training Negroes to pilot airplanes. In late 1940, for example, Brigadier General G. C. Brant expressed personal objection to "sending a colored company to the new flying school at San Angelo, Texas" because very few Negroes resided in that area and "recreational facilities in the city [were] non-existent for colored soldiers." Moreover, he contended, "[T]he City Bus Company operating the bus line to the field will not pick up Negroes unless the buses are almost empty."[43]

General Brant also was loathe to designate Ellington Field near Houston as a site for the aviation training of Negroes, citing in that case the "considerable feeling" of animosity among local whites

---

41 Memorandum for Chief of Staff, 14 April 1942, 145.81.84-91, 1942-APR 1943, AFHRA.
42 John Duff to Major General Walter Weaver, AAF Technical Training Command, 10 June 1942, 168.7061-30–71, 13 July 1945, 26 April 1941–10 Jun 1942, Gropman, A. L. Col., AFHRA.
43 Brigadier General G. C. Brant to Chief of Air Corps, 18 November 1940, 145.93-80–92, Jan 1936–April 1936 Jun 1941-Sep 1941, AFHRA.

resulting from a 1917 armed mutiny that involved Negro troops stationed there. He argued that the city of Houston already provided Blacks with adequate recreational facilities and that placing budding Negro aviators there "can end only in trouble" He also claimed that African Americans, many of whom did not own cars, surely would face immense transportation challenges making the 18-mile journey to the airfield from the city.[44]

Advocates for a Negro flight training school next turned their attention to Eglin Field in Florida, about 60 miles from Pensacola. However, Lieutenant Colonel W. A. Maxwell was as resolute in his opposition to that idea as Brigadier General W. C. Brant was to the Ellington Field proposal. Maxwell formally requested that "no colored [personnel] be assigned" to his air base, writing that it was sited in "a very isolated section which is popular with vacationists [sic] during the summer month[s]." Since "no recreational facilities for colored people" could be found closer than Pensacola, he claimed it would be, at best, awkward to pursue desegregation in his locale: Understatedly, he added:

> ...colored personnel are very unpopular in the immediate vicinity. Very few Negroes have been allowed to remain in this section and then only as servants living on the premises of their employers....[T]he attitude of the lower caste white population is that Negroes will not be permitted to live in this community.

Officer Maxwell expressed fear over what might happen if the local Jim Crow norms were violated: "Intimidation tactics by certain elements of the white population will sooner or later lead to serious conflicts and possibly desertion." Negroes, he believed, would have to flee for their lives. He also mentioned other supposedly niggling issues such as "the establishment of a separate mess [hall] for such a small number" of Negroes and deemed the related expenses "not feasible nor

44 Brigadier General G. C. Brant to the Chief of Air Corps, 19 November 1940, 145-.93–80–92, Jan 1936–April 1936, June 1941–September 1941, AFHRA.

practical because of the necessity for using a full complement of white personnel for the preparation of food, which is a very undesirable factor."[45] Maxwell and Brant were not alone in their views. As Jackson, Mississippi, Mayor Walter A. Scott preemptively proclaimed: "[W]e definitely do not want any Negro soldiers located in Jackson."[46]

To escape the strictures of Jim Crow and southern opposition, proponents of the Negro flight school even considered the Caribbean island of Antigua as a possible site.[47] Yet, the amount of animosity and opposition encountered in Dixie and elsewhere should have been a boon to Willa Brown and other advocates for the Chicago location. As Major Robert F. Reynolds of the U.S. Air Corps, who was based at Maxwell Field in Alabama, stressed in 1943: "[A] movement is underway *to make Chicago the hub* of Negro flying, which includes the establishment of a sizeable and complete modern Negro airport." Reynolds crowed that the Chicago proposal had "attracted the interest and possible backing of important capital and personnel" including such titans of industry as Henry Ford and Marshall Field. Though he admitted that the airport then in use by the Coffey School (Harlem Airport) was "inadequate," he declined to say that bolstering the aviation infrastructure of Black Chicago, arguably the most important Negro community in the nation, was yet a bridge too far for Jim Crow.[48]

Meanwhile, Willa Brown, still in league with Coffey and Waters, was coordinating what U.S. authorities termed an "approved primary and secondary flying school" at Harlem Airport. She was also

45 Lieutenant Colonel W. A. Maxwell of Air Corps Commanding, Headquarters, Air Corps Specialized Flying School, Eglin Field, Valparaiso, Florida, to Commanding General, AFHRA.
46 Mayor Walter A. Scott to Senator Pat Harrison, 4 March 1941, 145.93-80–92, January 1936–April 1936, June 1941–September 1941, AFHRA.
47 J. Todd Moye, *Freedom Flyers: The Tuskegee Airmen of World War II*, (New York: Oxford University Press, 2010), 44, 128.
48 Major Robert Reynolds to Commanding General, Army Air Force Base, Southeast Training Center, Maxwell Field, 17 August 1945, 220.765-2, 229. 8635, 1, 1943, Volume 4, Volume 2, AFHRA.

negotiating, with the support of De Paul University and the Chicago Board of Education, for a "larger airport...as long as the federal government" agreed to reimburse those supporters.[49]

The reimbursement caveat was only one of a number of stumbling blocks Brown faced while advocating for the Chicago training location. Months earlier, Harlem Airport had been closed, with a prime reason being its failure to have armed guards on duty, a decision that reportedly affected about 150 Negroes.[50] That adverse decision did not seem to affect the operations of the Coffey School[51]—that is, not until Major Reynolds inspected the site and concluded that its "barracks, messing facilities and latrine conditions [were] unsatisfactory."[52] His report tended to override the endorsements of even stalwart supporters like Ford and Field and sank Brown's prospects. By 1943, the once-vibrant Coffey School was on the verge of becoming defunct, one of several defeats suffered by what were then termed the "Negro Flying Schools."[53]

The Associated Negro Press's Claude Barnett did not seem displeased to learn that the Coffey School was going down in flames. He was busy touting the prospects of yet another school designed, as he stated, "to train Negro cross-country fliers at Flint, Michigan." Thus, he peremptorily dismissed the Coffey School, claiming that "far from being a school training men to become cadets," it was "training men who could not pass the rigorous army flying test." In his view, the school richly merited its imminent extinction. As for the woman he dismissively called the "attractive Miss Brown," he argued that her eminence was attributed largely to her assumed privileged

49 Willa Brown, Coordinator of CAA War Training Service, Coffey School of Aeronautics, 14 August 1943 and attached: President M. J. O'Connell, De Paul University, to Willa Brown, 27 April 1943, 220.765-2, 220.8635, 1, 1943, Volume 4, Volume 2, AFHRA.

50 Press Release, June 1942, Reel 24, #327, Part I, Press Releases, CAB-NCSU.

51 Press Release, August 1942, Reel 24, #628, Part I, Press Releases, CAB-NCSU.

52 Major Robert F. Reynolds to Commanding General, 17 August 1943, 220.765-2 220.8635.1 1943 Volume 4, Volume 2, AFHRA.

53 Press Release, March 1943, Reel 25, #682, Part I, Press Releases, CAB-NCSU; see also Press Release, October 1942, Reel 24, #1025, Part I, Press Releases, CAB-NCSU.

position with certain Negro press organs, aided immeasurably by her pulchritude.[54]

Yet even Tuskegee Institute's most diehard supporters were hard-pressed to see the subsequent "victory" of the Alabama HBCU (historically Black college/university) site over Chicago as a victory for the U.S.—or Black America. By the time flying instruction began at Tuskegee Institute, its president, Dr. Frederick D. Patterson, pointed out that "there were only twenty-five black pilots in the whole of the United States."[55] This was, of course, an underestimation, but it was suggestive of the larger problem faced by the nation.

Tuskegee had other HBCU competitors. Virginia Union University was viewed by one selection official as presenting a "good location" for aviation training where the "racial problem would be minor."[56] Hampton Institute was also in the running. Though Hampton already had a "colored officers' candidate school," other problems, unnamed by the selection team, hampered its ability to supplant or even complement the Tuskegee location.[57] When the dust settled, Tuskegee Institute emerged triumphant. Barnett's news agency trumpeted that news in August 1944, boasting that only three years before the first 500 troops arrived at Tuskegee Institute's air base—"the first in history to train Negro pilots"—was "but a huddle of tents."[58]

Indeed, lots of work needed to be done, and done quickly, to bring the Tuskegee flight training program up to speed to meet the demands

---

54   Claude Barnett to Ernest Johnson, 20 March 1943, Reel 6, #551, Part II, Organizational Files, CAB-NCSU.

55   Dodson, *Chronicles of Faith*, 73.

56   Lieutenant Colonel H. R. Maddux, Air Corps to Commanding General, Air Forces Technical Training Command, 19 August 1942, 220.765-2, 220.8635, 1, 1943, Volume 4, Volume 5, AFHRA.

57   Lieutenant Colonel H. R. Maddux to Commanding General, 8 August 1942, 220.765-2, 220.8635, 1, 1943, Volume 4, Volume 5, AFHRA.

58   Press Release, August 1944, Reel 29, #153, Part I, Press Releases, CAB-NCSU. Barnett's pivotal role in the formation of the Tuskegee Airmen also may have benefited his then influential Associated Negro Press, providing him a pipeline that transmitted "scoops" to his news service.

of the impending war. Earlier, a government report asserted that the government needed to train the following:

> …250 Negro airplane mechanics, 4 Negro aircraft machinists, 4 Negro aircraft welders, 6 Negro parachute riggers, 7 Negro teletype operators, 4 Negro weather observers, 20 Negro aircraft armorer students, 40 Negro technical and administrative clerks, 30 Negro radio operators and mechanics….These men must be trained and graduated no later than September 15, 1942" (not to mention a raft of pilots).[59]

The government's "outline of [a] plan for colored training" also included the need for 16 radar specialists to be trained in Boca Raton, Florida; 580 air mechanics at "Lincoln" (presumably the historically Black university in Missouri); 12 "parachute riggers" at Chanute Air Base in Illinois; and 35 "propeller specialists," also to be trained at Chanute.[60] The authoritative study on the Tuskegee Airmen states that the initial quota imposed upon the program was to train no more than 100 aviators at a time—or 200 per year.[61]

A post-war study by the U.S. Air Force, which listed 1,044 Negro "flying personnel" in the U.S. military in September 1944, confirmed that only "a very small percentage" of Negro airmen received aviation training at Tuskegee.[62] Yet another calculation, which claimed that 72 Negro pilots were killed in action during the war, seems also to undercount the total number of Black airmen.[63] It nonetheless confirms the need, unaddressed at the time, to replenish the diminishing and valuable supply of Negro aviators.

---

59 Lieutenant Colonel Perry C. Ragan, Technical Training Command to President, Board of Offices, 18 March 1942, 220.765-2, 220.8635, 1, 1943, Volume 4, Volume 2, AFHRA.

60 Memorandum, 15 January 1943, 220.765-2, 220.8635, 1, 1943, Volume 4, Volume 2, AFHRA.

61 Moye, *Freedom Flyers*, 123. 93, 124.

62 "Negroes in the AAF," no date, circa 1956, K239.0441-1, K239.046.9, 1910-1960, 1956, AFHRA.

63 Undated Clipping, Box 8, Gubert Papers.

Given the rancor directed at Negroes generally and at proposals to train Negro pilots in Texas, Mississippi, and Florida particularly, it is not surprising that the African Americans who wound up at U.S. air bases often reacted in kind. During the height of the war, for example, a man described as "young Negro flying officer, Lt. Milton Henry" and his like-minded comrades strode boldly into the officer's club at Selfridge Field in Michigan—from which they were barred— and wreaked havoc. Henry was later court-martialed, but proclaimed during his hearings that he was no longer committed to fighting for democracy because the country for which he was fighting was hardly democratic.[64] Henry's woes were ascribed to Major General Frank O'Donnell, a top leader of the army air force, a supervising officer, and a product of Dixie, Savannah in his case. Irrespective of the culpability of this leader, resting such difficulties solely at his doorstep neatly elides the institutional and societal racial problems festering in the U.S. at that time.[65] (Intriguingly, Henry became a premier Black Nationalist after the war, a comrade of Malcolm X, and a militant advocate of reparations for the unpaid labor of enslaved Africans in the U.S.[66])

In apparent emulation of Lieutenant Henry and his comrades, 60 disgruntled Negro officers—all aviators—were arrested at their base in nearby Franklin, Indiana, after defying a ban on their admittance into an officers' club.[67] Some of the pilots were transferred to a base in South Carolina, where their morale sank further. None was ever permitted to fly military planes there.[68] The Palmetto State's Jim Crow twin—Mississippi—was similarly intransigent. As the mayor of Biloxi, Mississippi, curtly informed his Congressman, William Colmer: if the government brought "more" Negroes to the air base in

---

64 Press Release, July 1944, Reel 28, #1054, Part I, Press Releases, CAB-NCSU.
65 Press Release, May 1945, Reel 30, #1223, Part I, Press Releases, CAB-NCSU.
66 *New York Times*, February 5, 2010; *New York Sun*, September 18, 2006.
67 Press Release, April 1945, Reel 30, #755, Part I, Press Releases, CAB-NCSU.
68 Press Release, July 1944, Part I, Press Releases, CAB-NCSU.

his jurisdiction than the local whites could "handle," "trouble" was surely in the offing.[69]

The conflicts between Negro airmen and their Euro-American counterparts extended beyond U.S. shores. Across the Atlantic, in Bristol, England, an investigation was opened during the war into what was called a "riot"—that is, yet another fracas between African American aviation personnel and their air corps antagonists.[70] The proliferation of confrontation across racial lines left impressions both contrary to and congruent with Jim Crow. For instance, Negro pilot George Watson was stationed at Tuskegee during the war but later was sent to Camp Patrick Henry in Virginia to await assignment overseas. While at Camp Henry, he noted, German prisoners-of-war served him food every time he dined in the mess hall—a putative violation, and puzzling contradiction, of Jim Crow dictates.[71] The heavens did not fall as a result of this putative violation of segregationist policy, which provided a rationale for a postwar retreat of this Jim Crow etiquette.

Another Tuskegee Airman, Woodrow Crockett, exposed an analogous conundrum, confiding that his Euro-American fellow citizens showed more respect to German prisoners-of-war, the presumed enemy, than to him.[72] Alex Jefferson, a Tuskegee-trained Army Air Force Negro aviator captured by the Germans during the war, had a similar experience. As he recalled, those who interned him were infinitely more respectful toward him than both his Euro-American counterparts in the Corps or his fellow U.S. prisoners-of-war.[73]

69 Chester Delacruz to Congressman Colmer, 1 May 1944, Box 66, William Colmer Papers, University of Southern Mississippi, Hattiesburg.

70 Press Release, July 1944, Reel 28, #1108, Part I, Press Releases, CAB-NCSU.

71 George Watson, *Memorable Memoirs* (New York: Carlton, 1987), 60.

72 Megan McDonough, "Woodrow Crockett, 93, Valiant, Decorated, Tuskegee Airman," *Washington Post*, September 11, 2012, B5.

73 Moye, *Freedom Flyers*, 122, 114. See also William Alexander Percy, "Jim Crow, Uncle Sam and the Tuskegee Flying Units: Race Relations in the United States Army Air Force in Europe During World War II," (M.A. thesis, University of Georgia, Athens, Georgia, 1994).

These and other accumulated slights encouraged Watson and others to seek to inflict deathblows on the ramified system of indecent inequality after the war ended. These incidents further suggest that the U.S. pattern of racial differentiation was ripe for exploitation by U.S. adversaries. Those adversaries were well aware of the racial contradictions that beset the U.S. air corps and subsequently sought to exploit those tensions. German captors of Negro pilots, for example, often querulously asked their Black prisoners of war why they chose to fight on behalf of a nation that obviously despised them. Their query perhaps was motivated by the pilots' own reference to themselves, in mock derisiveness, as the *Spookwaffe*. It also may have been driven by the well-known skepticism of the pilots' own trainers, one of whom reportedly asked, with a similar querulousness, "How do Negroes fly?"[74]

Another Negro pilot prisoner-of-war recalled that his German captors often had complete files on their Negro captives, a finding that led him to question whether Berlin's agents possibly had penetrated the U.S. military and were sharing that information with the captors. Strikingly—and perhaps conversely—Alexander Jefferson, another Negro pilot captured by the Germans, reported that his fellow Euro-American prisoners trusted him precisely because he was Black, noting with disgust that those fellow prisoners were "scared to death of a strange white face. Ain't that a bitch?!"[75]

Jefferson may have had Raymond Burke in mind when he expressed the sentiments above. In 1946, Burke told Senator Theodore Bilbo of Mississippi: "[The] Nigger 99th Squadron in the Mediterranean Theater of Operations flew high cover for bomber operations and never engaged the enemy attacks, even though the bombers fought off repeated attacks." Burke insisted that "leading generals" were demanding that

---

74 Broadnax, *Blue Skies, Black Wings*, 116, 46.
75 Alexander Jefferson, *Red Tail Captured, Red Tail Free: The Memoirs of a Tuskegee Airman and POW* (New York: Fordham University Press, 2005), 60.

"no additional Nigger Fighting Squadrons be sent" into battle since, in his view, "they continually caused trouble, wrecking and destroying property" and exhibiting "inefficiency and cowardliness." Moreover, he added that if any whites objected to the Blacks' conduct, "right or wrong they cried 'Race Discrimination.'" Burke's diatribe did not end there, however. If they (Blacks) were assigned a "job," he said, and if they were not watched carefully, "they would take off." Continuing, he added, "There was only one way to keep them [Negro pilots] on the job—lock every door in the building. They were slovenly....impudent and careless about anything they were told to do...they are not and never will be of any value."[76]

* * *

Tuskegee Institute nonetheless prevailed, despite Willa Brown's best efforts and its advocates' tacit acceptance of racial differentiation, becoming by 1941 the prime site for the training of Negro aviators. Yet Tuskegee did not achieve its position without opposition. U.S. Senator Lister Hill of Alabama was among those who drafted a petition that raised "serious objection" to the placement of a "colored aviation camp" at Tuskegee. As Hill claimed, doing so "would cut off the expansion of Tuskegee in the only direction [available] for white people to expand."[77] The notion of aviation training for Blacks in that direction was repugnant to him, although a site closer to Tuskegee was deemed to be acceptable.

Tuskegee did not attain its status as the government's premier site for training Negro pilots without incident. Colonel Noel Parrish, a military official at the school, complained bitterly about the "unjust and sometimes brutal treatment of Tuskegee soldiers by white policemen

76 Raymond Burke to Senator Bilbo, 3 January 1946, Box 1084, Theodore Bilbo Papers, University of Southern Mississippi, Hattiesburg.
77 William Varner to John Bankhead and Lister Hill, 23 April 1941, 145.93-80–92, January 1936–April 1936, June 1941–September 1941, AFHRA.

in the nearby town of Tuskegee."[78] Chauncey Spencer, a Negro aviator stationed at the school during the war, likewise was displeased to find the city of Tuskegee "rampant with discrimination." He recalled that the local theater "had two box offices; one labeled 'colored', the other 'whites.'"[79] Nonetheless, Lieutenant General Benjamin O. Davis Jr., one of the highest-ranking African Americans in the U.S. military and a commander of the Tuskegee Airmen, quite possibly may have seen this tiny Alabama hamlet, with all its misery, as a respite from what he had faced as a student at West Point in the early 1930s. There, Davis claimed, not one of his white peers or instructors spoke directly to him during his entire four-year tenure. When he later applied to fly with the Army Air Corps in 1935, he was blocked on racist grounds; thus, his role at Tuskegee must have seemed more than a consolation prize.[80]

The publisher of the *"Negro* Travel Guide," essential for beset travelers in the Jim Crow U.S. seeking lodging, food, and the like during long automobile journeys, was inspired to produce this valuable compendium after receiving aviation training at Tuskegee and encountering all manner of obstacles while traveling in the region.[81]

During the war, a white Alabama mother assailed the federal government for permitting Negroes to fly after her son's plane collided in mid-air with an army pursuit plane piloted by a Negro pilot. Over a dozen individuals perished in that crash. In her missive to the authorities, she prefaced her statements with the disclaimer that hers was "not a letter of hate," then added with surging fury:

> My boy [was] sacrificed to the fanatical idea that all men must be allowed to perform on the same level regardless of background...
> .I resent our government's apparent determination to raise the

---

78   Press Release, October 1944, Reel 29, #572, Part I, Press Releases, CAB-NCSU.
79   Spencer, *Who is Chauncey Spencer?* 46.
80   Davis Jr., *Benjamin O. Davis Jr., American*, 44.
81   Press Release, July 1948, Reel 8, #216, Part III, Series I, Subject Files on Black Americans, CAB-NCSU.

Negro overnight…to a place in civilization which he is as yet unprepared to assume [since] his mind is not prepared.

Unanimity of opinion about the feasibility of training Negro pilots was not evident nationally, and the question of Negro preparedness for flight was raised sharply whenever a Negro pilot performed at what was seen as a less-than-optimal level.[82]

Given such opposition, it should not be surprising that, as one commentator ascertained during the war, many felt that it was "almost impossible to find colored youth capable of qualifying for training as army aviators in the country." In early 1945, a government report concluded that efforts to fill Tuskegee's quota for such young men "almost met with failure" as "barely 20 were secured." The "output" from Tuskegee, that report noted, "average[d] roughly 10 percent of the total flying program…conducted by the army."[83] By September 1945, as the war was winding down, even Tuskegee Institute's President F. D. Patterson was requesting that the training program be relocated from the Alabama HBCU, a move purportedly endorsed by some aviators themselves.[84]

* * *

The continuing odyssey of Hubert Julian was further symptomatic of the impediments encountered by Negro pilots during the war. By 1943, Julian was on his way to Lincoln, Nebraska, where he was assigned to a U.S. air facility.[85] By 1944, he had departed for greener pastures to fly—not for the U.S, nor for the RAF, for that matter—but rather as the director of publicity for popular jazz musician Earl "Fatha" Hines. At the time, Julian was overjoyed that he could work for such a cosmopolitan figure as Hines. Hines, referring to his signature tune,

---

82 Press Release, December 1944, Reel 29, #1136, Part I, Press Releases, CAB-NCSU.
83 Press Release, March 1945, Reel 30, #701, Part I, Press Releases, CAB-NCSU.
84 Press Release, September 1945, Reel 30, #831, Part I, Press Releases, CAB-NCSU.
85 Press Release, March 1943, Reel 25, 594, Part I, Press Releases, CAB-NCSU.

was certain that Julian would "Straighten Up and Fly Right" as he was said to have done so many times before. "I know he'll do the same thing on the ground," the pianist was quoted as saying.[86]

It is unclear if the Tuskegee Airman Louis Purnell bumped into Julian in New York City after the latter's sojourn in Nebraska and before his tenure with Fatha Hines, but Purnell once claimed that he found the typically high-flying "Black Eagle" in bad shape during a visit to the renowned pilot's home. Reportedly, Julian had "no furniture in the living room and nothing but a big round oak tale in the dining room." Purnell concluded, however, that the senior pilot was "living in another world, still playing the role of a king in a cold, empty house." He also recounted that Julian was still espousing the motto, *per aspera ad astra*, or "to the stars through difficulties"—a slogan befitting the sage and the saga of Black aviation.[87] Julian had yet to be grounded permanently, and soon he was back in business, albeit not in the United States.

Quite tellingly, other Negroes who had been aviation pioneers before the bombing of Pearl Harbor did not see their talents drawn upon to any meaningful degree by Washington, despite the urgency of war. John Robinson, Julian's combative sparring partner from his East Africa days—who too had clocked many hours airborne and who presumably would have been helpful to the U.S. Air Corps, instead returned to East Africa.[88] Willa Brown also suffered setbacks during the war, despite her demonstrated competency as a pilot. Eugene Bullard, another pioneer of Black aviation, likewise was unable to contribute his piloting skill directly to Washington. After ascending to notoriety in France during the previous world war, by the time the Germans occupied his adopted homeland he was considered a leader of the resistance.

---

86   Press Release, August 1944, Reel 29, #228, Part I, Press Releases, CAB-NCSU.
87   Louis Purnell, "The Flight of the Bumblebee," *Air & Space*, October 1989, Technical Files, NASM.
88   Claude Barnett to John Robinson, 9 October 1943, Box 171, Folder 1, CAB-ANP.

Bullard had served in the French Foreign Legion and in the Lafayette Flying Corps of American volunteer pilots who flew for the French Air Force during World War I.[89] The Georgia-born flyer told a reporter, in a statement intended to rally U.S. Negroes to the war effort:

> Before Hitler came into Paris, we had men of color in the [French] government....do you know that for the first time in history, Negroes are now accepted as pilots in the RAF and in the Royal Navy Academy?

Though he did not admit it at the time for obvious reasons, Bullard, who had lost all to the Nazis' rapaciousness when they occupied Paris, joined the French underground and became a valued spy.[90]

James Peck, who had flown to great acclaim in Spain, added discouragingly that "color bars" had "blocked" his flying career and pushed him, out of necessity, out to sea. During the war years, he was a Chief Steward in the Merchant Marines. Like other Negro pilots, Peck's love of aviation began when he was a child; but finding difficulty obtaining employment in his chosen field, he worked variously as a drummer, a writer, and, ironically enough, as an elevator operator—one of the few routes for upward mobility for those like him during that era.[91]

The advent of the Second World War indeed placed the U.S. in a real bind. African Americans' pre-existing interest in aviation meant that they were primed to excel in this complex field, but the rigidity of Jim Crow made it difficult for the nation to violate its racist norms by recruiting Blacks to the air corps. What ultimately helped change the U.S. Department of War's resistance to the idea of involving Black pilots in the second global conflict was a far-reaching lawsuit brought by Wendell McConnell.

---

89 Brochure from "Free French in America," June 1941, Box 176, Folder 7, CAB-ANP.
90 *New York Amsterdam News*, 21 October 1961.
91 Press Release, January 1944, Reel 27, #580, Part I, Press Releases, CAB-NCSU.

McConnell was an attorney and member of the faculty at the law school at Howard University, a historically Black institution of higher education in Washington, DC. His litigation ensued after the war department refused to permit a young Negro to enter the aviation corps. The case won national attention and, according to one observer, was the "breaking point" that forced a change to the "discriminatory practices used against Negroes in that branch of the service."[92]

The War Department should have been thankful that their discriminatory hand was forced, for complicating matters further was the sheer difficulty of flying a plane—particularly when opponents were shooting at it with the aim of forcing a fatal crash landing—and an array of other factors impelling the demise of Jim Crow. Collapse from psychological pressure was a constant in the experience of combat pilots. Often-insupportable demands were placed on their psychological equilibrium, and a great many reported that fear was the primary emotion they faced while in the air. As one former pilot recalled: "I was scared all the time." Additionally, air casualties were high, not only because of combat but also because of routine flying accidents. No small number of those may have been initiated by the pre-existing miasma of fear-generated errors resulting from fear-induced anxiety. All perhaps contributed to the heavy drinking, psychosomatic disorders, and long periods of depression and enervation quietly noted among the nation's then-segregated flying corps—psychological maladies that sometimes combined with severe weight loss, insomnia, and operational fatigue, all of which contributed to a loss of efficiency.[93]

In late 1940, Major General H. H. Arnold of the Army Air Corps asserted that it took "from 5 to 7 years to train a good crew chief and from 5 to 9 years to train a good line or hangar chief."[94] He neglected

---

92   Press Release, April 1946, Reel 32, #1056, Part I, Press Releases, CAB-NCSU.

93   Overy, *The Bombers and the Bombed*, 163, 164, 167.

94   Major Ralph F. Stearley, Air Corps to Commanding General, Southeast Air Corps, 8 May 1941, 220.740, 220.765.2, 1940-1945, 1942, Volume 2, Volume 3, AFHRA.

to include in his estimates the assumption that a substantial number of aviation recruits might have to take a leave of absence at some time during their training—or drop out entirely—due to the resultant various pressures they would be forced to endure. This realization only reinforced the U.S.'s need for Negro pilots—actually, for more pilots generally—but formidable barriers were tossed in the path of this laudable goal.

The democratic deficit in Washington gave Berlin good reason to pay special attention to the *Spookwaffe*. As one wartime report acknowledged, "Negro flyers down[ed] 11 Nazi [fighter planes] in [a] furious air battle."[95] (Interestingly, that report credited a "Chicagoan" with downing three of the German planes, but it did not confirm whether Brown and Coffey trained the pilot.) Another reporter confessed his amazement when he visited a "mobile aviation" unit stationed in France during the war and "discovered…23 Negro officers including six captains," dubbing it "the largest concentration of Negro officers I have seen on the western front."[96]

Perhaps that observer encountered Lieutenant Felix Kirkpatrick, a Tuskegee-trained Negro fighter pilot from Chicago, who completed 70 missions in Greece, Romania, Austria, Hungary, Yugoslavia, Germany, and Southern France.[97] He also might have met Tuskegee Airman Lee Archer Jr., one of ten children, born in New York and raised in Harlem. "From childhood I had loved airplanes," Archer recalled in a 2001 interview, adding that "flying came naturally" to him and that Bessie Coleman was one of his "heroes"—all of which led him to the Army Air Corps.

To get into the Corps, however, Archer recalled that he had to take an entrance test covering "language, mathematics, history, geography,"

---

95   Press Release, July 1944, Reel 28, #1127, Part I, Press Releases, CAB-NCSU.
96   Press Release, November 1944, Reel 29, ##793, Part I, Press Releases, CAB-NCSU.
97   Press Release, January 1945, Reel 30, #114, Part I, Press Releases, CAB-NCSU.

and the like. He also recalled that of the 98 test takers who sat for the exam with him, only two were Negro, yet those two were the only ones monitored during the testing session. Still, he passed with flying colors and became a fighter pilot, arriving in Italy in January 1944 after training in Alabama. "I flew a lot of missions with a fellow by the name of Wendell Pruitt from St. Louis," Archer recollected. "In fact," he continued, "the nickname for the two of us was the 'Gruesome Twosome.'" He called Pruitt, with whom he conducted 169 missions, "one of the greatest pilots in the world."

Another of Archer's Tuskegee comrades, Roscoe Brown, was the first Negro pilot to engage and destroy an enemy jet plane.[98] After the war, Archer went on to fame and fortune as a corporate executive while his comrade Pruitt, who racked up an enviable aerial record, died young—killed, along with a student pilot, during a training exercise in Tuskegee in 1945. Pruitt was honored posthumously when a massive public housing project in his hometown of St. Louis was named after him—before being destroyed ignominiously years later.[99] Brown later earned his doctorate, becoming a professor at New York University and then director of its Institute of Afro-American Affairs. He later was a president of Bronx Community College and directed the Center for Education Policy at the City University of New York.[100] Archer, on the other hand, went on to fame and fortune as a corporate executive.

Yet Archer was not altogether pleased with his Air Corps experience. As he speculated in 2001, the U.S. military "became southern" after

98 Clipping, 31 March 1945, Technical Files, NASM. See also Oral History, Lee Archer (cited below).
99 Press Release, November 1944, Reel 29, #1034, Part I, Press Releases, CAB-NCSU. See also Henry J. Schmandt and George D. Wendel, *The Pruitt-Igoe Public Housing Complex, 1956-1976* (St. Louis, MO: Center for Urban Programs, St. Louis University, 1976); John J. Bauman et al., eds., *From Tenements to the Taylor Homes: In Search of an Urban Housing Policy in Twentieth-Century America* (University Park: Pennsylvania State University Press, 2000).
100 Sam Roberts, July 7, 2016, "Roscoe C. Brown, Jr., 94, Tuskegee Airman and Political Confidant." *New York Times*, A17.

the Civil War. Although the white southerners "lost the war," he stated, they nonetheless continued to fight for their white supremacist way of life and against Black progress on the ground and in the air—up to and through World War II. Even by the 21st century, he feared that white southern militarists were still planning for what he dubbed "the big battle" to achieve their poisonous objectives[101]

Despite the many hurdles the Tuskegee Airmen had to overcome—racist and otherwise—many were not dissatisfied with their service. This included the late Virgil Richardson of Texarkana, Texas, who, before becoming a pilot, was an actor and one-time understudy for the talented actor Canada Lee in the classic play "Big White Fog." Perhaps it was the perceived nobility of combating a foe as pestiferous as fascism; or maybe it was the simple, liberating feeling of sailing through the skies; perhaps it was the despair of knowing the U.S. forces were enmeshed in a bloody conflict with a formidable foe, some of whom realized that Negro aviators were needed desperately, causing divergences from routine maltreatment. Whatever the case, Richardson observed, "[A]ll the bitterness I had toward the army left me when I got [into] the air force." He added, "[F]or the first time I was treated like a good American soldier....It seems everybody has respect for any individual, white or black, who can fly a plane."[102]

Louis Purnell, another Tuskegee Airman, argued that his early dreams of flying were a form of escape for him. His later ability to soar through the heavens as a pilot was, in his view, therapeutically engaging.[103] Other Tuskegee Airmen held their Air Corps service as a more romantic alternative to the meat-grinder existence experienced by Army ground troops. As a 17-year-old in Lancaster, Kentucky, for example, future Tuskegee Airman Julian Freeman recalled that he

---

101 Oral History, Lee Archer, 13 March 2001, K239.0152-2580, 01156065, AFHRA.
102 Press Release, November 1945, Reel 32, #49, Part I, Press Releases, CAB-NCSU.
103 "AARP Bulletin," March 1991, Technical Files, NASM.

watched with awe a newsreel of the invasion of Normandy. Afterward, he exclaimed excitedly: "That's one of the reasons I went into the Air Force. I saw what happened when you went into the infantry."[104]

Whatever the motivation for their joining the U.S. Air Corps, the Tuskegee-trained Black aviators were indispensable in the victory over fascism and, as is now well known, many of them excelled both during the war and afterward. The ingrained tradition of aviation among African Americans paid substantial dividends for their homeland, even while Black aviators continued to be subjected to various forms of discrimination and harassment. Many returned home from aerial fighting overseas determined to redeem the promise that had been made to them implicitly and, at times, explicitly: that given the blood sacrifice they and others endured, conditions in the U.S. would improve for all. Across the ocean, their African counterparts in the air, many of whom had been conscripted by London, felt and acted similarly toward colonialism, as will be discussed in the next chapter.

---

104 *New York Amsterdam News*, 6 June 2014.

Claude Barnett. This founder of the Associated Negro Press used his news agency to share opportunties available for African Americans in East Africa.
(Courtesy Moorland-Spingarn Research Center, Howard University)

CHAPTER 5

JIM CROW AND APARTHEID: FLYING HIGH?

James Peck was optimistic. Months after the end of World War II, his analysis revealed that there were "more than 3,000 licensed Negro pilots" in the U.S. The assiduous Negro aviation pioneer concluded that these positive findings were an outgrowth of the reality that "600 Negro pilots and 3,800 aviation mechanics were trained during the war."[1] Soaking up much of this aviation talent was a new airline—Universal Skyways—which billed itself as one of the first "Negro airlines" to climb aloft, flying routes between Houston, Chicago, and Atlanta.[2]

In a similarly optimistic vein, by 1949 the Coffey School's Willa Brown was seeking federal aid for what was termed a "Negro airport" in Chicago.[3] In comments shared with the Associated Negro Press's Claude Barnett during this era of change, Ashby Carter, president of the heavily Negro National Alliance of Postal Employees, maintained that he was looking forward to seeing that Negro postal employees were "included and integrated" into the newly created "air crews" that were delivering increasing amounts of the nation's mail.[4]

---

1 Press Release, March 1946, Reel 32, #907, Part I, Press Releases, CAB-NCSU.

2 Press Release, November 1945, Reel 31, #1226, Part I, Press Releases, CAB-NCSU.

3 Press Release, January 1949, Reel 39, #1007, Part I, Press Releases, CAB-NCSU.

4 Ashby Carter to Claude Barnett, 22 September 1946, Reel 13, #717, Series A, Part III, Subject files on Black Americans, CAB-NCSU.

The pressure of an anti-fascist World War combined with the full-throated protests of African Americans to create a new environment for those demanding the right to fly. As mighty as those factors were, they alone were insufficient to deliver the kind of equality U.S. Negroes demanded. Assuredly, the progressive currents uncorked by the global war bolstered a strong, international anti-colonialism movement, which in turn buttressed anti-Jim Crow crusades in the U.S.[5] and immeasurably aided Negro initiatives in many nations and realms, including aviation. The emphasis placed on aviation by African Americans, for example, also had Pan-African repercussions, as evidenced by the fact that some of Haiti's first pilots were trained at Tuskegee Institute in Alabama, deep in the heart of Dixie.[6]

A survey of post-war aviation plans at historically Black land-grant colleges in the U.S. happily reported, "all children, even the youngest" among African Americans "are interested in planes and what makes them go." "Aviation instruction in public schools," the survey authors claimed, as a subject was "introduced as a result of demand on the part of the pupils." Thus, by early 1944, they noted, "more than half of the nation's 28,000 Negro-serving high schools had introduced pre-flight aeronautics courses as an integral part of the curriculum." The survey's findings led a number of Black land-grant institutions to expand their instruction in aviation. They subsequently encouraged officials and committees to "keep abreast [of] aviation developments in their state designed for whites."[7]

The trend toward aviation instruction for U.S. Negroes did not unfold neatly or smoothly, however. In the immediate aftermath of the

---

5   See, e.g., Gerald Horne, *Mau Mau in Harlem? The U.S. and the Liberation of Kenya* (New York: Palgrave, 2009).

6   Clipping, April 1943, Reel 3, #363, Series F, Part III, Subject Files on Black Americans, CAB-NCSU.

7   G. L. Washington, "The Negro Land Grant College and Full Postwar Employment: Survey of Postwar Aviation Possibilities in Negro Land Grant Colleges," paper presented at the 23rd annual session of the Conference of Presidents of Land Grant Colleges, October 23, 1945, Chicago; Library of Prairie View A&M University, Prairie View, Texas.

war, Willa Brown felt compelled to take the cause of Black aviation to a political level. She made a quixotic run for Congress—as a Republican—and lost.[8] Symbolically, her losing effort was seen by many as a reflection of the fact that her ambitious aviation dreams were crashing rudely to earth. The ANP's Barnett, for example, who had been so instrumental in aborting Brown's earlier, more capacious plans, reported that her political loss was further indication of Washington's decision to "[squeeze] Negroes" out of the aviation corps. "[T]he army wanted no more Negro pilots," the ANP reported.[9]

In short, there was a clash between the erstwhile national goal of solidifying Jim Crow and the newer goal driven by antifascist currents and relentless criticisms from Moscow of eroding U.S. apartheid. Nevertheless, aviation was shrinking the world, bringing distant nations ever closer and exposing internal national deficiencies to international scrutiny. Outsiders thus were able to gain an astringent view of Jim Crow as it was practiced in the United States. By the same token, aviation also allowed the primary victims of the nation's most iniquitous system of segregation—namely, African Americans— to escape the wrath of U.S. segregation more easily. As Universal Skyways was taking off, a Haitian visitor to the U.S. confessed that he was "never without anguish" whenever he landed in Miami. He explained that he feared "contemptuous treatment" at the hands of southern whites and felt as if he had to "risk his life and limb" merely to walk that city's "streets full of sunshine"[10]

As the post-war climate was evolving and anti-Jim Crow crusades were gaining steam across the U.S., a contrary tail wind began blowing west, across the Atlantic, from the newly *apartheid*-driven South Africa. The advent of that nation's violent and rigidly separatist regime

---

8 Press Release, January 1946, Reel 32, #480, Part I, Press Releases, CAB-NCSU.

9 Press Release, February 1947, Series F, Part III, Subject Files on Black Americans, CAB-CHM.

10 Press Release, November 1946, Reel 54, #92, Part I, Press Releases, CAB-NCSU.

tremendously complicated the U.S. movement toward desegregation. The apartheid tailwind propelled and strengthened more than Jim Crow, however. It also propelled anticommunism and served to undermine stalwarts like Paul Robeson and W. E. B. Du Bois. It lifted the ideology of "free enterprise" and hampered those Negroes of a socialist persuasion who were often the most resolute anti-apartheid and anti-Jim Crow fighters. It also undermined Negroes like John Robinson, whose pioneering aerial efforts did not fit neatly into the ascending free-enterprise mantra.

Helen Nash, described in court papers as a "Negro citizen," was among the anti-Jim Crow crusaders. She sued the airport in Washington, DC, for damages after being refused service in a dining room there. Her case snaked slowly through the courts until 1949, when it was dismissed without cause. In their ruling against Nash, the federal jurists concluded thusly: "[S]egregation is not violative of the Federal Constitution or of any act of Congress."[11] Undeterred, another Negro, Edgar Brown, took matters into his own hands. He and his son engaged in an eight-hour, sit-down strike at the airport to protest the Jim Crow ruling in Nash's case.[12] Yet neither Nash nor Brown should have been shocked by her case's outcome. If the U.S. had allowed Jim Crow to fester during wartime, when national security hung in the balance, why would anyone expect it to change course after its combative adversaries were vanquished? A few years later, the city of Houston—soon to be crowned the nation's aerospace center—approved plans to have segregated, Jim Crow toilets installed in its main airport.[13]

As the drums of anti-colonialism began to beat in Africa, the colonizers saw the need for more aviators, not just for military

---

11 *Nash v. Air Terminal Services, Inc., et al.*, 85 F. Supp. 545 (1949), University of Houston Law Center. See also *Air Terminal Services v. Rentzel*, 81 F.Supp. 611 (1949); *Henderson v. American Airlines*, 91 F. Supp. 1950.

12 Clipping, January 10, 1949, Box 1, Edgar Brown Papers, Tulane University, New Orleans.

13 Press Release, December 1951, Reel 8, #461, Series I, Part III, Subject Files on Black Americans, CAB-NCSU.

purposes but also for civilian travel, flying for carriers such as Wilson Airways of Kenya.[14] As the war dragged on, it seemed evident to John Robinson, the U.S.-born Negro aviator, that his fungible skills as a pilot were far more valuable in Ethiopia than at home. Robinson was growing increasingly frustrated by the lack of opportunity available to him in his homeland. When a visiting Ethiopian official invited him to return to East Africa in 1943, he gathered a group of like-minded pilots and pilots-in-training and headed back to East Africa, where opportunities to fly for persons of his ancestry appeared to be more abundant.[15] Robinson did not depart alone for Ethiopia. At least seven other African Americans left under his leadership and at his behest; however, Claude Barnett of the ANP reported that as many as 30 men accompanied Robinson.[16] All were talented, and they were mostly aviators.

Fearing attack by Axis submarines, the exiles took a circuitous route by sea to Ethiopia. They departed from New Orleans, stopping in Cuba, Haiti, Trinidad, and Brazil before heading around the Cape of Good Hope and then up the coast of eastern Africa.[17] After a grueling 105-day journey[18] that involved dodging Japanese submarines near Durban[19] and a layover in Kenya, the group reached the Horn of Africa, from which they traveled by lorry to Addis Ababa.[20] Along the way, the men reported that Kenya was a worse place on the racial front

---

14   Beryl Markham, *West with the Night* (San Francisco: North Point, 1983 [originally published 1942]), 187.

15   "East African High Commission, Report of an Inter-Territorial Committee on Ground Services for Civil Aviation in East Africa, Nairobi," December 1948, Duke University.

16   Claude Barnett to John Robinson, 22 October 1945, Box 171, Folder 1, CAB-CHM.

17   Press Release, August 1946, Reel 33, #546, Part I, Press Releases, CAB-NCSU. The emigrants included Andrew Hester, David Talbot; Thurlow Tibbs; Joe Muldrow; Edward Jones; and James Cheeks. Simultaneously, an influx of Ethiopians and East Africans was then reaching Harlem. See, e.g., Press Release, July 1946, Reel 33, #453, Part I, Press Releases, CAB-NCSU.

18   Press Release, October 1946, Reel 33, #1126, Part I, Press Releases, CAB-NCSU.

19   Press Release, August 1946, Reel 33, #694, Part I, Press Releases, CAB-NCSU.

20   Press Release, September 1946, Reel 33, #893, Part I, Press Releases, CAB-NCSU.

than even South Africa.[21] They also found the conditions in the Horn to be very difficult. On land, they encountered challenges of biblical proportions, including a swarm of locusts so thick that it turned the skies pitch black in its wake.[22] Most of the men persisted and chose, like their leader Robinson, to stay. Others eventually departed.

The Ethiopian planes were in bad shape, and Robinson was tasked to oversee not only their repair and upkeep but also to supervise his fellow U.S. Negroes and about a thousand others in the budding Ethiopian aviation enterprise. The larger group of trainees included Ethiopians, Italians, Egyptians, Sudanese, Somalis, and Eritreans. "As a result of our ability and ingenuity in accomplishing work," said Andrew Hester, one of the U.S. emigrants, speaking of his fellow African Americans in particular, "we won the admiration and respect of everyone who knew us."[23]

Barnett, who by that time had reconciled with Robinson, continued to tout through his news agency the opportunities available to U.S. Negroes in East Africa. Another advocate for overseas opportunities for African Americans was Dr. T. Thomas Fortune Fletcher, director of a school in the Ethiopian capital. Fletcher was a professor on leave from Lincoln University in Missouri, and he was seeking to recruit African American teachers to Ethiopia in much the same way as Robinson was seeking to recruit Black pilots.[24] These and other prospects for U.S. Negroes coincided with a time when distance, due to aviation, was becoming less of a factor in the separation of nations. They provided African Americans with opportunities to lobby abroad more effectively and elevated their efforts to shine a light on as well as turn the tide against U.S. injustices.

Robinson soon established a commercial airline in Ethiopia, Sultan Airways, which deployed Douglas DC3 passenger and cargo planes

21 Press Release, August 1946, Reel 33, #759, Part I, Press Releases, CAB-NCSU.
22 Press Release, September 1946, Reel 33, #1064, Part I, Press Releases, CAB-NCSU.
23 Press Release, October 1946, Reel 33, #1199, Part I, Press Releases, CAB-NCSU.
24 Press Release, August 1947, Reel 35, #515, Part I, Press Releases, CAB-NCSU.

in its service. The ANP hailed his achievement, declaring that, due in no small part to Robinson's energy and ingenuity, Addis Ababa was quickly becoming "the greatest air hub in East Africa." Soon, flights were taking off and landing inside the nation from one node to another. Ethiopian planes then began traveling outward—to Somalia, the Arabian Peninsula, India, and France. By the late 1940s, Robinson was fully in charge of Ethiopia's aerial enterprise, employing experienced flyers from around the globe and continually soliciting the involvement of African American pilots whose skills were woefully underutilized in the States. His recruitment missives, which urged recipients to respond and helpfully included his return address in Addis Ababa, proclaimed that Ethiopia represented "an excellent opportunity for some of our air veterans of World War II."[25]

As Robinson was reaching out to his peers in the U.S., a convention of Negro aviators was taking place in New York City. At that meeting, members of the curiously named Warhawk Aviation Club lamented: "[A]lthough Negro pilots had an excellent war record, only about 30 colored pilots are employed throughout the nation."[26] Around the same time (spring 1948), members of the Chavis Wing Flying Club—which included Charles Foxx of Norfolk, Virginia, a former Tuskegee Airman, and other top U.S. Negro pilots—were decamping to Greensboro, North Carolina. There, in an effort to keep their aerial skills sharp, they staged their first annual air exhibition, which featured, as per usual, a number of death-defying parachute jumps.[27]

Airplane manufacturers' records with regard to hiring Negro aviators and otherwise engaging Blacks in the aviation field had not improved appreciably. Northrop Aircraft, for example, remained as recalcitrant as its peers. The good news was that they hired their first

---

25 Press Release, February 1948, Reel 36, #887, Part I, Press Releases, CAB-NCSU.
26 Press Release, August 1948, Reel 38, #512, Part I, Press Releases, CAB-NCSU.
27 Press Release, April 1948, Reel 37, #650, Part I, Press Releases, CAB-NCSU.

Negro—among 1,300 workers in its employ. The bad news was that the man was hired by a kind of accident in that he did not reveal his racial identity on his application and was able to slip through the mesh before he was exposed.[28]

The sad reality of under-recognition and under-employment may have inclined African American pilots and pilots-in-training to test the occasionally locust-laden skies of East Africa. Unfortunately for Colonel Robinson and those who accompanied him to Ethiopia, Addis Ababa was not exactly the idyll its promoters represented it to be, thus further circumscribing opportunities for U.S. Negroes who wished to climb into cockpits. Nevertheless, Robinson's fellow expatriate, Professor Fletcher, who had the added and sensitive assignment of teaching English to members of the Soviet legation in Ethiopia, claimed that Robinson was doing "well." "[H]e is still in aviation," Fletcher wrote, "but not doing one-tenth of what he could and would do were he given a chance."[29]

Moreover, just as Robinson had engaged in fisticuffs with his fellow aviator Hubert Julian in the previous decade, he did the same during his second sojourn—this time mixing it up with Carl Gustaf von Rosen, a Swedish count then serving as head of an aviation training program in Ethiopia. Both men held the rank of Colonel in the Ethiopian Air Force, and during the 1930s war with Rome they had been collaborators. As a result of the fight, the Scandinavian wound up in the hospital with a concussion while the African American wound up in court charged with assault and battery. As one commentator reported, however, the future for Robinson, who notably "received his private civil pilot's license in 1928," seemed highly "uncertain."[30]

Homer Smith, an ANP journalist posted to Ethiopia by Barnett, concluded differently. He suggested that the Swede's future, not

28 Press Release, October 1948, Reel 38, #1062, Part I, Press Releases, CAB-NCSU.
29 T. Thomas Fortune Fletcher to Claude Barnett, 12 February 1947, Box 171, Folder 2, CAB-CHM.
30 Press Release, August 1947, Reel 35, #811, Part I, Press Releases, CAB-NCSU.

Robinson's, was the "uncertain" one because of the thrashing the former had suffered. "[Robinson] certainly did sock that Swede," Smith marveled, "I saw [the Swedish pilot] in the hospital and he looked as if Joe Louis had been fumbling with him."[31] In court, Robinson admitted that he leveled his fellow pugilist with a powerful haymaker, but he argued that he did so in self-defense. He claimed that his opponent had pulled a pistol on him on more than one occasion, thus leaving him with few options beyond forceful retaliation. He also objected to being tried as a subject of the British Empire pursuant to an archaic Italian code, and he demanded a new trial under Ethiopian law.[32] His request was honored, but he later deemed the Ethiopian court a travesty as well and alleged that the judge was biased against him.[33]

Homer Smith predicted rightly that the judge would order Robinson to pay a light, $300 fine[34]; but perhaps because of the embattled pilot's sour comments about Ethiopian justice, the fine was boosted later to $1,000.[35] The judge also gave Robinson a three-month jail sentence, which apparently Robinson never served. The pilot later was exonerated by Judge Nathan Marein, a Palestinian educated in the U.S., who was appointed to the Ethiopian bench by His Imperial Majesty Haile Selassie I himself.

As one observer present in Marein's courtroom asserted, immediately after the judge's ruling Robinson was "almost mobbed" by jubilant Ethiopians, many of whom, perhaps vicariously, were sharing the experience of knocking out a European and escaping punishment. Robinson, however, remained displeased, alleging that "certain European and other foreign circles [in Addis Ababa] have been doing their damnedest to have me railroaded into prison." He maintained that

---

31 Homer Smith to Claude Barnett, 19 November 1947, Box 172, Folder 1, CAB-CHM.
32 Press Release, September 1947, Reel 35, #994, Part I, Press Releases, CAB-NCSU.
33 Press Release, October 1947, Reel 35, #1088, Part I, Press Releases, CAB-NCSU.
34 Homer Smith to Claude Barnett, 19 November 1947, Box 172, Folder 1, CAB-CHM.
35 Press Release, May 1948, Reel 37, 802, Part I, Press Releases, CAB-NCSU.

those unnamed forces had long resented his aviation prowess and his ability to break the pattern of other expatriate technicians, who were tied to the apron strings of the major North Atlantic powers.[36]

That Colonel Robinson was saluted by the Ethiopian people after his brutal encounter and exoneration may have been a reflection of the state of justice in that nation at a crucial point in its history. Soon after Robinson's victory, Emperor Selassie ordered the hanging of any Ethiopians found to have "incited [a] riot against whites" in that country. The deceased among those thus convicted included many leaders of Ethiopia's organized railway workers' union, who were accused of injuring dozens of Europeans.[37]

Despite his travails, by late 1947 Robinson had managed to organize Sultan Airways and was seeking to interest the ANP's Barnett in some of his more ambitious plans. As Robinson confided then to Barnett, he constantly was trying "to interest some of the most important [people] here in Ethiopia to sponsor some kind of big industrial and agricultural program that would encourage the financial support, technical skill and cultural background of American colored people." He offered leadership of the initiative to Barnett and claimed that the Ethiopian authorities had agreed to set aside a stunning 320,000 acres for it. Plus, he indicated: "the entire stock of the corporation [would] have to be owned by Ethiopians and colored Americans"—51 percent and 49 percent, respectively.

Yes, the Ethiopian climate was hot, Robinson conceded euphemistically, but the East African nation had "plenty of water," a resource he posited could be harnessed into hydroelectric power and diverted to support the raising of livestock. "Select about eight or twelve good colored American engineers who could lay out a modern industrial city," Robinson challenged Barnett, and the project could

36 Press Release, May 1948, Reel 37, #857, Part I, Press Releases, CAB-NCSU.
37 Press Release, August 1949, Reel 41, #492, Part I, Press Releases, CAB-NCSU.

become a profitable reality. He warned the newsman, however, that his interest would "have to be kept absolutely secret until we can secure the land" because "European influence will try and block the plan." Robinson could have added that said influence would also be a factor in blocking the takeoff of his airline,[38] a condition precedent to his broader project.

Barnett was blunt in informing Robinson that his relationship with former Secretary of State Edward Stettinius, who in turn was tied to Juan Trippe of Pan American Airways, made it virtually impossible for him to collaborate with the ambitious expatriate. He already was allied with those powerbrokers "in a fashion somewhat similar" to the Ethiopia plan that was unfolding in Liberia—the other ostensibly independent African nation—which was more subject to U.S. penetration.[39] What Barnett did not share with Robinson was information that, despite his own high-level relationships, the Liberian venture was encountering as many headwinds as the one in Ethiopia.

Barnett had been compelled to protest to the Civil Aeronautics Board after Pan Am suspended service to Liberia in early 1947. As he testified then, it was "indefensible" to "leave Liberia without air transportation," particularly when he was just about to travel to Monrovia. "I am a stockholder of Pan American and proud of its record," he stated proudly, "but a storm of protest will descend around our heads if this discontinuance of service to Liberia goes through."[40] Despite his insider status, Barnett seemed to be no more effective in delivering aviation to the continent than did Robinson, the consummate outsider.

* * *

38 John Robinson to Claude Barnett, 12 November 1947, Box 171, Folder 2, CAB-CHM.
39 Claude Barnett to John Robinson, 11 February 1948, Box 171, Folder 2, CAB-CHM.
40 Claude Barnett to Civil Aeronautics Board, 22 March 1947, Box 208, Folder 1, CAB-CHM.

With anti-colonial stirrings and the democratic rhetoric that had accompanied the war yet to be stanched by the late 1940s, expatriates like Robinson had reason to suspect that the Jim Crow status quo would stiffen reflexively. In 1948, Pan American Airways inaugurated a new direct air service between Johannesburg and New York City.[41] As an official on Washington's Civil Aeronautics Board, Oswald Ryan, argued, his government "authorized this service because it found there was a genuine public need for uniting this nation with the Union of South Africa," which then accounted for "50 percent of all the United States foreign trade with Africa."[42] Ominously, this pact was inked just as apartheid was being inaugurated in that benighted land.

This closer relationship with apartheid was no step forward for anti-Jim Crow forces in the U.S. In 1948, John Ewing, the editor and publisher of the *Shreveport Times* in Jim Crow Louisiana, traveled by air to South Africa, where he hailed the "new frontier" he had just traversed. [43] He was accompanied by Roy Howard of the Scripps-Howard news organization, James Stahlman of the *Nashville Banner*, Charles McCabe of the soon-to-be defunct *New York Mirror*, and Juan Trippe of Pan American Airways. Newspaper executives from Miami and Hartford were also part of this delegation. Ewing effusively praised General Jan Smuts, the southern African nation's premier leader, as "one of the greatest leaders of our time."[44] As he added with a tinge of accuracy, though not in the way he envisioned: "I predict that the Union of South Africa is destined to play a vastly more important role on the stage of history in the future than in the past." [45] Smuts was more accurate in his response to the U.S. visitors, stating: "[Y]ou know

---

41   Press Release, 1948, Box 200, Folder 19, Pan Am Papers.

42   Statement of Oswald Ryan, circa 1948, Box 200, Folder 19, Pan Am Airways.

43   Brochure, 1 October 1848, Box 54, Folder 5, Pan Am Papers. In the same collection, see also List, 1948, Box 320, Folder 7. The delegation of about 22 also included Hugh Baillie, head of United Press International; and Norman Chandler of the *Los Angeles Times*.

44   Ibid.

45   Ibid.

there's a lot in common between us old Afrikanders [sic] and you old, unreconstructed rebels of the South." The only difference being, Smuts added bluntly, that the Afrikaners "didn't kill Indians."[46] Ewing later noted that the general's latter "meaningful statement" was "delivered with a hearty laugh," which did not obfuscate the wider point that "Smuts seemed to find a kinship between our problems of the native in South Africa and the Negro in our South."[47] As Ewing added:

> I could not help but think at this point, as Smuts spoke that a statesman like him would bring much understanding to our own Southern Negro problem, that he might be a leavening influence on those professional do-gooders in our own country who think that decrees and laws on paper can abruptly bring about a solution to the basic differences between white and black men.[48]

The U.S. newsman's ensuing pointed remarks, offered in light of the ongoing tumultuous events in Eastern Europe, were garnished with a generous dollop of anticommunism.

Much to the chagrin of anti-Jim Crow advocates, the growth of aviation, which brought them closer to like-minded advocates overseas, did the same for their opponents. The latter, who were decidedly more financially endowed, were perhaps even more empowered than their antagonists by the advent of aviation. It may not have been accidental that Ewing and his high-powered delegation landed in South Africa just as apartheid was being installed and as Jim Crow was facing a stiff postwar challenge.

From southern Africa, Ewing's delegation headed north to the Belgian- and French-colonized areas of the Congo, where he noticed that "the large number of natives in proportion to the whites create[d]

---

46 Ibid.
47 Ibid.
48 Ibid.

a difficult problem," which, he posited, could not be solved easily. He nonetheless optimistically concluded that "the same situation exists, of course, in the entire South African Union," which seemed, in his view, to be evolving nicely. "Everywhere we went in South Africa," Ewing claimed nervously, "the white citizens expressed concern, feeling that the United States might object to racial policies existing in South Africa, and attempt to interfere." "I told them," he asserted with bravado, "that the United States is not worried over their native problems and that we had no idea whatever of trying to dictate or influence their policies." The other members of his delegation, he added, "gave them the same answer, but it is interesting to note," he declared with a hint of angst, "that this anxiety existed in their minds.[49]"

The *Miami Herald*'s Lee Hills detected the same creeping sense of panic. "I hadn't been among South Africans 24 hours," he stated wondrously, "before I realized these people are completely on the defensive and hypersensitive about one issue. They're still hopping mad about the criticism flung around the United Nations about their handling of the race problem."[50]

Outnumbered by Africans perhaps 10 to 1 and locked in a system of crude repression that was unsustainable, the anger and implantation of apartheid that was the Afrikaner elite's response was, in the U.S. delegation's view, completely understandable. Moreover, news of that elite's actions could be whisked across the ocean by air at rapid speed by human couriers as opposed to winding its way laboriously. Hills was stunned nonetheless, pointing out that he had barely deplaned when "at least 20 persons brought up this question" of global pressure. "Even Prime Minister Jan Smuts brought up the question," he said, seemingly baffled, noting that the ruling elite "pleaded" so much for sympathy from the party of North Americans until finally he told one

---

49 Ibid.
50 Lee Hills, "Flight to Africa," 1948, Box 344, Folder 1, Pan Am Papers.

official: "We're in no position to throw stones. You know we have racial problems of our own." Dismissively, Hills concluded, "It's very easy smugly to indict distant sins 10,000 miles away" while ignoring the mote in one's own eye. Nonetheless, he found the anxiety of this European minority all the more staggering given that, he surmised, there were "probably more zillionaires per capita in Johannesburg than in any other city" and status anxiety was not the normal companion of elite wealth—or so he thought.[51]

If the angst-ridden defenders of apartheid had consulted with their comrades in Portugal, who were then presiding over neighboring Angola and Mozambique, consolation would not necessarily have been the result. As a Pan Am official based in fascist Lisbon, which was to become an important base for that airline, confided "off the record" in 1948, the Portuguese Prime Minister angrily claimed that "every time he roll[ed] out a red carpet for anyone connected with newspapers or magazines," the media representatives reciprocated by penning "slanderous articles about him."[52] The colonial leaders did not seem to realize the U.S.'s dilemma: although Washington was eager to encroach on their preserves, it was nervous that the despised Communists might rise up in the wake of a successful anti-colonial revolt.

According to B. S. Murphy of the *Hartford Times,* this dilemma was evaded, at least in one instance, in the so-called Belgian Congo. In an article he happily titled, "We fly high to Africa!" he wrote enthusiastically that "Leopoldville is a surprisingly modern city of 140,000 of whom only 7,000 are whites" and, strikingly, "of these 1,100 are Americans." He did not add that of those worldwide who might be defined as "white," a plurality was to be found in the U.S., with the second-largest number in Russia or, as was said then, "behind

---

51 Ibid.
52 W. H. Lyons, Regional Director, Iberian Peninsula & Africa to Vice President Smith, 20 February 1948, Box 29, Folder 10, Pan Am Papers.

the Iron Curtain" in Eastern Europe. This provided an advantage to the U.S. as it moved to encroach on territory otherwise occupied by the declining European powers' embattled "white" minority regimes, who had been battered during the war in any case. Deftly, Murphy asserted, "The Belgian Congo was and still is of tremendous values to the United States in the production of atomic bombs for it is here that is found and produced the largest supply or uranium in the world." Indeed, he concluded, it was "the most important source in the world" for this increasingly valuable commodity.[53]

Lee Hills of the *Miami Herald* also was not displeased to find that his homeland was the recipient of "the output of the closely guarded [uranium] mines at Shinkolobwe," where exploitation of African laborers was known to be shameless. "U.S. Marines guarded the operations during the war, and nearby Elizabethville boomed" as a direct result, he exulted. Moreover, he reported, "shipments were made back to the United States by plane," thus facilitating and speeding the development of atomic weapons used to level Hiroshima and Nagasaki.[54]

Hills, who seemed to be the most class-conscious newspaperman of the group, represented a chain of periodicals that included the *Chicago Daily News*, the *Detroit Free Press*, the *Akron Beacon Journal*, and his own Miami newspaper. He therefore arranged to have his musings on his Africa tour published in all those papers. Befitting his residence in a bastion of Jim Crow, however, he heartily endorsed the land of apartheid, enthusing that this mournful nation was the "bright spot on the dark continent." "*It is one of the last few spots on earth that practices free enterprise*," he noted, emphatically. Ironically and contradictorily, he stated this after he sang the praises of the state-owned enterprises there.[55] Such rhetoric was in the vanguard of the early defense of

---

53 B. S. Murphy, "We Fly High to Africa!" circa 1948, Box 320, Folder 18, Pan Am Papers.
54 Lee Hills, "Flight to Africa," circa 1948, Box 344, Folder 1, Pan Am Papers.
55 Editorial by Lee Hills, 21 March 1948, Box 344, Folder 1, Pan Am Papers.

apartheid as not just a headquarters of anti-communism but also as a citadel of capitalism in the face of the sturdy challenges provided by Nelson Mandela's African National Congress and its stalwart ally, the Communist Party of South Africa.

The fact that Pan Am's Juan Trippe accompanied this group of editors and publishers indicated that newsgathering was not the sole province of this delegation. As Ewing suggested, the uniting of apartheid and Jim Crow was also part of their agenda, and Trippe's airline was uniquely suited to act as matchmaker. "American business has long had its eye on South Africa," wrote one of the journalists, "[S]uch companies as Ford, General Motors, Chrysler, Studebaker, Goodyear and Firestone either have plants or formed subsidiaries in the Union [of South Africa]."[56] Certainly, the ability to fly with relative ease between New York and Johannesburg—as opposed to a lengthy sea voyage—facilitated the postwar tie between the lands of apartheid and Jim Crow.

This Pan Am knew well. "South Africa's boom, incubating before the war, is now a bouncing lusty youngster bearing striking resemblance to America's industrial expansion of the years following 1900," stated one of the airline's publicists. He continued: "Immigrants attracted by the sound of construction but caught by transport shortages, are trekking down the length of the African continent from Europe practically on foot"—though Pan Am was more than willing to fly them to Cape Town. "South Africa, at the end of the world's longest line of communication, once weeks away from Europe or the United States, has been tied closely to the rest of the world by [Pan Am]." The post-war boom meant that by 1947, "approximately 13,000 new cars coming from the U.S." had arrived in South Africa, and "in the past year Ford, General Motors, Chrysler and Studebaker [had] erected assembly plants" there. Thus, U.S. products that had "become outmoded for the

---

56 Clipping, 24 February 1948, Box 320, Folder 7, Pan Am Papers.

American market [found] ready markets in the hinterland of South Africa." This too gave a boost to both apartheid and Jim Crow, and Pan Am justifiably took some credit for this trend. By "eliminating the stop in Europe altogether and cutting six hours off the trip" from the U.S. to southern Africa, Trippe's airline was critical to the expansion of this trade.[57]

Befitting an airline that considered itself an arm of Washington, Trippe had coordinated this important journey of U.S. opinion molders in league with the U.S. legation in South Africa. However, casting a pall over their voyage, he bemoaned, was "a number of strikes in the publishing business" that barred the powerful Robert McCormack of the *Chicago Tribune* from traveling with the group. Trippe also lamented that "Gannett of the Gannett chain and Mr. David Hearst of the Hearst group" were unable to join them. He nonetheless was justifiably confident that those who did travel with him to the land of apartheid would "present to their readers a picture of South Africa which should give the American public a better appreciation of that great country." "Their initial enthusiasm," he opined, "spurred us on and tipped the scales of proceeding with this program."

Trippe did not mention, of course, that such favorable publicity would serve multiple purposes such as increasing travel to Cape Town to the benefit of his own coffers while connecting this African nation closer to his on the basis of anticommunism and defense of "free enterprise."[58] Apartheid's U.S. envoy chortled with delight at the prospect of the newspaper delegation's visit, noting that "[W]e South Africans sometimes like to refer to our country as 'THE OTHER U.S.A.'" He added, with satisfaction, that his "white settlement at the foot of the African continent is practically as old as the white settlement

---

57 Press Release, circa 1948, Box 344, Folder 1, Pan Am Papers. A version of this release can also be found in Box 320, Folder 18 of this collection.

58 Juan Trippe to T. Holcomb, 18 February 1948, Accession II, Box 29, Folder 10, Pan Am Papers.

of America itself [and] there are a great many historical parallels in the growth and development of our two countries."[59]

South Africa had moved from Dutch to British colonialism by the beginning of the 19th century, then fought a brutal (and unsuccessful) war with London at the end of that bloody century before moving in succeeding decades to a quasi-colonial status. By the late 1940s, the war had weakened the European powers and the world was shrinking steadily due to increasing travel by air. The U.S., aided by its vibrant airline industry, was on the verge of forging solid ties with the land of apartheid as its newly crowned champion and moving to dethrone London as the regime's premier supporter.

Meanwhile, the ANP's Barnett was chiding Trippe about the continued encroachment of apartheid policies on his airline. "Will you describe for us the policy on handling Negro passengers on Pan American who are en route to South America?" he asked curtly. "Does the company have a policy affecting races in the matter of seating and accommodation?" The latter possibility seemed unbelievable to the Chicagoan, who insisted that "even in the southern part of the United States there is no segregation on passenger airplanes and there has been little or no difficulty *to my knowledge*" [60]—with the italicized words being an important qualifier.

Barnett raised these questions because, he said, the bard of Harlem, Langston Hughes, who also happened to be an inveterate traveler, had just informed him that "airplanes going to South America separate even individual members from the rest of their own families because of color." As the Negro newsman cautioned Trippe, "I happen to be one of Pan American's small investors and am a booster for our line." He could have pointed out that Jim Crow was not enforced as rigidly on domestic planes as it tended to be, for example, on buses in the U.S. South. He also

---

59 Speech by Harry T. Andrews, 25 February 1948, Box 320, Folder 18, Pan Am Papers.
60 Claude Barnett to Juan Trippe, 22 June 1946, Reel 8, #431, Series I, Part III, Subject Files on Black Americans, CAB-NCSU.

could have added that he had refused to back an East African challenger to Pan Am—namely, Robinson's Sultan Airways carrier.[61]

Hughes, thus roped into this dispute, denied the statement attributed to him; he did, however, accuse Pan Am of subjecting passengers arriving in Miami from Latin America to Jim Crow dictates, which Haitians traveling by air contemporaneously asserted. In 1946, Hughes wrote that he had endured a "tour entirely by air" from Seattle to Mississippi, and when he returned in March he reported finding pervasive "evidence of Dixie prejudice at airports." That prejudice, he noted, increased the further South he flew:

> In previous seasons I have not seen any Jim Crow signs in airport waiting rooms but during Negro History Week, I notice[d] they [had] a tiny colored waiting room at the Birmingham Airport; and at Nashville they [had] a single bench marked 'colored.' I paid no attention to either one and no one said anything to me.[62]

Roger Wolin, who was authorized to respond to Hughes on Pan Am's behalf, claimed that while his employer did not countenance "discrimination as to the color, creed or race of its passengers," policies then being formulated for South Africa did not necessarily accord with those lofty words. Wolin nevertheless praised his supervisor, Trippe, for having "the foresight to establish this policy when the airline was formed" in 1927. He added that Pan Am's policy was "also observed in our employment of personnel" in that "several hundred colored men and women are employed by this organization in the Miami area alone." Tactfully, he did not specify what level—beyond the menial, that is—those "colored men and women" occupied.[63]

---

61 Claude Barnett to Juan Trippe, 22 January 1946, Reel 2, #654, Series D, Part III, Subject Files on Black Americans, CAB-NCSU.
62 Langston Hughes to Claude Barnett, 4 March 1946, Reel 2, #657, Series D, Part III, CAB-NCSU.
63 Roger Wolin to Claude Barnett, 7 February 1946, Reel 2, #634, Series D, Part III, CAB-NCSU.

Hughes' experience was informative because he violated Jim Crow norms without retaliation. At the conclusion of the previous World War, Jim Crow advocates drowned in blood any African American with the gumption to object to segregation.[64] That Hughes lived to tell of his rejection of Jim Crow norms suggests that segregation in aviation, an industry that was expanding in the aftermath of the antifascist war, was being tugged in opposing directions and responding accordingly. Air carriers were seeking simultaneously to adhere to segregation while realizing that this ideology and praxis was under siege by its opponents. Apparently, in the aftermath of World War II, many believed that anti-Jim Crow advocates had to be instructed to expect no meaningful changes in the status quo. The weight of antifascism, however, was translating rapidly into anti-Jim Crowism.

During the war, Southern Air Lines had the effrontery to seek the aid of the NAACP to help them "Jim Crow" Negro passengers. R. L. Heininger, the Chicago-based general traffic manager for that airline, went so far as to ask for a "list of homes in Memphis to which we could send Negro passengers who needed accommodations because of flight delays" or instances when they might be removed from a flight to accommodate white travelers.[65] As Negroes were shedding blood in copious amounts on the war's battlefields, the NAACP's Roy Wilkins was both dumbfounded and disgusted to learn of the plight of a Negro doctor from Corpus Christi, Texas, who found himself on a plane that was forced to touch down in Memphis. Given Jim Crow, the doctor was put up overnight at a "colored hotel" that he described as "a bedbug heaven."[66]

---

64 See, e.g., Cameron McWhorter, *Red Summer: The Summer of 1919 and the Awakening of Black America* (New York: Holt, 2011).

65 R. L. Heininger to Roy Wilkins, 2 July 1943, Box II: A9, NAACP Papers.

66 Roy Wilkins to E. J. Miller, Manager, Passenger Relations, Transcontinental and Western Airlines, circa 1945, Box II: A9, NAACP Papers.

After the war, this pattern continued in a manner that affected members of the NAACP staff as well. Wilkins, for example, recalled that he once was headed from Knoxville to Atlanta on Delta Airlines when the flight attendant on duty asked him, without explanation, to wait at the door of the plane. "She then went to the front of the cabin," the irked leader stated, "and whispered to a white man who was sitting in the first single seat. He moved to another seat and she smilingly conducted [Wilkins] to the seat [the white man] had vacated." Wilkins also recounted an earlier flight he took from Chicago to Kansas City on Braniff Airlines. On that flight, he explained, the attendant seemingly wanted to place him, in Jim Crow fashion, in the front of the cabin— the functional equivalent in the air of sitting in the back of the bus.[67] Future Supreme Court Justice Thurgood Marshall recalled being treated similarly. Once, while he was heading from Little Rock to New York on American Airlines, he sighted the word "Negro" on the bottom of his reservation card. He rightly determined that mark to be one "designed to facilitate Jim Crow treatment" on the incorrigible carrier.[68]

Dixie was not singular in its maniacal pursuit of enforcing apartheid norms. During the war, Wilkins told Mayor Fiorello La Guardia of New York City that "colored employees" were "not permitted to eat in the dining room with other employees" but instead had to eat "in a separate room far from the cafeteria;" naturally they had "separate locker rooms" too.[69]

* * *

Meanwhile in Africa, John Robinson was busily trying to organize an Ethiopian airline that—potentially—could drain business away from Pan Am and more easily transport anti-apartheid fighters continentally. For its part, Pan Am was looking to acquire airlines that already were

67 Roy Wilkins to Thurgood Marshall, 4 March 1946, Box II: A9, NAACP Papers.
68 Thurgood Marshall to American Airlines, 24 September 1945, Box II: A9, NAACP Papers.
69 Roy Wilkins to Mayor La Guardia, 30 March 1942, Box II: A233, NAACP Papers.

operating out of Addis Ababa, which was located in one of the few zones on the continent yet to be colonized. Pan Am officials were convinced that a carrier with operations in Ethiopia "should be very profitable" given that "business is good and rates are relatively high." Pan Am's competitor, Trans World Airlines (TWA), which cooperated contractually with local Ethiopian carriers, was not well run and, according to Pan Am vice president H. M. Bixby, was plagued by "excessive overhead" and "wholly unreasonable" charges. Bixby recommended that Pan Am take steps to undercut TWA and use that approach as a template by which other carriers such as the fledgling Iranian Airways could be undermined similarly.[70]

As the imperialist deck was being reshuffled in colonial societies in Africa and around the world, the U.S. sought to take the place of its erstwhile allies. Competing U.S. airlines battled for overseas markets in the formerly colonized territories after the war. Harold Ickes, one of the late President Roosevelt's top aides, assailed "British attempts to thwart American economic interests in the Middle East," citing postwar London's efforts to block TWA's entry into Egypt as a typical example. "The Americans," Ickes contended, "offered to hand over to the Egyptians the largest and most modern airfield in the Middle East—the Payne Field." In exchange, TWA was "to have been accorded necessary flying rights." According to the irate Ickes, however, London "objected strenuously," as it was intent on "sabotaging American commercial transactions."[71] Both TWA and Pan Am were unhappy when London sought to restrict their operations in its far-flung jurisdictions.[72] British opposition only enhanced the attractiveness of destinations like Ethiopia and South Africa to U.S.

---

70 H. M. Bixby to Vice President Ingalls, 18 September 1947, Box 469, Folder 21, Pan Am Papers.
71 Harold Ickes to T. Arazi, 17 September 1946, Box 45, Harold Ickes Papers, Library of Congress.
72 *Jamaica Daily Express*, 3 May 1949, Box 324, Folder 1, Pan Am Papers.

carriers, much to the detriment of Colonel Robinson and other anti-Jim Crow and anti-colonial champions.

"With the outbreak of the war," Juan Trippe proclaimed, "Pan Am became virtually an adjunct of the United States armed forces."[73] The war's conclusion hardly altered this reality. Pan Am was a major tool in the extension of U.S. influence into British colonial domains as London continued to reel postwar from the dual battering administered by Berlin and Tokyo. When the airline lifted off in 1927, it acknowledged that it could have added "many of Great Britain's colonies in the Western Hemisphere" to its routes, as they "were isolated lands." By 1949, Pan Am had its sights on British Guiana, located "2,268 miles away on the South American continent" yet "less than 19 hours [by air] from the United States." Jamaica and Trinidad too were brought closer to the U.S. as a result of aviation and the weakening of London. Pan Am's fleet of Boeing 314 Clippers, the airline announced proudly,

> ...have been playing a vital role in the economic growth of Great Britain's once remote possessions [for] through Pan American's phenomenal expansion in 1929 and 1930 these colonies attained fast transportation to and from the United States and more than half of the Latin American countries.

Pan Am's first pioneering flight into British territory took off on January 2, 1929, when "an S-38—a trim, eight passenger twin motor amphibian flew into Nassau from Miami." By 1949, the airline was offering "24 flights between Miami and Jamaica and 34 weekly flights between Miami and Trinidad."[74]

Pan Am's base in Jamaica was not just important for their Caribbean operations generally. The 600-mile stretch of open water between Jamaica and Panama was, according to an employee, Pan

---

73 Press Release, no date, Box 357, Folder 6, Pan Am Papers.
74 Press Release, 15 January 1949, Box 372, Folder 21, Accession II, Pan Am Papers.

Am's "flying laboratory." The ocean navigation and direction-finding techniques that its pilots and crews learned in the Caribbean enabled them to conquer first the Atlantic, then the vaster Pacific. After five years of flying the Kingston-Panama route, then billed as the "longest nonstop overwater route in the world," Pan Am had the know-how to send its planes winging over the 2,400-mile hop from San Francisco to Honolulu in 1935. A year later, it pushed on 5,400 miles over the vast Pacific to Manila.[75]

What was not openly discussed was that as these heavily Black islands became ensnared in the U.S. ambit, with Pan Am playing an instrumental role, their residents were brought into even closer contact with African Americans, thus allowing them to better compare anti-colonial and anti-Jim Crow notes.[76] It also meant that more travelers from the Caribbean would have a bracing confrontation with Jim Crow Miami—a difficult situation for Washington to handle as the Caribbean nations surged toward independence, thus creating additional momentum for desegregation.

Pan Am, with the politically savvy Trippe at the helm, was well disposed to sideline TWA in Africa given that both airlines operated in an environment where Washington connections were essential even to garner simple landing rights in foreign climes. Ethiopia was a uniquely sizeable independent nation on a continent dominated by European colonizers, where "imperial preference" or preferential treatment for London, Paris, Lisbon, and Brussels was the norm. It therefore offered a tantalizing treat to Washington. First, TWA moved to block Pan Am in Addis Ababa, and apparently—Trippe notwithstanding—it succeeded. Then, a Pan Am executive, in a supposedly confidential message, issued the following warning: "The last thing that the Ethiopian Government

---

75 Press Release, 24 October 1955, Box 372, Folder 22, Pan Am Papers.
76 See, e.g., Gerald Horne, *Cold War in a Hot Zone: The United States Confronts Labor and Independence Struggles in the British West Indies* (Philadelphia: Temple University Press, 2007).

wants is to have the State Department mad at them." Referencing nations such as Somalia and Eritrea, the message continued: "The question of the disposition of the former Italian colonies and a seaport for Ethiopia are vastly more important than any airline," including the fortunes of Pan Am. It concluded by confiding that this situation was "delicate" and "must be handled with caution" given that "remarkable potentialities" could be in store for Pan Am "if the deal goes through." To resolve this dilemma, Pan Am was instructed to contact John Spencer, "an American advisor to the Foreign Office" who was close to the Addis regime and a "person not to be overlooked."[77]

Robinson's fledgling venture, which later was to become Ethiopian Airways, was being squeezed by two U.S. giants. Moreover, according to Pan Am, TWA was looting the infant carrier. It accused its U.S. competitor of overcharging Robinson's carrier a hefty $1,000 each for three simple compasses. It further claimed that, like other U.S. manufacturers and corporations generally—which were sending their inferior products to African markets—TWA was "bleeding" Ethiopia specifically. Pan Am also accused TWA of sending personnel "of low caliber" to the exploited continent.[78] Try as they might, Robinson and the African American expatriates who accompanied him to Addis Ababa found it difficult to overcome the combined strength of the two U.S. airlines, who were backed by the potency of state power and determined to capture and dominate the region.

* * *

All these tumultuous events were unwinding as Moscow and Washington were trapped in what quickly became a nuclear standoff. Bomber pilots would become an essential part of a possible U.S.

---

77 "John" to "Dear Ed", "Confidential," 13 November 1947, Box 469, Folder 21, Pan Am Papers.

78 Assistant Vice President of Pan Am to Vice Present Ingalls, 20 October 1947, Box 624, Folder 17, Pan Am Papers.

nuclear strike, which would have led to as many as 80 million casualties among Soviet citizens.[79] In late 1949, Lieutenant General Curtis Le May of the U.S. Air Force elatedly discussed the need to accelerate U.S. "readiness to conduct effective atomic warfare," even though he knew Moscow had "the capability of penetrating all [U.S.] Strategic Air Command stations," thus guaranteeing enormous counter-damage to his homeland.[80] As during the World War, a number of the nation's Euro-American pilots were paralyzed with fear, indecision, or revulsion at such a prospect. Arguably, the *de facto* exclusion of African Americans from the cockpit compromised the U.S. plan for national security by delimiting the aviator ranks and depriving the nation of flying talent. Even Le May acknowledged the impact of an increasing number of suspended pilots among the segregated flying forces, including "36…voluntary request[s] for suspension" and a "net reduction through suspensions [of] 464 active duty officers and 8 reserve officers."[81]

Unfortunately for Washington, its problems in the air were due to more than just paralysis and vacancy in the cockpit. In late 1947, an official inspection by the Air Force found dismayingly high court-martial rates "due to immature youths committing minor offenses." The inspectors also reported that the incidence of venereal disease was "a major problem" among youthful service personnel. Further, they found that "aircraft maintenance [was] barely satisfactory due to lack of properly supervised systems and lack of knowledge." They regrettably concluded that the U.S. mission abroad of "supporting military occupational force by air power [was] impractical because of lack of combat units."[82] Another source concluded that the crucial

79 Overy, *The Bombers and the Bombed*, 200.

80 Lt. General Curtis Le May to Hoyt S. Vandenberg, 12 December 1949, Box 192, Curtis Le May Papers, Library of Congress.

81 Office of the Vice Chief of Staff to Lt. General Le May, 21 April 1950, Box 192, Curtis Le May Papers.

82 Office of the Vice Chief of Staff of the U.S. Air Force to General McKee, 9 December

position of aerial engineer was also critically short of personnel, yet African Americans continued to be excluded from entering the ranks of aviators and aeronauts.[83]

By 1948, the Secretary of the Air Force and future U.S. Senator W. Stuart Symington pointed out that in the peak year of U.S. plane production, the automotive industry produced most of the nation's aircraft engines, 10 percent of its complete aircraft, and the major portion of aircraft accessories and component assemblies. This meant that a great deal of his division's funds was spent in Detroit—a bastion of union and Negro militancy. That city, Symington told an audience at Selfridge Air Base, which recently had been the site of protests by Black pilots, was "the world center of hard-line production." As he proclaimed: "[A]ny enemy of America in all probability would consider [Detroit] his No. 1 target."[84] Detroit was also a center of Communist Party activity, not the least of all in the auto industry.[85] It thus would have been understandable if Washington had taken such militancy into account when plotting national security.

General Muir S. Fairchild, who then was the Air Force's vice chief of staff, brought a different message to a California audience in what was perhaps a more prophetic analysis than that delivered by Secretary Symington. The West Coast states, Fairchild announced, were "more closely linked to the future of aviation than any other region." "Important aircraft factories stretch along the Coast from Boeing at Seattle to Consolidated at San Diego," he claimed. Coincidentally enough, neither of those cities was then as renowned for Black militancy as Detroit. According to Fairchild, the Air Force had "very largely centered its experimental development flights in West Coast

---

1947, Box 36, Vandenberg Papers.

83   Colonel Henry Huglin to Assistant Secretary Griffith, 13 September 1949, Box 60, Vandenberg Papers.

84   Speech by W. Stuart Symington, 18 September 1948, Box 35, Vandenberg Papers.

85   Roger Keeran, *The Communist Party and the Auto Workers Union* (New York: International, 1986).

areas, due not only to climate but to the unique advantages of desert terrain." He added that the trend westward additionally was buoyed by simple economics, noting that as late as 1935, the Air Force paid less than "$7,000 per pound for the B-18 bomber" while the B-50 bombers under production by the late 1940s were "costing us approximately $30.00 per pound."[86] Even Secretary Symington admitted in 1949 that the Pacific Coast was overwhelmingly the epicenter of U.S. airplane production.[87]

The development of what was to be termed the "military-industrial complex" had enormous consequence for the Golden State particularly, helping to advance a conservatism that later contributed to the election of actor-turned-politician Ronald Reagan as governor.[88] That California-style conservatism was not necessarily helpful to anti-Jim Crow advocates.[89] The same could be said for the decline of Detroit as industry fled in the decades following Symington's remarks.[90]

* * *

Aviation brought advocates of apartheid and Jim Crow together just as easily as it congregated the opponents of both systems. The problem for the former was that decolonization and desegregation were proceeding apace to the point where they were becoming unstoppable. In such a context, aviation provided powerful tailwinds to propel the latter onward and upward.

---

86 Speech by General Muir S. Fairchild, 17 September 1948, Box 35, Vandenberg Papers.

87 Secretary Symington to A. J. Hayes, President of International Association of Machinists, 19 August 1949, Box 51, Vandenberg Papers. Boeing, headquartered in Seattle, employed 25,800 workers, a "considerably greater number of employees than any other airplane plant" in the nation.

88 Roger W. Lotchin, *Fortress California, 1910-1961: From Warfare to Welfare* (New York: Oxford University Press, 1992); Gerald D. Nash, *World War II and the West: Reshaping the Economy* (Lincoln: University of Nebraska Press, 1990).

89 Dan T. Carter, *From George Wallace to Newt Gingrich: Race in the Conservative Counter-Revolution, 1963-1994* (Baton Rouge: Louisiana State University Press, 1996).

90 Thomas J. Sugrue, *The Origins of the Urban Crisis: Race and Inequality in Postwar Detroit* (Princeton, NJ: Princeton University Press, 2005).

Colonel Benjamin O. Davis. Air base at Rametti, Italy.
(Courtesy Library of Congress, Prints and Photographs)

CHAPTER 6

MORE TURBULENCE

In early 1950, Claude Barnett and his spouse, the actor and singer Etta Moten, were visiting Haiti. At the time, the island was just 4.5 hours from Miami by air, with a stop in Cuba or Jamaica, and flights took off and landed daily at a round-trip cost of $110. While there, they encountered James Plinton, a former Tuskegee Airman who was notorious for flying his plane so low that he terrorized the earthbound. After the war, Plinton, a college graduate, tried to start an aircraft company in Liberia, but the venture collapsed when Pan Am and Firestone Rubber—the latter being the giant of that nation's economy—balked at training African pilots. He then moved to Haiti and started an innovative dry-cleaning business. According to a dazzled Barnett, Plinton, with his staff of 20 Haitians, had "one of the most successful businesses imaginable." "He still flies an airplane which he use[s] to pick up and deliver garments to the various towns within a range of 25 miles," reported the newsman.[1]

Barnett was surprised to find so many African Americans on the island, all "doing worthwhile things" as they reveled in the many "possibilities" offered there. Barnett claimed that the Haitian president told him that "he was especially anxious to have American Negro

1 Article, 2 April 1950, Reel 8, #816, Series B, Part III, Subject Files on Black Americans, CAB-NCSU.

business people come to Haiti." In addition to Plinton, the Barnetts spotted other Negroes such as Giles Hubert, formerly of the faculty at Fisk University; James Johnston of Seattle, a forester trained at the University of Washington; Elle Griffin of Massachusetts, then with the United Nations Educational, Scientific, and Cultural Organization (UNESCO); and Griffin's UNESCO colleague, Barrington Dunbar. Also present on the island were Edzier Carter, an artist from Chicago, and many more.[2]

As this episode involving Barnett suggests, aviation provided a unique form of upward mobility for African Americans. Piloting was a fungible skill that could be deployed in Africa as easily as in the Caribbean, and planes could easily transport those willing to depart the land of Jim Crow to places far away from its ordinary terror. Abroad, U.S. Negroes also could exert influence on independent nations, who could then pressure Washington in anti-colonial and anti-racist ways. Additionally suggestive of aviation's increasing grip on the African American imagination was the name Chicago publisher John H. Johnson's gave to his wildly popular weekly magazine launched in 1951. Appropriately, the affluent Black businessman called the publication *Jet.*[3]

As the walls of Jim Crow began to crack and crumble, Plinton, who organized a successful airline venture in Ecuador after his sojourn in Haiti,[4] eventually was hired by a U.S. airline.[5] Tellingly, a few years after he left Liberia, that neo-colonial nation hired yet another African American aviator—Leon Jordan of Kansas City—to supervise the training of its first pilots.[6] Around the same time, Pan Am's Juan Trippe, in a bow to commercial if not racial reality, resumed his active

2 Press Release, March 1950, Reel 42, #1123. Part I, Press Releases, CAB-NCSU.
3 John H. Johnson, *Succeeding Against the Odds: The Autobiography of a Great American Businessman* (New York: Warner, 1989), 3.
4 Moye, *Freedom Flyers*, 1.
5 Broadnax, *Blue Skies, Black Wings*, 144-145.
6 Press Release, May 1951 and August 1951, Box 188, Folder 5, CAB-CHM.

business interests in Liberia, initiating direct flights between New York and Monrovia.[7]

That the legendary pilot Hubert Julian and his exploits continued to be newsworthy well into the 1950s was another exemplar of the value of aerial mobility. After congratulating President Truman on his inauguration in 1949,[8] Julian flew off to Europe under a cloak of mystery. How, asked a baffled reporter, did Julian "get to Europe to inspect Negro Troops in Germany," and then how did he get to meet with U.S. General Lucius Clay while there? Abetted by a White House aide, General Harry Vaughn Julian was representing the Crescent Trading Company overseas, selling cigarettes at a nifty profit.

Soon thereafter, the man described as "one of the world's most fantastic characters"[9] wound up in Guatemala, which was then in the throes of a civil unrest that would culminate with a U.S.-backed coup a few years later. Julian next reportedly requested a U.S. export license to ship bazookas and ammunition to Central America and somehow became the purchasing agent for Guatemala's Minister of Defense.[10] He adamantly denied, however, that his armaments would be supportive of "Communist influence" in that region.[11] Flummoxing those who believed him to be a toady of reactionaries, Julian was viewed as all too close to a Central American regime that the U.S. wanted to subvert. He blasted the U.S. refusal to sell arms to the regime. Reportedly, just before the coup, he spent $91,000 of his own money on arms for Guatemala and wanted to spend more, so he traveled to Manhattan to meet with U.S. officials about breaking the arms embargo. When it looked like no deal could be made, the frustrated Julian suddenly

---

7 Press Release, November 1951, Reel 47, #301, Part I, Press Releases, CAB-NCSU.

8 Memorandum, 21 January 1949, Box 235, 811.001 Truman, H. S., 1-2149, PI 537, E200, HM 1992, Decimal Files, NARA-CP.

9 Press Release, August 1949, Reel 41, #288, Part I, Press Releases, CAB-NCSU.

10 See Memoranda, 3 October 1950 and 13 August 1952, Box 242, 411.148/10-350, 414598/8-1352, Pi-157 E200, HM 1992, Decimal Files, NARA-CP.

11 Press Release, October 1952, Reel 49, #1228, Part I, Press Releases, CAB-NCSU.

departed, shouting and crying this loss would also mean the loss of his Rolls-Royce.[12]

Julian nonetheless was insistent on removing the racial barriers that sometimes impeded his progress on land and in the air. As he told a journalist, "[U]pon my return to Guatemala my primary project will be seeing that Negroes are no longer debarred from entering this country where one is measured by his brain and ability and not [by] the color of his skin."[13] As Barnett and his wife were arriving in Haiti, Julian's "charming wife, Essie Julian," as she was described by Barnett's Associated Negro Press, was being flown to Guatemala on Black Eagle Airlines, her worldly husband's own airline. Reportedly, given Julian's status as the independent carrier's president and general manager, she was treated "with all the pomp and ceremony usually reserved for a Barbara Hutton [wealthy heiress]." Later, Julian's colorful image, if not his marriage, was polished further when he was named as a party in what was described as a "lurid" divorce suit. The jealous husband who filed the suit, prominent Los Angeles attorney Walter Gordon, charged that his spouse had "spent the night in a hotel with famous flyer, Hubert Julian."[14]

Due east, in Jamaica, Pan Am continued to flex its muscles as more African Americans streamed onto that island, which was then on the verge of its own independence. On the eve of Sputnik's launch, Pan Am had the largest payroll of any foreign carrier servicing Jamaica, with 98 local employees and 5 from the U.S. Additionally, up to 10 cargo flights took off weekly from the island, guaranteeing an influx of U.S. goods and the continuous edging out of the airline's British competitors. Pan Am's flights helped Jamaica secure U.S. markets for its local products, which included seafood, furniture, and so forth—

---

12 Press Release, May 1954, Reel 54, #645, Part I, Press Releases, CAB-NCSU.
13 Press Release, September 1950, Part I, Press Releases, CAB-NCSU.
14 Press Release, December 1951, Reel 47, #459, Part I, Press Releases, CAB-NCSU.

tying the island nation ever more closely to Uncle Sam. Pan Am staffers had to be trained in Miami, however, which meant that Jamaicans would be subject to a kind of Jim Crow with which they were hardly familiar. The increasing numbers of tourists from the U.S. also brought many Euro-Americans into contact, often for the first time, with Black people whose circumstances were not mandated by Jim Crow.[15]

Claude Barnett remained a major promoter of aviation throughout its early decades of advances and expansions. He was especially supportive of aerial links between the Caribbean and the U.S. mainland, for more than simply moral or philosophical reasons. Ever the savvy businessman, he wanted to position his news agency, the Associated Negro Press, to take full advantage of the growth of Caribbean tourism by enticing air carriers to advertise in the pages of his syndicate's growing stable of newspapers.[16]

* * *

Though Jim Crow encountered a bout of turbulence after the end of World War II, it remained largely intact as war erupted anew in Korea. Although President Truman issued a formal proclamation mandating desegregation of the armed forces, the actual implementation of that decree proceeded fitfully for several years after its passage. The U.S. air corps, for its part, seemed still intent to block African Americans' path to the future, as it held on tenaciously to its dearly won reputation as a paradoxical companion of the past. Anticipating possible objections to the presence of U.S. Negro servicemen by host nations, the Air Force's Colonel Harlan C. Parks wrestled with the knotty issue of where—and whether—Negroes should be posted overseas.[17] Weeks

---

15   M. C. Arner, Director, Latin American Division to Division P.R. Manager, 9 October 1956, Box 372, Folder 22, Pan Am Papers.

16   Joseph Albright to T. M. Miller, 10 March 1953, Reel, #621, Series C, Part III, Subject Files on Black Americans, CAB-NCSU.

.

17   "Confidential" Memo from Colonel Harlan C. Parks, 7 September 1949, 168.7061-30-71, 13

before war erupted in Korea in 1950, Assistant Secretary of the Air Force Eugene Zucker moved to rescind "the previous conditional restrictions on the assignment of Negro personnel to Greenland, Canada (including Newfoundland), Bermuda and the British possessions in the Caribbean." For some reason, however, Iceland continued to be off limits for African American Air Force personnel.[18]

Army leaders seemed likewise aligned with Jim Crow, despite the observation by one historian who concluded that "the wartime experience of the all-black 92nd Infantry Division in northern Italy...ultimately provided the best argument for desegregating" the U.S. military. Yet, Jim Crow advocates were not necessarily paying close or careful attention to anti-Jim Crow results.[19] In 1950, Eddie Rickenbacker, formerly a challenger to Charles Lindbergh for the mantle of chief U.S. aviator, was president of Eastern Airlines. He had the temerity that year to write the NAACP directly as he sought to justify his use of the term "old darkies" to refer to the few African Americans working for his company.[20]

The NAACP's Walter White upbraided the armed forces for not implementing President Truman's desegregation mandate forcefully. "When I was in Japan in 1949," White noted, "I saw little evidence of any compliance with the integration order." His comrade Thurgood Marshall, who traveled to Japan and Korea in 1951, detected a similar pattern.[21] A scant year later, circumstances had not improved significantly. In December 1952, the left-led National Negro Labor Council launched a campaign to get six of the nation's air carriers to hire Black personnel, including pilots. Leading the campaign were the singer-activist Paul Robeson and future Detroit mayor Coleman

---

July 1945, 26 April 1941–10 Jun 1942, Gropman, A. L. Col., 42, AFHRA.

18 Memorandum from Eugene Zucker, 23 April 1950, 168.7061-30–71, AFHRA.

19 Moye, *Freedom Flyers*, 149.

20 Press Release, April 1951, Reel 45, #789, Part I, Press Releases, CAB-NCSU.

21 Press Release, June 1951, Reel 45, #1136, Part I, Press Releases, CAB-NCSU.

Young. Robeson was under siege politically at the time, as were his various crusades, which led to predictable results. Convening in Cleveland, members of the Council nonetheless took time out from their deliberations to march to the offices of American Airlines. There, they waved placards that read, "Negro Pilots Fly in Korea—Why Not in America?" and "We Want Negro Stewardesses."[22]

Unavoidably, Washington had to contend with regressive attitudes abroad that pushed the U.S. rightward. By mid-1953, commercial airlines in Panama, seeking to attract U.S. tourists, proclaimed rudely that "Negroes are not wanted."[23] Apparently this applied to Negro pilots as well. As Claude Barnett lamented in a letter to his star reporter Alice Dunnigan in early 1955, "For some time I have told you that colored boys are not becoming pilots. The ratio has dropped greatly since the establishment of the flying school at Tuskegee."[24] By 1955, the NAACP was complaining to the Pentagon, asserting that "racial discrimination in the assignment of quarters [was] flourishing" at Air Force bases overseas. Moreover, it claimed that Jim Crow was being "abetted by the Air Force's continued use of racial designation in its billeting registration card."[25] NAACP officials also pointed out a persistent problem that had especially deep roots, denouncing the recent "firing of French female employees for association with colored airmen" that was reported at the U.S. base in Chaumont, France.[26]

The military's Jim Crow tendencies were abetted by domestic policies. For example, in 1956, Negroes stationed at Finley Air Force Station in North Dakota, a key node in the protection of the homeland,

22 Press Release, December 1952, Reel 10, #620, Series C, Part III, Subject Files on Black Americans, CAB-NCSU.
23 Press Release, August 1953, Reel 52, #829, Part I, Press Releases, CAB-NCSU.
24 Claude Barnett to Alice Dunnigan, 19 February 1955, Reel 2, #943, Series F, Part III, Subject Files on Black Americans, CAB-NCSU.
25 J. Francis Poulhaus to James C. Evans, Assistant Secretary of Defense, 8 September 1955, Box IX: 58, NAACP Papers.
26 J. Francis Poulhaus to James C. Evans, 28 November 1955, Box IX: 58, NAACP Papers.

complained irately about their maltreatment. Airman Charles Tillman spoke on behalf of the group:

> There are six Negro airmen here at this radar site. We are not wanted here on the base. The white airmen don't even speak, except in the line of duty. And the few that did speak before have been beaten up and called 'niggar [sic] lovers.' The townspeople are just the same...we are called 'darkies, niggers and blackboys'...[and]we have been told by a certain police chief that he has seen some of us [Negroes] hanging before and would like to see a couple...hang now.

Understandably, Tillman continued, "we are kind of worried, because if we stay here any longer, they will find some way in which to court-martial each and every one of us."[27]

This disturbing trend was taking shape as the U.S. became embroiled in the war on the Korean peninsula against Communist-led forces who were not averse to underscoring U.S. frailties in the racial arena.[28] This in turn placed pressure on the U.S. to improve its sorry record in this hotly contested realm. The anticommunism that buoyed the war simultaneously undergirded an illiberal attitude that was congenial to Jim Crow. African Americans were buffeted vigorously by the clashing of these contrasting approaches.

One unique factor that pressured Washington to batter down the walls of Jim Crow in aviation was the persistent fear of flying evidenced among the pool of potential pilots in the United States. Hoyt Vandenberg, who served as both Secretary of the Air Force and as the second director of the newly formed Central Intelligence Agency, was acutely aware of this phenomenon. During the height of the war with Korea, he strained to "insure [sic] that the emotionally sick" among air corpsmen were "identified and given proper medical consideration"

27 Charles Tillman, et al., to NAACP, 11 August 1956, Box IX: 58, NAACP Papers.
28 See e.g. Horne, *Black Revolutionary*, passim; Horne, *Black Liberation/Red Scare*.

so that they could be excluded from service in Air Force cockpits. "Psychoneurosis" and what was viewed as a related trend—namely, "fear of flying" among U.S. aviation trainees—were notable concerns of his. Vandenberg also expressed alarm about the number of pilots who sought to "avoid hazardous duty and in particular training for and actual combat," which he believed contributed to "a contagious aspect" as other pilots also tried to shirk active duty. "Trial by court-martial is not precluded," he warned, adding that living behind bars was preferable to perishing in a burning stew of petroleum and twisted metal—a very real possibility feared by too many pilot candidates.[29]

Air Force Colonel Emmett Cassady echoed Vandenberg's concerns. As he pointed out, "the 'jet age' around which all Air Force publicity is built, is so completely new" that "its very newness [was a] source of apprehension to those who might otherwise be interested in aviation cadet duty." That tendency, Cassady posited, affected those who had "no wish to experiment or pioneer." It was also, in his view, a "guinea pig fear" akin to that experienced "by the thought control exercised by the mate or the prospective bride."

What then was the U.S. Air Force to do? Cassady's recommendation was to enlist cartoonists and song writers to create propaganda that would refute this trend.[30] A more comprehensible response would have been to expand the pool of recruits by drawing upon a vast reservoir of untapped potential talent among African Americans.

It would take more than adroit propagandists to resolve this pervasive problem. After all, an official 1952 report concluded morosely that it required a good deal of "time for people to acquire know-how" necessary to operate a jet fighter.[31] As the U.S. was

---

29 Hoyt Vandenberg to Wright-Patterson Air Force Base, Dayton, Ohio, 16 April 1952, Box 84, Vandenberg Papers.
30 Colonel Emmett Cassady to General Grussendorf, 25 March 1952, Box 84, Vandenberg Papers.
31 Report on "Manpower Requirements for Expanded Air Force Structure," 25 March 1952, Box 51, Vandenberg Papers.

moving to threaten Pyongyang, Air Force Major Joseph Connor groaned that the "reserve of young combat ready pilots is not large" and that this formidable issue was exacerbated by a stunning reality— that "70% of the aircraft accidents were caused by 5% of the pilots." Moreover, he noted, "older aircrew members, many of them combat veterans…revealed an apprehension regarding their flying careers and concern with the increasing hazards of aerial combat." Major Connor was distraught: "[W]e probably [could] muster a first string varsity team, but beyond that we may find ourselves in the same position for replacements as did the Japanese and the German Air Forces in World War II." By way of "contrast," he lamented that Communist nations were "utilizing the Korean Air War as a combat training school for jet fighter pilots."

Such conclusions did not augur well for Washington. Major Connor viewed "with alarm the disinclination among the youth of this country to participate in the flying activities of the Air Force."[32] He advised General Omar Bradley that the "Air Force needs to do a thorough job of re-evaluation and soul searching" as a result.[33] This apparently precluded aggressive recruitment of "soul" brothers and sisters as pilots and aviation crew members.

Interpretation matters here, for in 1953 a Negro journalist gleefully observed that "integration" was a "fact in [the] Air Force." By May of that year, the airborne branch of the U.S. armed services counted among its ranks 1,140 commissioned officers, 60 warrant officers, 106 aviation cadets and 69,900 enlisted men, for a total of 71,376 Negroes in that branch. In September 1951, only 173 Negro pilots could be counted among that number, which, in retrospect, seems sparse, but apparently it was not viewed that way then.[34]

---

32 Memorandum from Major Joseph Connor, 5 March 1952, Box 84, Vandenberg Papers.
33 V. Bush to General Omar Bradley, 13 April 1950, Box 192, Curtis Le May Papers.
34 Press Release, August 1953, Reel 52, #504, Part I, Press Releases, CAB-NCSU.

Besides a possible dearth of pilots, Washington faced other intractable issues as the Korean War unfolded. Earlier, Secretary of Defense James Forrestal decried the public's perception of "leaders of the aircraft industry...as warmongers for profit."[35] This view, he claimed, was not helpful insofar as securing ever-larger appropriations for the U.S. Air Force was concerned. In 1949, Air Force Secretary Symington pointed out that Boeing—one of the nation's and the world's chief suppliers of aircraft—"anticipate[d] little additional commercial business in the near future." This made the Seattle behemoth even more dependent upon an Air Force that was facing peculiar problems all its own.[36]

The Air Force's problems in securing pilots served to increase the momentum behind its recruitment efforts among a community— African Americans—that long had evinced interest in aviation. That community had persisted in its interest, often under the most adverse conditions, that made operating jet fighters seem plush and comfortable by comparison. Tuskegee Airmen notwithstanding, that shift would involve a reversal of centuries of encrusted and inured policies of slavery, racism, and Jim Crow, thus making the most feasible recruitment remedy the most difficult to pursue.

Certainly, Frank Petersen, who billed himself as "America's First Black Marine Aviator," could attest to that. A proud Marine born in Topeka, Kansas, in 1932 (whose father hailed from St. Croix in the U.S. Virgin Islands) Petersen unabashedly acknowledged that his branch of service was the last to desegregate. Still, he flew numerous combat missions in northern Korea, where he dropped napalm on civilians, and received the Distinguished Flying Cross. He also felt, as he recounted years later, the "searing heat" on the back of his neck after flying his plane near Yucca Flats, Nevada, after an atomic blast.

---

35 Address by James Forrestal at "Air Force Day Dinner," 17 September 1948, Box 35, Vandenberg Papers.
36 W. Stuart Symington to A. J. Hayes, president of the International Association of Machinists, 19 August 1949, Box 60, Vandenberg Papers.

None of this saved him from feeling another kind of coruscating heat from his erstwhile marine comrades. Despite his heroic feats in the cockpit as a frontline warrior, he could not escape racist harassment at the hands of his fellow pilots. Upon returning home from war and attaining the rank of Lieutenant General, Petersen bitterly recalled the continued difficulty he and his family experienced finding decent hotels in which to reside while traveling in the States.[37]

Petersen was joined in his ennui by Colonel Benjamin O. Davis Jr., the son of a renowned military officer, who by late 1951 was the air corps' highest-ranking Negro officer. In that role, Davis controlled the deployment and operations of U.S. fighter planes globally, a post that required him to personally log 100 hours yearly in the air. He annually met this metric with flying colors, typically flying B-25 twin-engine bombers or C-47 and C-45 cargo transport planes.[38] Despite his many military accomplishments, this exceedingly talented and mobile officer later confessed openly that after he and his family visited Brazil (he was stationed there on assignment), they "dreaded the return to the racist atmosphere of Washington."[39] Indeed, Davis recalled, his stated preference was for overseas assignments:

> In a foreign country, racism would not be nearly the problem it was at home....I always felt freer outside the United States. In this country I was treated as a black man first and a human being second....I found the respect [abroad] I had been denied at home in other countries.[40]

At age 16, Davis recalled that he had visited France, France, Belgium, and Switzerland as a result of his famous father's international tours of duty. "For the first time in my life," he wrote of those travels,

---

37 Frank E. Petersen, *Into the Tiger's Jaw: America's First Black Marine Aviator—The Autobiography of Frank E. Petersen* (Novato, CA: Presidio, 1998), vii, 62-63, 69, 80, 88.
38 Press Release, November 1951, Reel 47, #357, Part I, Press Releases, CAB-NCSU.
39 Davis, Jr., *Benjamin O. Davis, Jr., American*, 183.
40 Ibid., 188

"I was not a black American"[41]; rather, he was viewed simply as an "American". Such realizations led the young Davis to contemplate emigration. Later, as a soldier-pilot, he repeatedly found that Euro-Americans treated Negroes like himself more humanely abroad. Only when he returned to the United States, he recalled, did he feel the ugliness of racism. As he claimed: "[M]y relationships with the Chinese in general, as with the Koreans and Filipinos, transcended any consideration of race, which was not always true of my relationships with American officers."[42] In Davis' view, "[I]t seemed ridiculous and totally unnecessary that, for non-whites, life outside the United States could be equal and free for all, which at home it was so frequently painful."[43]

Davis' conclusions, though offered retrospectively, raise enormous questions. What was the impact and what were the national security implications of leading Negro military men such as General Davis feeling more comfortable consorting with the "Chinese"—although Davis was more likely referring to the Taiwanese—than with U.S. nationals? What did it mean when those considered to be among the nation's staunchest patriots—namely, African Americans—seized every opportunity to flee their homeland?

Davis was joined on the frontlines in Korea by Jesse L. Brown, a Negro bomber pilot. Brown was the first African American to serve as an aviator in the U.S. Navy, a branch of service that resembled the Marines in its reluctance to accept Black recruits. Born in Hattiesburg, Mississippi, Brown attended The Ohio State University. During the war, he flew numerous attack missions both in northern Korea and across the border in China. He died in battle, crash- landing into the mountains five miles behind enemy lines. The unfortunate accident occurred in

41   Ibid., 190.
42   Ibid., 191.
43   Ibid., 207.

the aftermath of a brutal snowstorm, when temperatures had fallen to a bone-chilling 25 degrees below zero (Fahrenheit).[44]

Brown's death was a big loss to the U.S. military. On his first sortie, he destroyed 5 railroad cars and damaged 15 others on North Korea's east coast. He also strafed two warehouses and damaged a vehicle on that run.[45] Not perishing with him, however, was the idea borne by his fellow Black aviator, General Davis, who believed that "air power was the decisive factor in the Korean War."[46] Davis also insisted that but for the presence of the likes of pilots like Brown and Petersen, the U.S. setback in the Korean conflict would have been more substantial than it was.

Despite the importance of pilots like Brown, when U.S. forces in the 1950s conceived the largest war game exercise since World War II, a new secret society in Baton Rouge, Louisiana—where the maneuvers were to occur—objected to the presence of Black Air Force personnel among the 140,000 troops there assembled.[47]

Eventually, the inevitable occurred: a 26-year-old Air Force veteran, Howard B. Spears Jr., applied for Soviet citizenship because he was fed up with Jim Crow.[48] Beginning in 1952, Louis Wheaton of New York City, a 38-year-old former Air Force officer and former Tuskegee instructor, began broadcasting radio programs from China that accused the U.S. of germ warfare during the Korean War. After being repatriated, Wheaton was brought before an angry congressional panel in Washington, where one member flatly branded him "guilty of treason." The deposed airman, who possessed a law degree from Fordham University and previously seemed poised for a comfortable

---

44 *Navy Times*, 16 December 1985; *Naval Aviation News*, March 1951, Technical Files, NASM.
45 Press Release, October 1950, Reel 44, #468, Part I, Press Releases, CAB-NCSU.
46 Davis, Jr., *Benjamin O. Davis, Jr., American*, 183.
47 Press Release, November 1955, Reel 58, #554, Part I, Press Releases, CAB-NCSU.
48 Press Release, January 1956, Reel 59, #17, Part I, Press Releases, CAB-NCSU.

life, eventually was accused of the ultimate sin: being a Communist leader—and one from Harlem, no less.[49]

Later during the Korean War, two Negro Air Force servicemen were hung in Guam after being accused and convicted of the rape and murder of a 27-year-old white civilian employee.[50] At a time when the talents of Negro pilots should have been held at a premium, Senator John Stennis of Mississippi did not hesitate to force the resignation of Air Force Lieutenant Titus Saunders in 1956. At 25 years of age, Saunders was a rarity—a Black officer in the Air Force. He was arrested in the Magnolia State on what many deemed spurious charges of drunk driving and forced to resign from the service.[51]

These and other seemingly random incidents all pointed in a similar direction. A conflict between the poisonous rigidity of Jim Crow and the demands of national security in the so-called jet age was evident. Looming large in the skies above was yet another challenge, and Washington soon would have to choose between the logic of the "space race" and the demands of the "race race."

True to the proverbial adage, old habits die hard. The flight school at Tuskegee Institute turned out to be more an indicator of the exigency of war than a precursor of things to come. Once the emergency dissipated, the nation regressed to the meanness of Jim Crow.

* * *

As aviation was shrinking the planet, bringing previously far distant sites into the close purview of the U.S.—and vice versa—Washington and U.S. airlines alike had to grapple with the consequences of greater transparency. The increasing global competition made possible by aviation complicated matters considerably. In southern Africa, for

---

49 Press Release, May 1956, Reel 60, #121, Part I, Press Releases, CAB-NCSU.

50 Press Release, February 1954, Reel 3, #305, Series F, Part III, Subject Files on Black Americans, CAB-NCSU.

51 Press Release, November 1956, Reel 61, #494, Part I, Press Releases, CAB-NCSU.

example, Pan Am was competing for business not only with TWA but also with KLM, Sabena, Scandinavian, BOAC, South African Airways, and other carriers. As W. H. Lyons, an executive vice president at Pan Am, enviously observed in 1953: "TWA has been unusually active in the Union of South Africa." By then, this competitor also had solidified its ties to Ethiopian Airways and was operating from Mozambique as well. Nonetheless, executives at the well-connected Pan Am believed they had an advantage—or so thought Lyons, who bragged that his airline's "representatives in Johannesburg are in good standing both with the United States Embassy and the Union Government." Moreover, since "stepped-up mining activity" was then occurring in "Nyasaland [Malawi] and Southern Rhodesia [Zimbabwe]," Lyon wrote, the future for air carriers in that part of the world seemed rosy indeed. "The number of U.S. citizens now in the copper area amount to approximately 50," he reported while also predicting that "something like 500 U.S. technicians," maybe more, soon would be in the vicinity. Thus, he boasted with pride that Pan Am had "carried seventy-nine more passengers from Johannesburg to the USA in the first four months of this year than in 1952."[52]

Lyons thought Pan Am held the trump card in the region. In late 1954, he commented on a notorious architect of apartheid, J. G. Strijdom, who had been elected that year as prime minister of the Union of South Africa. "His [Strijdom's] first public statement confirmed his aim to establish the Union of South Africa as a republic. The ultimate result could well bring about greater community of interest with the USA than with the British Commonwealth," he asserted, insisting that this could only spell increased profits for his airline. There was, he contended, "tremendous growth and development in this large area," including Pretoria's neighbors in his projections, and that expansion

---

52 W. H. Lyons, Regional Director, Iberian Peninsula & Africa to Executive Vice President, 12 May 1953, Box 320, Folder 40, Pan Am Papers.

was "accompanied by a rapidly increasing demand for international air transportation."

What Lyons did not report was that this trend was two-edged— that is, as apartheid's architects got closer to the U.S., they also became targets for anti-Jim Crow crusaders. Likewise, as Washington competed for "hearts and minds" in Africa in the context of its Cold War competition with Moscow, both apartheid and Jim Crow became albatrosses around the neck of the U.S. Secretary of State.[53] This dilemma was hardly the concern of Pan Am. Instead, Lyons was dreamily contemplating the apparently rich prospects of doing business with apartheid South Africa. "[I]n spite of the over-emphasis given to various local problems by the international press," he noted waspishly, "the country seems to be developing in a very healthy fashion." He lauded the many "reasonably priced U.S. products in the shops and showrooms" of that nation, an outgrowth of the fact that South African "produced nearly all of the world's gold" while its uranium-mining operations were "rapidly expanding,"[54] much of which was in the illicitly occupied territory that became the independent nation of Namibia.

Elsewhere, clouds of pessimism were gathering. After Lyons visited the U.S. ambassador to South Africa in 1955, the latter "predicted increasing stability and prosperity" for the land of apartheid. "Off the record," however, Lyons was informed that the staff of the embassy "were having some difficulty…convincing their colleagues in Washington of this point." They further were "somewhat hampered, at times, by the attitudes generated due to the press campaign in the USA" against the apartheid regime. That allegation, if true, might have undermined the positive results gained from the press junket to South

---

53 W. H. Lyons to Executive Vice President, 7 December 1954, Box 320, Folder 40, Pan Am Papers.
54 W. H. Lyon to Executive Vice President, 5 April 1955, Box 320, Folder 40, Pan Am Papers.

Africa of leading editors and publishers facilitated by Pan Am's Juan Trippe a few years earlier.

Although Lyons reported counting only 3,000 visitors from the U.S. who had traveled to South Africa in 1954, he predicted those numbers would see a "steady increase" in subsequent years.[55] In Durban alone, he noted, speaking of the metropolis hugging the Indian Ocean coast 250 U.S. nationals, with about 250 more elsewhere in the vicinity resided, most of whom were missionaries. He also revealed that U.S. visitors to this region were second only to those visiting the "Rhodesias" (Zambia and Zimbabwe).[56] As he further surveyed the business landscape in his report, Lyons scanned the profit projections and nervously eyed the competition—TWA, Sabena, KLM, BOAC, and others—whom he fretted might cause a "saturation of service to Africa" and possibly drive his airline out of business in the region.[57]

While Lyons was focusing on Pan Am's affairs in southern Africa, the airline was reducing its service to West Africa—the latter could have served as a hedge against potential challenges in Southern Africa. This cost-cutting maneuver angered the U.S. and European missionaries who relied heavily on Pan Am for their international travel.[58] Harold Gray, a Pan Am executive, argued that the "west coast of Africa bulges out and offers an important point of access, not merely to the continent of Africa but also to portions of Africa, to the Middle East and to Asia… [and had] provided the access point for a very large military operation to and through Africa during the last war." He also argued that West

55 W. H. Lyons to Executive Vice President, 20 July 1955, Box 320, Folder 40, Pan Am Papers.

56 W. H. Lyons to Executive Vice President, 10 February 1956, Box 320, Folder 40, Pan Am Papers.

57 W. H. Lyons to Executive Vice President, 14 December 1956, Box 320, Folder 40, Pan Am Papers.

58 George Carpenter, Executive Secretary, National Council of Churches of Christ in USA to Ross Rizley, Chair of Civil Aeronautics Board, 1 February 1956, Box 141, Folder 17, Accession II, Pan Am Papers.

Africa was "considerably more remote from the sphere of Communist influence" than were other regions.[59]

But Pan Am would not be turned away easily from the richness that southern Africa seemed to portend. The feeling, apparently, was mutual: "We have a very high regard for your Pan American service in South Africa," wrote one apartheid bureaucrat, who also mentioned the "kindness" the carrier seemed to exude toward (melanin deficient) persons like himself.[60] Pan Am had been flying to Pretoria via Lisbon and Madrid, but by 1955 it had reconsidered that route, concluding that it was logistically cumbersome to rely on those two citadels of fascism as stopovers.[61]

If Pan Am's leadership had scrutinized the big picture more closely, they might have reconsidered their Africa strategy. In northern Africa, for example, Lyons had detected as early as 1954 "greatly increased terrorist activities by Arab Nationalists." He sadly reported that "an assassination is reported almost every day in Casablanca or the adjacent areas and this has caused a marked drop in tourists both from Europe and the U.S."[62] Pan Am nonetheless pushed on, expanding its services into southern Africa and capitalizing on U.S. efforts to secure landing rights in the Belgian Congo and the French Congo too.

According to Congressman Carl Hinshaw, a Republican from California, Pan Am's Africa stops were "of great national interest—and are certain[ly] of great commercial interest to the United States suppliers and buyers of raw materials." He observed that the "predominance of the American automobile in that area" was an indicator of the

---

59 Testimony of Harold Gray, Executive Vice President in Charge of the Atlantic Division of Pan Am, 1 February 1954, Box 141, Folder 17, Pan Am Papers.

60 J. A. Gibson, Secretary for Transport, Department of Transport-South Africa to Russell Adams, Vice President of Pan Am, 7 August 1953, Accession II, Box 141, Folder 16, Pan Am Papers.

61 John C. Leslie to Vice President Adams, 27 April 1955, Accession II, Box 141, Folder 17, Pan Am Papers.

62 W. H. Lyons to Executive Vice President, 29 March 1954, Box 141, Folder 17, Pan Am Papers.

tremendous amount of business African nations did with the United States, adding enthusiastically that such trade came "replete with dollar exchange" and "great tourist potential." Additionally, he indicated, U.S. visitors "would be welcomed by the South Africans [meaning, of course, Afrikaners and those otherwise defined as "white"] who feel a very close affinity for the United States."[63]

***

By the mid-1950s, as Black pilots dropped bombs from military planes in northeastern Asia and their white counterparts jetted between the Jim Crow U.S. and apartheid South Africa, Negroes back home were still encountering grave difficulty in their efforts to help construct planes, board civilian aircraft, or even get a decent meal at an airport. In 1953, Hays King Aircraft Company in Birmingham, Alabama, simply refused to hire even "qualified Negro applicants."[64] Douglas Aircraft of El Segundo, California, even then one of the nation's largest aviation companies, at the time employed only one Negro engineer.[65] By 1956, African Americans were still largely barred from securing employment in what would soon become a leading growth engine of the economy— that is, the sector that came to be known as the "military-industrial complex." Perhaps unsurprisingly, African Americans who generally leaned to the left were not embraced by the sector of the economy that tended to undergird illiberalism.

At Lockheed's sprawling plant in Marietta, Georgia, Herbert Hill of the NAACP reported on the following conditions:

> Negroes are completely denied admission into the apprentice programs which [are] conducted jointly by the Company and the

---

63 Congressman Carl Hinshaw to Chan Gurney, Chair-Civil Aeronautics Board, 2 February 1954, Box 141, Folder 17.

64 William Oliver, Co-Director, Fair Practices and Anti-Discrimination, UAW-CIO to Panfile Ciampa, Director of Region 8, UAW-CIO, Box 96, Herbert Hill Papers, Library of Congress.

65 Press Release, August 1949, Reel 41, #358, Part I, Press Releases, CAB-NCSU.

Union. In the past five years, there has not been a single Negro admitted into the apprenticeship training program even though Negroes have repeatedly attempted to secure admission.[66]

Hill claimed to have found "collusion between the Union and the Company in preventing Negroes from participating in the apprentice training program."[67] As a result, he reported, "with very rare exceptions Negroes are not hired above the classification of 'assembly helpers.'"[68] Thus, he charged:

> ...[the] seniority rights of Negroes are deliberately and systematically violated...when Negroes begin to approach a seniority rating that would qualify them for a higher classification the Company often reclassifies the job or moves the job operation completely out of the Negro work group...[69]

Hill further charged, the "practice of the Company" was to use a "code to racially identify every plant employee in the plant-wide seniority roster." He exposed what he called a "total pattern of racial segregation in every phase of the Company's operation," noting that "'White' and 'Colored' signs [were]...found throughout the plant, over water fountains, in the plant cafeteria and even in the medical dispensary." Job segregation also reigned at Lockheed, in that "all of the custodial workers such as janitors, washroom attendants, refuse collectors, etc." were Black. "For all practical purposes," Hill concluded, "the white and colored employees are in separate white and colored locals of the IAM [International Association of Machinists union]."[70]

Lockheed was not *sui generis*. In southern California, an area that rapidly was becoming known as the headquarters of U.S. aviation

---

66 Ibid. Oliver, Box 96, Herbert Hill Papers.
67 Herbert Hill to Roy Wilkins, 18 December 1956, Box 60, Herbert Hill Papers.
68 Ibid.
69 Ibid.
70 Ibid.

production, a local NAACP official named William Davis accused the Rohr Aircraft Corporation of Riverside with abject failure to comply with the nondiscrimination clause in its contract with the Pentagon. The NAACP reported that only 3 of Rohr's 3,000 workers were Black, even though "a large number of Negroes…made application for employment with this corporation, many of whom [possessed] extensive experience in their field."[71]

Negroes in Wichita, Kansas, were disenchanted similarly. According to, NAACP attorney Chester Lewis, writing in May 1957: "White students from the same school as Negro students were hired and placed in pre-production training, while the Negro applicants were informed that the only opportunities available were for porter jobs." Black job candidates were even sequestered in a racially discriminatory manner into "separate rooms" for "physical examinations."[72]

By August 1957, as the pivotal landmark events of Moscow's Sputnik launch and the desegregation controversy involving the Little Rock Nine in Arkansas crept closer, Boeing capitulated. Preceding all three occurrences was a pivotal anti-Jim Crow rally that took place in Washington, DC, and was attended by 25,000 people. "Since the investigation," in Wichita of racially biased practices, Lewis wrote approvingly, "Boeing has hired scores of Negro workers in almost every capacity" and was "literally begging for Negro workers." Additionally, he reported, "Negro workers who did not file complaints have been receiving promotions that they have been seeking for some time."[73]

Despite such advances, matters hardly improved for African Americans seeking to board U.S. airplanes for commercial or leisure travel. During the fall of 1951, an American Jewish Congress (AJC) investigator in Queens, New York, revealed that American Airlines

---

71 William Davis, President of Riverside-NAACP to Vice President Richard M. Nixon, 14 June 1957, Box 60, Herbert Hill Papers.

72 Chester Lewis to Herbert Hill, 28 May 1957, Box 59, Herbert Hill Papers.

73 Chester Lewis to Herbert Hill, 2 August 1957, Box 59, Herbert Hill Papers.

fired one of its agents after he refused to mark a Black ticket purchaser's reservation order with a code number designating the passenger as a Negro. This practice secretly identified Black passengers for possible disadvantageous treatment such as being bumped from a flight or accorded sub-par accommodations as the airline so warranted. Apparently, the practice was a long-standing one, as American's reservation agents-in-training routinely were instructed to mark tickets with a particular symbol if they identified a purchaser as Negro after in-person contact. Alternately, trainees were told to use their best judgment to discern if callers making a reservation by phone were Black and to mark those tickets accordingly.[74]

The AJC investigation further revealed that U.S. air carriers designated specific seats or rows for Negro passengers and that flight attendants routinely treated Blacks rudely. Negro celebrities were not exempt from such ill treatment. Singer Ella Fitzgerald, for example, successfully sued Pan Am for discriminatory treatment after they stranded her in Hawaii. Congressman Adam Clayton Powell Jr. of Harlem was outraged to find that a newly opened airport in Maryland forbade Negroes from entering its dining area. Of course, these experiences became additional grist for Moscow's propaganda mill. Ultimately, such external pressure, combined with mounting internal resistance, convinced the U.S. and its businesses to retreat from the more egregious aspects of Jim Crow.[75]

The internal forces against Jim Crow began to rally increasingly during the 1950s. In 1950, Negro plaintiffs filed damage suits against American Airlines and Sky Chiefs, Inc., after being refused service at an airport restaurant in Covington, Kentucky.[76] In 1951, Negroes refused admittance to the coffee shop and restaurant at the airport

74 *Chicago Defender*, 6 October 1951, Box IX, NAACP Papers.
75 Victoria Vantoch, *The Jet Sex: Airline Stewardesses and the Making of an American Icon* (Philadelphia: University of Pennsylvania Press, 2013), 63, 64, 69.
76 Press Release, April 1950, Reel 42, #1211, Part I, Press Releases, CAB-NCSU.

in Charleston, West Virginia, likewise pursued their case in court.[77] Suggesting the onset of racial retrogression in the U.S. propelled by the Korean War, the dining area at the airport in Norfolk, Virginia, was not segregated until suddenly, in 1953, a curtain was installed there to separate Negroes and those defined as white.[78] Congressman Powell did not indicate if he thought that as an outgrowth of the war in Korea, there was a resurgence in strength of anticommunism, a doctrine which historically had argued that anti-Jim Crow measures were largely inspired by Communists.

President Truman's attempt to desegregate the military did not magically eventuate in a nation free of Jim Crow, nor did the U.S. Supreme Court's decision to move in a similar direction on May 17, 1954, necessarily resolve the problem of Jim Crow conclusively. "Separate restrooms for whites and Negroes," for example, were slated for a Houston airport in 1955, according to one journalist.[79] In September of that year, the main dining room of an airport restaurant in that city reportedly continued to refuse service to African Americans.[80] A Negro pilot was treated similarly at a restaurant at the Birmingham airport around the same time;[81] and weeks later 11 Negroes in Louisville, Kentucky, filed suit against American and Eastern airlines after being barred from a dining area at that city's airport. Naturally, similar Jim Crow practices were in place at the airport in New Orleans, but these too met with increasing opposition.[82]

By 1953, NAACP executive Walter White had informed leaders of his group's local branches that incidences of "segregated restrooms and other facilities for Negro passengers at airports are spreading"

77 T. G. Nugger to Claude Barnett, 8 June 1951, Reel 1, #620, Series C, Part III, Subject Files on Black Americans, CAB-NCSU.

78 Press Release, February 1953, Reel 50, #908, Part I, Press Releases, CAB-NCSU.

79 Press Release, December 1951, Reel 8, #461, Part I, Press Releases, CAB-NCSU.

80 Press Release, September 1955, Reel 58, #84, Part I, Press Releases, CAB-NCSU.

81 Press Release, September 1955, Reel 58, #129, Part I, Press Releases, CAB-NCSU.

82 Press Release, November 1955, Reel 58, #1029, Part I, Press Releases, CAB-NCSU.

even though, he noted, "even in the Deep South there is no segregation in seating, feeding or otherwise handling of colored [airline] passengers."[83] White may have underestimated the extent to which Jim Crow prevailed among U.S. commercial carriers, and he may not have understood fully the patchwork nature of those carriers' racial policies and practices. However, it did seem that segregationists among the airline industry viewed the anti-Jim Crow decrees emanating from Washington as a tossed-down gauntlet that had to be confronted aggressively. Their approach met with a number of problems, however.

One such challenge emerged in August 1955, when India's ambassador was perceived as Negro by authorities at the Houston airport, who subsequently asked this eminent diplomat to move to a smaller, inferior dining area in the "colored" section of the facility.[84] Given that New Delhi was then moving closer to Moscow, U.S. diplomats viewed this error as being even more egregious. Before the unfortunate indiscretion occurred, Walter White had warned an executive at United Airlines about the "great deal of bitter anti-American feeling" he had perceived while on a recent trip to Asia "because distinguished dark-skinned Asians had been subjected to discrimination in American [venues there]."[85]

* * *

Once Negro diners escaped the indignity of Jim Crow airports by boarding their respective planes, chances were high that they would not encounter any Black flight attendants. In 1956, then-NAACP legal counsel Thurgood Marshall was informed by Ruth Weyand, a Chicago attorney, that due to a "shortage in the neighborhood of 500 hostesses," the nation's air carriers had lowered their hiring standards to the point

---

83 Walter White to Dear Branch Officer, 7 May 1953, Box II: A9, NAACP Papers.
84 Press Release, August 1955, Reel 57, #1070, Part I, Press Releases, CAB-NCSU.
85 Walter White to D. P. Magarell, Vice President of United Air Lines, 22 April 1952, Box II: A 233, NAACP Papers.

where they were employing "girls as young as 19." At the time, Weyand pointed out, no American airline employed Negroes as stewards or stewardesses, although Cordoba Airlines in Alaska had deigned to hire a Negro pilot. She accused Allegheny Airlines of "importing French girls" as flight attendants while ignoring the potential stewardesses of color virtually on their doorstep.[86]

Lorraine Keel was a young Negro woman who sought employment as a flight attendant with the most recalcitrant of the nation's commercial carriers, American Airlines. At her interview, she asked if American "employed any Negro girls." She was informed that some were working as stewardesses in Panama, but "none were employed in the U.S." Keel also recalled that she was asked if she had ever worked as a model. "When I replied affirmatively," she said, she was asked for "a demonstration." She responded by walking back and forth in the room several times. Fortunately, the interviewer, a man defined as white, made no comments about her physical appearance. Keel nonetheless was disposed to file a lawsuit and charge American Airlines with "refusing to employ" her because of her "color."[87]

If Keel had been able to confer with John Terry, an attorney who, like Weyand, also cooperated with the NAACP, she would have been able to ascertain that it was routine for so-called "airline personnel schools" to convey contracts with provisions stating that the training they provided was "available to persons of the white race only." She would also have discovered that just in case an applicant was able to evade that contractual filter by virtue of their having light skin and so-called European features, she or he was subject to being asked abrasively, "Are you of the white race?" A negative answer, of course, would invoke immediate dismissal.[88]

---

86   Ruth Weyand to Thurgood Marshall, 13 June 1956, Box III: A177, NAACP Papers.
87   Complaint of Lorraine Keel, 4 February 1957, Box III: A 177, NAACP Papers.
88   John Terry to Roy Wilkins, 18 February 1957, Box III: A177, NAACP Papers.

* * *

The remarkable confluence of 25,000 anti-Jim Crow advocates rallying in Washington in May 1957 was followed quickly by the desegregation crisis in Little Rock that September and—most importantly for the purposes of this book—by the launching of Sputnik, a Moscow satellite thrust into the heavens a month later in October. All led to a breakthrough for racial equality, which assuredly had a massive impact on aviation. In turn, aviation's ability to shrink the size of the planet facilitated a process whereby anti-colonialist forces came more acutely within the purview of anti-racist forces in the U.S.—and vice versa—with the productive exchanges redounding to the benefit of both.

Even before Sputnik, Dean Acheson, a leading formulator of U.S. foreign policy, shared with Associated Negro Press founder Claude Barnett a comment the latter knew well to be "obvious"—namely, that "the existence of discrimination against minority groups in the United States is a handicap in our relations with other countries."[89] In the wake of the satellite's successful launch, Barnett continued to warn against the insidious nature of Jim Crow discrimination. He and other U.S. journalists also warned about "Sputnik diplomacy," whereby Moscow would leverage its victories in aeronautics to woo African and other nations surging toward independence to its side—a fear repeatedly articulated by then U.S. Vice President Richard M. Nixon. As coverage of Sputnik quickly overtook news about the Little Rock Nine, this fear metastasized, and the nation's national security establishment sprung into action.

Flailing about for a solution, the Central Intelligence Agency lamely suggested the creation of an "African Center," to be located somewhere in the U.S., for the purpose of displaying cultural items from the colonized continent and promoting pro-U.S. propaganda throughout the continent and to African Americans. The agency

---

89 Dean Acheson to Claude Barnett, 25 March 1954, Box 208, Folder 1, CAB-ANP.

even proposed recruiting a "competent Negro scientist" to read a scientific paper at an important conference on atomic energy and then circulating a photograph from that event to the people in various African nations with the intent to impress them with Washington's (alleged) goodwill.

More concretely, U.S. thought and political leaders proposed more decisive steps away from Jim Crow in light of Sputnik.[90] Claude Barnett, who had been so instrumental in promoting opportunities for African Americans in aviation, unleashed his news agency, the Associated Negro Press, to that effect in the aftermath of Sputnik. The ANP's influential Negro columnist Gordon Hancock, posited, for example, that Sputnik and Moscow helped to "show the world a new moon" while the U.S., disgustedly showed the world "its disgraceful Little Rock situation." Continuing this invidious comparison, he argued that "while Russia struggles for scientific and technological supremacy, unfortunately too many Americans are concerned with white supremacy." In the U.S., he claimed, "[S]o much time is spent holding the Negro back, while Russia threatens to run away with the world....either this country must let the Negro go or succumb to the triumph of Communism. America must make its choice!"[91]

The threat, contended Hancock, "is upon us [the U.S.]. We are worried and alarmed, as well we should be." Perhaps recalling the Tuskegee Airmen, he spluttered that "this matter of rushing the Negro to the front in times of war and to the rear in times of peace" was absurd, as the U.S. was facing its "gravest peril since the founding of the nation." "With every Russian giving his best and with only the whites of our nation giving their best," he concluded, "we can never overtake Russia in the missile and space race."[92]

---

90 Yanke Mieczkowski, *Eisenhower's Sputnik Moment: The Race for Space and World Prestige* (Ithaca, NY: Cornell University Press, 2013), 80, 197.

91 Press Release, October 1957, Reel 63, #1127, Part I, Press Releases, CAB-NCSU.

92 Press Release, January 1958, Reel 64, #480, Part I, Press Releases, CAB-NCSU.

As another ANP columnist proclaimed: "Sputnik signals for all mankind to see and hear the end of colonialism and race and colour discrimination."[93] He suggested that, with its as-yet-unparalleled aeronautic achievement, Moscow—then seen as a major bulwark of anti-colonialism and anti-Jim Crow—had gained a decided advantage over its Cold War detractors and opponents in the U.S. Yet another ANP columnist wrote that Sputnik's launch was a "bigger defeat than Pearl Harbor. And that is an understatement."[94]

Earl Morris, an ANP correspondent stationed in Mexico, juxtaposed Little Rock as a site where "war" was being waged "against nine little Negro children," with Moscow, a nation engrossed with "preparing to launch her satellites." With asperity, Morris proclaimed: "The Russians, who are white people, will pay no attention to the fact that [Arkansas Governor Orval] Faubus is white, and should Russia bomb the United States, they will not try to single out the Negroes."[95]

Given that Barnett's columnists were published in Negro press organs nationally, the ANP's pungent opinions were guaranteed to reach a wide audience. The consensus of their views was that race hatred and discrimination were to blame for the lag behind Soviet Russia in scientific achievement. After all, one ANP reporter touted: the insidious apartheid of Jim Crow, which exalted and promoted the waste of valuable human capital, particularly the intellectual variety, "barred many Negroes from white colleges and schools in the South where courses in electrical engineering, electronics, physics and…. higher mathematics" were offered. The failure to make available such courses, "which cannot be secured in Negro colleges" thus was dubbed "partly responsible for Soviet Russia being ahead."[96]

---

93 Press Release, October 1957, Reel 63, #1125, Part I, Press Releases, CAB-NCSU.
94 Press Release, December 1957, Reel 64, #332, Part I, Press Releases, CAB-NCSU.
95 Press Release, December 1957, Reel 64, #282, Part I, Press Releases, CAB-NCSU.
96 Press Release, November 1957, Reel 64, #28, Part I, Press Releases, CAB-NCSU.

Benjamin Epstein of the Anti-Defamation League of B'nai B'rith echoed much of the ANP's commentary. His observations, summarized, warned the U.S. to "erase college bias or risk losing [the] science race."[97] W. E. B. Du Bois, whose increasing sympathy for Moscow had led, by the 1950s, to his being marginalized, also chimed in on the issue, declaring that his homeland had suffered a "vast intellectual waste of human ability in the past 60 years by depriving Negroes of equal educational advantages." He and his spouse, Shirley Graham Du Bois, and Paul Robeson and his spouse, Eslanda Goode Robeson, together celebrated the 40th anniversary of the Bolshevik Revolution— and Sputnik's success—as guests of the Soviet ambassador at the Soviet Embassy in Washington.[98] Harlem Congressman Adam Clayton Powell likewise was emphatic in his assertions about "the three evils facing America...Sputnik, Science and Segregation." As Powell warned, America would forever be "a second-class power as long as she tolerates the concept of a second-class citizenship."[99]

With Sputnik, the ANP's Gordon Hancock argued, Moscow had surged ahead in the "space race" because Washington had a "preoccupation with the race race."[100] Indeed, the years following the Russian space launch were characterized by a determined grassroots push, led by Negroes and their allies, against Jim Crow. That movement was complemented by pressure from on high, as exemplified by President Dwight D. Eisenhower's deployment of federal troops to push back segregationist forces in Little Rock. These and other pressures helped to open the cockpits of opportunity for U.S. Negroes generally; but for those Blacks interested in aviation and aeronautics, the forces that caused Jim Crow to free-fall thrust their soaring ambitions ever upward, higher than most could have imagined.

---

97 Press Release, November 1957, Reel 64, #29, Part I, Press Releases, CAB-NCSU.
98 Press Release, November 1957, Reel 64, #138, Part I, Press Releases, CAB-NCSU.
99 Press Release, January 1958, Reel 64, #480, Part I, Press Releases, CAB-NCSU
100 Press Release, May 1961, Reel 73, #736, Part I, Press Releases, CAB-NCSU.

CHAPTER 7

BUMPY LANDING

After the Sputnik shock, African Americans' decades-long efforts to gain a toehold in the expanding field of aviation began realizing some victories. Even Vice President Richard Nixon, not renowned as a friend of Negro progress, hailed the 1957 hiring of James Plinton as an assistant to TWA's director of personnel and industrial relations. Plinton—an enterprising former Tuskegee Airman who had developed an air service in Haiti to complement his dry-cleaning business and who later launched a commercial carrier that flew between Kingston, Jamaica, and the Turks and Caicos Islands—actually may have been overqualified for his new bureaucratic post. His aviation prowess, however, made it possible for him to abandon Haiti hastily after regime change made it dangerous to stay on the island. His return to the U.S. mainland and his hiring by TWA was indicative of the continuing ability of aviation to provide Blacks with opportunities for upward mobility.

News coverage of Plinton's barrier-crashing appointment did not mention the implications his new role held for TWA's ongoing attempt to gain a foothold in the burgeoning African market. The carrier's executives were certain that market, coincidentally bolstered further when Ghana achieved its independence in 1957, was bound to grow as colonialism continued to erode. Indeed, Ghana's liberation had itself been bolstered by African Americans, and there was no gainsaying that progress for U.S. Negroes seemed to be in motion.[1]

Soon after his pioneering appointment, Plinton was joined in commercial aviation by Perry Young, another former Tuskegee Airman. Although the South Carolina-born Young had been an instructor at the Alabama flight-training school and not a pilot, his first job with a mainstream carrier was to operate a helicopter, then to ferry passengers and cargo to and from New York City.[2] Young is viewed widely as being the first African American hired as a commercial pilot by a major airline. Like Plinton, after the Second World War, he too departed for greater opportunities in the Caribbean, flying between Haiti, Puerto Rico, and the U.S. Virgin Islands.[3] He accumulated an astounding 7,000 hours in the air as a result of his Caribbean experience. Until he began his job with New York Airways in late December 1956, not one Negro pilot, navigator, radio operator, or flight attendant was in the employ of any scheduled passenger airline in the U.S.[4]

This enhanced mobility was not just a one-way street. John Roach, whose roots were in Montserrat, could be included among a group of Caribbean aviators who were trained in the U.S. This trend indicated that when African Americans stormed the heavens, their victories did not redound to their benefit alone.[5]

As Plinton departed Haiti, his comrade, Claude Barnett, arrived there. The Chicago publisher had befriended Haitian president

---

1 Release, December 1957, Reel 63, #698, Part I, Press Releases, CAB-NCSU. On Ghana and African-Americans, see, e.g., Horne, *Race Woman*.

2 Broadnax, *Blue Skies, Black Wings*, 144-145.

3 Charlie Leduff, "Perry H. Young, 79, Pioneering Pilot, Dies," *New York Times*, November 19, 1998, B7. Other Negro pioneers in commercial aviation include David Harris, Jack Noel, William Norwood, Otis Young, Ed Daly, Baley Pendergrass, Jill Brown, Marcella Hayes and Shirley Tyus. See, e.g., Broadnax, *Blue Skies, Black Wings*, 144-145.

4 Press Release, December 1956, Reel 61, #663, Part I, Press Releases, CAB-NCSU.

5 Moye, *Freedom Flyers*, 1, 37. Note as well Mohamed Shaik, an airman who was the son of an Indian father educated in Britain who had migrated from Calcutta before decamping in New Orleans. Shaik's mother was a "Creole" from New Orleans with indigenous roots and a graduate of the historically Black Xavier University in Louisiana.

Francois Duvalier, who came to power in 1957, running on a platform of populist Black Nationalism. As he had done in East Africa, Barnett sought to promote the interests of Pan American Airways. He told the new leader—the man who later would be known as "Papa Doc," a brutal and autocratic dictator—that Pan Am could "be of tremendous aid to Haiti" and could "divert even more tourists" to the island. He suggested that Duvalier write the carrier's Juan Trippe directly, adding that he would time a corresponding letter to reach Tripp "at the same time."

Barnett additionally hoped to rope Duvalier into his West African ventures, explaining that he was "also a member of the Board of Directors of the Liberia Company." That company, he touted, "held a concession to develop all the natural resources" in that West African nation. He further promoted the company as controlling "several thousand of acres" there, on which it was "developing cocoa and bananas." Of course, he invited Duvalier to leap aboard this gravy train in a relationship that he claimed would be facilitated by the growth of aviation, which Barnett had done so much to promote.[6]

The pivotal year 1957 witnessed another important journey. That year, perhaps the most heralded Tuskegee Airman of all, General Benjamin O. Davis Jr., returned to Washington from a tour of duty in Taiwan. Davis later confessed that neither he nor the members of his family who had traveled with him to that distant post were thrilled at the prospect of resuming their lives in the States. "We were in no way eager to return," he recalled, "especially not to [the] segregation in Washington." His cautionary comments were illustrative of the mounting tensions that eventually compelled Jim Crow to retreat.

Davis, a staunch U.S. patriot, was nonetheless suitably impressed with Sputnik. The launch of the Soviet satellite, in his view, "gave many Americans, including me, a healthy new respect for Russian

---

6 Claude Barnett to Francois Duvalier, 30 November 1957, Box 206, Folder 1, CAB-ANP.

technological capabilities." Such grudging respect, in combination with U.S. Negroes' mounting displeasure with their homeland's racial-caste system, contributed mightily to the course correction that would lead to an erosion of Jim Crow.[7]

President Truman's executive order desegregating the U.S. armed forces was supposed to put to rest the substance of Jim Crow, at least insofar as the branches of the military were concerned, with this change thought to be rippling into the larger society. Yet, like the whiskers that continue to grow on the face of a corpse, Jim Crow persisted even when officially declared dead. During the tumultuous 1950s, the yawning gap between the President's missive from on high and state praxis was problematic. As late as 1958, the NAACP reported "an overt attempt has been made to bar Negroes"—even those who had "trained in the Air Force at public expense"—from "flying jobs as pilots, navigators, and stewardesses." It further insisted that, emblematic of a national trend, "no Negroes [were] employed" in the Pittsburgh sales offices of a major carrier. Resultantly, the organization contended that African Americans generally believed that "airline jobs [were] not available to them," an inference grounded in reality, even in the post-*Brown v. Board of Education* era.[8]

Joan King, a young Negro woman who was eager to work as a stewardess on one of the nation's major airlines, could have provided first-hand testimony affirming this fraught matter. An investigation by the New York State Commission Against Discrimination concluded that Negro women like her were routinely rejected by U.S. air carriers on such grounds as having a "large nose," "hips heavy," "ill-kempt" hair, or a poor figure. The subjective application of narrowly constructed beauty standards, the study concluded, meant that no Negro women could "meet the specifications" for flight attendant jobs. To make matters worse, the

7 Davis Jr., *Benjamin O. Davis, Jr., American*, 236.
8 Louis Mason, Chairman of "NAIRO Manpower Commission" to Herbert Hill, 28 February 1958, Box III: A177, NAACP Papers.

New York investigators found out that "in the case of not a few white applicants" for those positions, "opportunity was offered to correct defects [sic] in weight, teeth, speech, excessive weight," and so forth. Those options were not offered "to a single Negro applicant."[9]

More than a decade after Sputnik passed into the heavens, U.S. air carriers were still struggling to improve their employment records. By the end of 1972, Pan Am would report employing 2,834 "officials and managers," only 48 of whom were Negroes and only 5 of whom were women. Conversely, Negroes were overrepresented in the airlines' employee category denoted as "laborers, unskilled."[10] In 1958, however, Pan Am executives seemed intent on ducking and dodging as the National Urban League sought to place a sole "colored administrative assistant" within their ranks.[11] During the final quarter of that year, Pan Am hired and promoted a grand total of zero Negro workers.[12] The prospects for Black workers was no better in Pan Am's Latin American division in the late 1950s, even though, in 1957, the airline was commended for "employing Puerto Rican stewardesses."[13] That division, however, still had not hired any U.S. Negroes.[14]

Pan Am nonetheless was trying to run with the hares and hunt with the hounds in pursuing its capacious global plans. That is, while adroitly evading demands to hire Black workers at home, they were determinedly courting Black leaders in the Caribbean Basin and Africa. That duplicitous practice seemed unsustainable, however.

---

9 Elmer Carter to Joan King, 7 January 1958, Box III: A177, NAACP Papers.

10 EEO Report, 1973, "Data as of 12/31/72," Box 389, Folder 2, Pan Am Papers. Of "officials and managers," 144 were listed as "female," 46 as "Oriental," 4 as "American Indian," and 104 as "Spanish-surnamed."

11 Major General C. E. Ryan (retired), Executive Vice Chairman of President's Committee on Government Contracts to Everett M. Goulard, 2 December 1958, Box 474, Folder 6, Pan Am Papers.

12 Wilma Sivertsen, Personnel Manager to Manager, 14 November 1958, Box 474, Folder 6, Pan Am Papers.

13 Everett M. Goulard to Juan Trippe, 21 May 1958, Box 420, Folder 6, Pan Am Papers.

14 Thomas White, Industrial Relations Manager to Manager, 3 July 1958, Box 474, Folder 6, Pan Am Papers.

The year of Sputnik was also the year Pan Am—after 15 years of trying–won the right to provide air service to Barbados. A journalist captured the enthusiasm that accompanied the airline's arrival to this island, accurately reporting that while "most" of the jubilant Barbadians were indeed "colored," they were "showing the stirrings of colored races all over the world."[15]

When the newly installed Ghanaian Prime Minister Kwame Nkrumah arrived in Manhattan in 1958, Pan Am was among the first corporations to reserve a table at a gala dinner held in his honor at the posh Waldorf-Astoria.[16] Airline founder, Juan Trippe, invoked "the great threat of the Communist infiltration in Africa and particularly the Gold Coast" [17]—meaning Ghana, in justifying his rubbing shoulders with Nkrumah. Trippe's airline also donated heavily to a foundation that subsidized scholarships for African students to attend colleges in the U.S.[18]

Washington also sought to curry favor with Africa, consonant with its foreign policy obligations: the U.S. pressured Pan Am to improve its appallingly discriminatory hiring record. Jacob Seidenberg, executive director of President Dwight D. Eisenhower's Committee on Government Contracts, pushed the carrier to address its "flight, professional and executive positions" primarily, given that the company's minority hiring in that area was "virtually non-existent."[19]

Trippe was acutely aware of what was at stake. He worried that his stockholders might question his airline's responses to the sensitive interlocked issues of Jim Crow and colonialism. After all, Claude Barnett was among this elite group. At the 1957 gathering of shareholders, Trippe was blunt in underlining the challenges Pan Am faced on both fronts. As he noted, "We operate through 88 countries abroad....and

15 Clipping, 17-18 June 1957, Box 322, Folder 17, Pan Am Papers.
16 Memorandum, 21 July 1958, Box 474, Folder 6, Pan Am Papers.
17 Juan Trippe to Vice President, 23 March 1956, Box 751, Folder 1, Pan Am Papers.
18 Everett M. Goulard, Vice President of Industrial Relations, Pan Am to Emory Ross of the Phelps Stokes Fund, 14 July 1958, Box 474, Folder 6, Pan Am Papers.
19 Jacob Seidenberg to Juan Trippe, 18 July 1958, Box 420, Folder 6, Pan Am Papers.

we have problems which result which are not normal in companies operating solely in the domestic field." His competitor, TWA, which earlier had blared its intention to hire a Negro flight attendant for its international service, had surpassed Pan Am by adopting more open hiring practices. TWA's bold actions, Trippe feared, might "give rise to a specific inquiry as to whether Pan American plans to hire Negroes as flight crew members." In a defense that predated excuses invoked by similarly situated executives in the contemporary era, Trippe raised a straw man to undermine his carrier's critics by expressing his stout opposition to hiring quotas. He also was prescient in raising irrelevant red herrings in Pan Am's defense; mentioning, for example, that Pan Am sponsored a "Wheelchair Basketball Team" coached by a "disabled Negro basketball star."

The Congress of Racial Equality (CORE) was another civil rights organization that took up the mantle of addressing Jim Crow's persistent presence in the aviation industry. As CORE officials told the members of the Civil Aeronautics Board in 1957, they were "very concerned over the racial discrimination which exists in the field of airlines flight-crew employment." The rising organization offered a strategically targeted recommendation, that a "no airline be considered for the award of a new route without investigation of its flight-crew employment policy."[20] CORE knew that such a decision could be devastating for all airlines but particularly troublesome for Pan Am, which at the time was seeking access to choice global routes in formerly colonized territories that were mushrooming as colonialism was decomposing.

Apparently, the airlines were hesitant to hire Negro hostesses for fear of alienating certain customers in Dixie. Alice Howland of Santa Fe, New Mexico, was among those questioning the hiring practices of major airlines, observing in 1958:

---

20 Joel B. Slocum, Chairman of CORE-New York City to James Durfee, Civil Aeronautics Board, 2 May 1958, Box 420, Folder 6, Pan Am Papers. On the shareholders' meeting, see Everett M. Goulard to Juan Trippe, 21 May 1958, in the same box and folder.

> In these difficult times where the *Eastern World* [original emphasis] is watching us closely, I feel we want to help the Negroes to secure education & better economic opportunities. I urge that you place Negro girls on your Northern, Western, & Foreign planes. Also Negro co-pilots or pilots.[21]

The growth of aviation facilitated increasing global pressure against Jim Crow. This, in turn, had ramifications for the hiring of Negroes in the U.S. aviation industry as well as significant repercussions for how African Americans would be treated on commercial air carriers. Pan Am, for example, was forced to compete with global competitors, many of whom were not as enamored with Jim Crow as was the U.S.-based carrier. Similarly, as Pan Am adapted to the global standard, other domestic carriers (i.e., TWA, Eastern, etc.) that flew beyond U.S. shores, were forced to conduct themselves likewise in a virtuous circle. A similar process spelled doom for colonialism too.

In early 1958, TWA announced its intention to hire its first Black flight attendant.[22] This preemptive move put Pan Am in a considerable bind. The latter airline had bet heavily on the continuing viability of apartheid South Africa, but it did not take an oracle to see that the rise of an anti-colonial Africa, as embodied by Ghana's Kwame Nkrumah and Jomo Kenyatta of Kenya, held grave consequences for Pretoria. "Relations between South Africa and most of the independent Africa nations continue to be severely strained," asserted one Pan Am executive euphemistically. "In air transport this opposition has been expressed in what may be termed a 'boycott' of direct air services between South Africa and other African nations."[23]

Several African nations were seeking to "withdraw landing rights from South African and Portuguese airlines and not to operate services

---

21 Alice Howland to "Dear Sir," 23 January 1958, Box 420, Folder 6, Pan Am Papers.
22 Press Release, February 1958, Reel 64, #775, Part I, Press Releases, CAB-NCSU.
23 Russell B. Adams to Richard O'Malia, Civil Aeronautics Board, 21 July 1966, Box 761, Folder 13, Pan Am Papers.

to South Africa."²⁴ If such restrictions had been put into place, they would have broad ramifications for Pan Am, which by then had hitched its wagon to the star of those polecat nations. As a result, air transport service between South Africa and other independent African countries, which was provided by carriers such as Pan American, was becoming an increasingly unsustainable proposition. After the Organization of African Unity, the continental grouping of independent nations, called for a "secondary boycott" of Pan Am in 1964, the carrier's vice president, Russell B. Adams, responded that the action "would obviously jeopardize seriously or force the termination of Pan American's present flight to Johannesburg."²⁵

Increasingly under siege in Africa, Pan Am opted for cosmetic reforms. Perhaps to solidify its ties to the "colored races," as early as 1956, the airline became a "charter subscriber" to the *Chicago Daily Defender*, which served that city's important and ever-growing African American community. Reciprocally, the paper gave the carrier an award, with a golden seal no less.²⁶ Nevertheless, as the coming years were to reveal, Pan Am's problems with Africans and African Americans could not be resolved with mere palliatives. This lesson was a difficult one for Pan Am to absorb. It proved similarly difficult for the carrier's peers.

* * *

The 1960s saw a continuing pattern of pressure and resistance, both to and from Jim Crow. At the beginning of that decade, Marlon Green, the Negro who later was hired by Continental Airlines, was still in court trying to win the legal battle to become that carrier's first Black pilot. Continental, for its part, was continuing to pay expensive lawyers to bar this result.²⁷ Cross burnings and racial clashes erupted at an Air

24 Ibid.
25 Ibid.
26 Press Release, 6 February 1956, Box 279, Folder 5, Pan Am Papers.
27 Press Release, September 1960, Reel 71, #775, Part I, Press Releases, CAB-NCSU.

Force base in New Mexico that same year—yet another indication of the still-forbidding climate endured by Negro aviators.[28] The walls of Jim Crow were nonetheless showing signs of erosion by 1960, when the airport in Greenville, South Carolina, halted the segregation of Negro passengers in its waiting room.[29] Still, the patchwork pattern of Negro progress predominated. The Civil Aeronautics Board, in the decade's same inaugural year, claimed it did not have jurisdiction to compel the Montgomery, Alabama, airport to retreat from its Jim Crow practices.[30]

Another strong tailwind pushing the U.S. toward greater racial reform was the increasingly nagging perception that the U.S. was lagging behind the U.S.S.R. in exploration of the heavens because of the obdurateness of Jim Crow. In 1961, the NAACP categorically offered Jim Crow as the reason why the U.S. was playing "second fiddle" in the cosmos, a result with sobering national security implications.[31] Thus, rather dramatically, it was announced portentously that "the Soviets could land a rocket on a dime anywhere in North America."[32]

Carl Rowan, who would go on to serve the U.S. as ambassador to Finland before becoming a top-ranking Negro commentator in the mainstream press, added more fuel to the debate, declaring that "Russia's space achievements" were made possible because that nation, unlike the U.S., used all its available human resources. Yet in conferring with India's top jurist he found that this eminent lawyer had been denied service in a dining car in the U.S. because of his dark skin, a reflection of what had befallen visiting African diplomats and their families seeking meals in Maryland. In other words, Jim Crow was compromising national security quite dangerously by hampering the

---

28 Press Release, March 1960, Reel 69, #1140, Part I, Press Releases, CAB-NCSU.
29 Press Release, December 1960, Reel 71, #508, Part I, Press Releases, CAB-NCSU.
30 Press Release, May 1960, Reel 70, #618, Part I, Press Releases, CAB-NCSU.
31 Press Release, May 1961, Reel 73, #682, Part I, Press Releases, CAB-NCSU.
32 Press Release, October 1959, Reel 68, #860, Part I, Press Releases, CAB-NCSU.

ability to challenge Moscow, while alienating potential allies in New Delhi.[33]

As exploring the cosmos became the new reality, Washington too came to view the decidedly earthbound policy of Jim Crow as a hindrance. After being prodded by Vice President Lyndon B. Johnson, Lockheed, a prime contractor in the emerging aeronautics field, actively began seeking Negro workers in 1961. Soon, 530 of the giant corporation's workforce of 11,000 was Negro—a small percentage still, but a great leap forward from previous years.[34]

In 1961, NASA, the newly created National Aeronautics and Space Administration founded in 1958, sited an important U.S. tracking station for one of its key space exploration programs in Zanzibar in East Africa. That country, once a prime depot for enslaved Africans, was by then a seething cauldron of anti-colonial sentiment. NASA's Project Mercury base in Zanzibar, which hired African personnel, was heralded as a signal of the U.S.'s desire to improve its relations with Africa.[35] Another U.S. tracking station was sited soon thereafter in Kano, northern Nigeria. In direct violation of Jim Crow norms, NASA stationed a number of African American personnel at that installation.[36] When future U.S. Senator John Glenn of Ohio made his journey in outer space in 1962, the stations in Kano and Zanzibar proved to be critical for his mission.[37]

The Associated Negro Press was harshly censorious of any who mocked Washington's space-age desegregation practices, castigating, for example, a local periodical in Jackson, Mississippi, that lampooned the dearth of Negro astronauts by mocking and ridiculing the prospect of "A Freedom Rider in the Sky." What was intended as

33 Press Release, November 1961, Reel 75, Part I, Press Releases, CAB-NCSU.
34 Press Release, July 1961, Reel 74, #177, Part I, Press Releases, CAB-NCSU.
35 Press Release, October 1961, Reel 75, #40, Part I, Press Releases, CAB-NCSU.
36 Press Release, November 1961, Reel 75, #396, Part I, Press Releases, CAB-NCSU.
37 Press Release, February 1962, Reel 76, #141, Part I, Press Releases, CAB-NCSU.

mockery and ridicule, however, masked the reality that for decades the equivalent of freedom riders had been storming the heavens in pursuit of justice.[38]

The year 1963 saw a replay of the confluence of Sputnik and Little Rock. As U.S. astronaut Gordon Cooper was exploring the outer reaches of the universe, police dogs were attacking Negro children protesting in Birmingham, Alabama. The ANP did not hesitate to point out that the "strongest denunciations of the racial trouble came from Moscow [and] Peking."[39] Strident condemnations were also the order of the day at the founding convocation of the Organization of African Unity (OAU) in Ethiopia. Attending that meeting was the U.S. Negro activist-intellectual, Shirley Graham Du Bois, Also present was James Plinton, by then a public-relations executive at TWA. Akbar Muhammed, yet another African American activist, attended in order to lobby the African delegates to assert a stronger reproach of U.S. Jim Crow.[40] Not coincidentally, in 1964, Zanzibar staunchly opposed a multi-million dollar expansion of the NASA tracking station located in this former slave trading emporium—a powerful blow to the U.S. space program,[41] but a sacrifice replete with poverty and other dire consequences for the East African island nation.

As the 1960s unwound, the barrier of Jim Crow, which had barred African Americans from aviation for so long, seemed to recede. Another barrier arose to take its place, however; and this time, the obstacle loomed higher in the cosmos. By 1965, for example, Edward Dwight Jr.'s curious denial that he had been eliminated as an astronaut due to racism was not accepted universally.[42] Since Dwight had said in 1963

---

38 Press Release, April 1962, Reel 76, #561, Part I, Press Releases, CAB-NCSU.
39 Press Release, May 1963, Reel 79, #661, Part I, Press Releases, CAB-NCSU.
40 Press Release, June 1963, Reel 79, #991, Part I, Press Releases, CAB-NCSU.
41 Press Release, April 1964, Reel 82, #283, Part I, Press Releases, CAB-NCSU.
42 *New York Times*, June 3, 1965.

that he was "ready to leave for outer space right now,"[43] his denial was doubted. The skepticism that greeted Dwight's denial may have been connected with a broader dubiousness among African Americans more broadly about the origins and leadership of NASA.

The experiences of Ruth Bates Harris of Harlem also affirm the presence of new barriers to Black progress in the cosmos. Harris was an early employee of NASA, and it was while working there that she confronted the agency's leader, Wernher von Braun, with articles detailing his role in slave labor camps during the tenure of the Nazi regime he served so faithfully. "Please tell me, is it true?" she asked plaintively. Von Braun's answer was evasive: "Certainly not as it's written here."[44]

*   *   *

As both the old and new Jim Crow obstacles receded, those Black aviation pioneers who earlier stormed the heavens began to fade from the scene. In 1954, the same year that saw the U.S. Supreme Court stride away from Jim Crow, Colonel John Robinson, whose aerial exploits in Ethiopia had done so much to interest African Americans in aviation, passed away in Ethiopia. During his funeral, Ethiopians lined up for miles to pay homage to him in a remarkable display of Pan-Africanism. His Imperial Majesty Haile Selassie I, visiting Chicago later that year, insisted on stopping at the deceased pilot's former church to pay homage to him.[45] During that epochal visit, His Imperial Majesty awarded a medal to Janet Harmon Waterford Bragg, yet another pioneering Negro aviator, who had assisted Ethiopian students in the U.S. at Robinson's suggestion. When Bragg visited Addis Ababa later that year, she discovered that she was wildly popular there because of

---

43   Press Release, April 1963, Reel 79, #158, Part I, Press Releases, CAB-NCSU.
44   Ruth Bates Harris, *Harlem Princess: The Story of Harry Delaney's Daughter* (New York: Vantage, 1991), 254, 258.
45   Tucker, *Father of the Tuskegee Airmen*, 257.

her altruism. When she returned, she was appointed Ethiopia's Consul in Chicago.[46]

Old nostrums died hard, however. According to Claude Barnett, a purpose of the visit of the high-level delegation from Africa was to dispel the persistent idea that "Ethiopian royalty looked down its nose at American Negroes."[47] Homer Smith, Barnett's correspondent in Ethiopia, begged to differ. He claimed that the Africans still "worship[ped] white people" and worse, they "look[ed] down" on Black Americans."[48] Robinson apparently was exempted from their disdain. During a 1957 visit to Addis Ababa, Barnett reported finding "the memory of Col. Robinson very green," suggesting that the aviator "had been highly thought of by many" there. That same year, however, when Smith was seeking to raise funds for the pilot's headstone, which by then had deteriorated tremendously, he got little financial support for that effort from the Ethiopian government.[49] Reflectively, Barnett recalled Robinson's plan from years before to teach aviation at Tuskegee, a dream that fell through and led to his being offered a lesser job as a teacher of "sheet metal or automobile shop instructorship," which led to his departing in frustration for greener pastures in East Africa.[50]

Robinson's legacy includes the creation of Ethiopian Airlines, which today is Africa's largest and most profitable carrier, earning more revenues than any of its rivals on the continent combined. By 2015, the airline was servicing 82 international destinations, and it added 11 more in 2016. This venerable indigenous East African airline is expected soon to become the continent's first Pan-African carrier, aligning with its smaller rivals to open additional hubs in Togo and Malawi. After 70 odd

46 *Chicago Defender*, circa 1954, Box 2, Gubert Papers.
47 Claude Barnett to Charles Hanson, 14 June 1954, Box 171, Folder 2, CAB-ANP.
48 Homer Smith to Claude Barnett, 15 July 1957, Box 172, Folder 1, CAB-ANP.
49 Press Release, April 1957, Reel 62, #406, Part I, Press Releases, CAB-NCSU.
50 Claude Barnett to Luther Foster, 8 April 1957, Box 171, Folder 2, CAB-CHM.

years of operation, Ethiopian Airlines is indeed a viable expression of Colonel Robinson's pioneering Pan-African spirit and vision.[51]

Eugene Bullard, who left Georgia as a youth to make his way to France, where he became a World War I flying ace, died in 1961 at the age of 67.[52] Despite his and others' yeoman-like service, by 1969, the number of Negro pilots out of the U.S. total was—reportedly—a paltry 100 compared to almost 33,000.[53] By 1988, that number had doubled—reportedly—to 200 out of 45,000. Where the lengthy collaboration between Jim Crow and the pernicious "old boys' network" had failed to completely bar African Americans from the future and modernity that aviation was believed to represent, the two insidious forces had succeeded in suppressing Black participation in the skies.[54]

Robinson's former sparring partner, Hubert Julian, survived him, continuing his colorful career well into the latter part of the 20th century. As a result of his association with the pre-coup regime in Guatemala, France even prevented Julian from leaving his plane when he landed in Paris thereafter.[55] At that point, however, Julian was considering returning to the land of his birth: Trinidad.[56] His reputation was deteriorating rapidly. By 1958, a Julian antagonist asked rhetorically, "Is Hubert Julian a clown?" Answering his own question to the negative, that writer claimed that Julian's shenanigans were a ruse. The once-heralded pilot, who was by then a world-class arms dealer selling his wares in Cuba and Haiti, was also, according to the reporter, "as smart as a whip"—"intelligent, dapper, quick-witted," and multi-lingual (conferring easily in French, Spanish, and English), but decidedly a "mystery man, not only of Harlem but [an] international mystery man."

---

51 *The Economist*, October 22, 2016.
52 Certificate of Death of Eugene Bullard, 12 October 1961, Box 4, Gubert Papers.
53 *St. Paul Pioneer Press*, 18 May 1969.
54 Don Phillips, "Study Finds Few Black Airline Pilots," *Washington Post*, August 1, 1988, A6.
55 Press Release, March 1955, Reel 56, #826, Part I, Press Releases, CAB-NCSU.
56 Press Release, September 1955, Reel 58, #70, Part I, Press Releases, CAB-NCSU.

"Whenever there is the possibility of a revolt," the observer concluded, "Colonel Hubert Fauntleroy Julian pops up."[57]

By 1962, Julian was serving as an envoy for Congolese secessionists from Katanga, but he was arrested when his plan to sell millions in arms there was exposed. He was then flown under United Nations guard to the city then known as Leopoldville, where, quite customarily, he was seen fashionably attired, sporting his signature monocle.[58] Miles away in Chicago and Newark, four planes bound for Katanga were seized. The finger of accusation was, of course, pointed at Julian.[59]

The following year, the peripatetic pilot was in Haiti. He was spotted by a reporter at a fashionable watering hole, attired in a silk shirt and white trousers but apparently not in good health. "I am a sick man," Julian confided, claiming to have been hospitalized recently due to a stroke. Despite his ill health, few viewed his presence in Haiti as benign, surmising that arms trading in neighboring Santo Domingo was the real reason for his Caribbean sojourn.[60]

By 1983, Hubert Julian was dead. Perishing with him was his once-colorful legend, as his passing went virtually unnoticed.[61]

Willa Brown survived Robinson, Bullard, and Julian, reaching the ripe old age of 86 before she died in 1992. Unlike her male compatriots, however, she abandoned piloting while relatively young, while they pursued their aviation dreams to the very ends of their lives. By 1960, an inquisitive journalist went looking for her and found that she was living the life of "an ardent church worker and wife of a minister." Though she had won her pilot's license in 1937 and had trained many others to fly—often jetting from college to college to recruit flight trainees—

---

57 Press Release, August 1958, Reel 65, #1046, Part I, Press Releases, CAB-NCSU.
58 Press Release, May 1962, Reel 76, #782, Part I, Press Releases, CAB-NCSU.
59 Press Release, May 1962, Reel 76, #1013, Part I, Press Releases, CAB-NCSU.
60 Press Release, September 1961, Reel 80, #553, Part I, Press Releases, CAB-NCSU.
61 Caroline M. Fannin, "Hubert Julian," in *Harlem Renaissance Lives*, ed. Henry Louis Gates Jr. and Evelyn Brooks Higginbotham (New York: Oxford University Press, 2009), 316-318.

by 1950, her activity in the celestial realm had come to a close. Her churchly activities increased and, as her former sponsor Enoch Waters claimed: "where once she crusaded for converts to aviation," her mission subsequently evolved to winning "souls for Christ."[62] Brown also taught shorthand at Chicago's Crane High School. In the early 1930s, he recalled that she became obsessed with speed, initially with automobiles, and she was injured seriously in a car wreck before she switched to planes. In her later years, her need for speed was assuaged by racing through text as an expert in shorthand.[63] Waters inferred that her ultimate retreat from aviation marked a kind of descent from her heady days in the clouds. It also may have been symbolic of the still-turbulent journey of Black women in the field of aviation.

* * *

In a pattern that stretched back to the birth of modern aviation, African Americans continued to view planes as vehicles of liberation. This realization dawned rudely in the 1960s, when persons described as "Black militants" began to seize—or "skyjack"—commercial airplanes and demand that they be flown to destinations unaligned with the U.S., Cuba and Algeria in particular. Between 1961 and 1972, 159 commercial flights were commandeered in this rough fashion. Though only a few of the plane skyjackings were perpetrated by Negroes, the public imagination increasingly linked Black faces with that new trend. Tellingly, President Richard Nixon chose Lt. General Benjamin O. Davis Jr., who by then was retired and entering the final phase of his storied career, as the nation's first anti-skyjacking czar.[64]

The intense emotions aroused by flight have long sparked the imaginations of Negro creative writers. The idea of taking to the air,

---

62 Press Release, August 1960, Reel 71, #423, Part I, Press Releases, CAB-NCSU.
63 Press Release, May 1962, Reel 76, #796, Part I, Press Releases, CAB-NCSU.
64 Brendan I. Koerner, *The Skies Belong to Us: Love and Terror in the Golden Age of Hijacking* (New York: Crown, 2013), 8, 37, 77.

either as pilots or passengers, continues to provide fertile fields for fiction, prose, and poetry by Black authors. It likewise has provided literary impetus for writers of other ancestries such as Japanese American writer William Hayashi. One of Hayashi's short stories tells of the discovery of a fictional group of African American separatists whose disgust with racial disparity in the U.S. leads them to create a new society on the moon long before Neil Armstrong's arrival there.[65]

What this spiraling story of aviation suggests as it has ascended through the decades to the 21st century is that the right to fly—which involved "storming the heavens"—has been an essential element in explicating the retreat of both Jim Crow and colonialism and of their dual progeny. This story is part of a wider story involving the advance of the scientific and technological revolution and how these forces of production ultimately were in conflict with the relations of production. As a result, Washington was forced to acknowledge that advancing in the "space race" meant eroding the cruel diktat of the "race race" and, at the very least, being seen as unleashing the untapped human capital that was embodied in African Americans. Unfortunately, it appears that this simple and illuminating lesson about the deleterious import of seeking to bar African Americans from modernity and the future itself has yet to be learned altogether, even as our small planet faces ever stiffer challenges.

---

65 Ytasha L. Womack, *Afro-futurism: The World of Black Sci-Fi and Fantasy Culture* (Chicago: Lawrence Hill, 2013), 9, 24.

Eugene Bullard. As a youth, Bullard moved to France where he bacame a Flying Ace in World War I.
(Courtesy National Air and Space Museum Archives, Smithsonian Institution)

INDEX

A

Abbott, Robert Sengstacke 33, 89, 91
Acheson, Dean 205
Adams, Russell B. 217
aerial bombing 7, 8, 30, 32, 36, 37
aerial performances 11, 15, 29, 35, 40, 51, 86
Aeronautical Union Local 751 121
aerospace industry
  African Americans in the 17
Africa. *See under* individual countries
African American military
  treatment of 135
African American pilots
  and commercial licenses 55
African National Congress (ANC) 5
African Slave Trade 23
Afro-American Texas-to-New York Air Derby 86
Afro-Futurism 10
aircraft manufacturing
  automobile industry and 176
  employment discrimination and 17–19, 118–122, 155–156
  growth of 117–118
  military-industrial complex and 19, 177, 198
  national security and 17–18
  postwar business and 165
  South Africa and 165–167
  unionized factories 118
  wartime production and 117

229

C

Dr. Gerald Horne holds the John J. and Rebecca Moores Chair of History and African American Studies. His research has addressed issues of racism in a variety of relations involving labor, politics, civil rights, international relations and war. He has also written extensively about the film industry. Dr. Horne received his Ph.D. in history from Columbia University and his J.D. from the University of California, Berkeley and his B.A. from Princeton University. Dr. Horne's undergraduate courses include the Civil Rights Movement an U.S. History through Film. He also teaches graduate courses in Diplomatic History, Labor History and 20th Century African American History. Dr. Horne uses a variety of teaching techniques that enrich his classes and motivate students to participate. Dr. Horne is the author of more than thirty books and one hundred scholarly articles and reviews. Horne is also a guest contributor on MSNBC.

130418-300-4-60W